Country Food

COUNTRY
F·O·O·D

A Seasonal Journal

MIRIAM UNGERER

VINTAGE BOOKS
A DIVISION OF RANDOM HOUSE
NEW YORK

Most of this material was originally published in Miriam Ungerer's column "Long Island Larder" in the East Hampton *Star* (East Hampton, New York).

Grateful acknowledgment is given to the following for permission to reprint previously published material:

Chappell Music Company and Cahn Music Co.: Excerpt from lyrics to "Let It Snow! Let It Snow! Let It Snow!" by Jules Styne and Sammy Cahn. Copyright 1945 by Cahn Music Corp. Copyright renewed; assigned to Producer's Music Corp., Inc. and Cahn Music Corp. for the U.S.A. only. Jules Styne administered in the U.S.A. by Chappell & Co., Inc. International Copyright secured. All Rights Reserved. Used by permission.

Dover Publications, Inc., Illustrations from *Food and Drink: A Pictorial Archive from Nineteenth-Century Sources*, by Jim Harter, 1979 Dover Publications, Inc., NY.

Harcourt Brace Jovanovich, Inc. and Faber & Faber Ltd. (London): Two-line excerpt from "Little Gidding" in *Four Quartets*. Copyright 1943 by T. S. Eliot; renewed 1971 by Esme Valerie Eliot. Reprinted by permission of the publishers.

Holt, Rinehart and Winston, Publishers: From "Loveliest of trees, the cherry now" from *A Shropshire Lad*—authorized edition—from *The Collected Poems of A. E. Housman*. Copyright 1939, 1940, © 1965 by Holt, Rinehart and Winston. Copyright © 1967, 1968 by Robert E. Symons. Reprinted by permission of Holt, Rinehart and Winston, Publishers; The Society of Authors as the literary representative of the Estate of A. E. Housman; and Jonathan Cape Ltd., publishers of A. E. Housman's *Collected Poems*.

Little Brown and Company: Six lines from "The Shad" by Ogden Nash from *Verses from 1929 On*. Copyright © 1957 by Ogden Nash. First appeared in *House and Garden*. Excerpt from *Beautiful Swimmers* by William Warner. Copyright © 1976 by William W. Warner. Used by permission of the publisher.

Harold Ober Associates Incorporated: Excerpt from *French Provincial Cooking* by Elizabeth David (Penguin Books). Canadian rights administered by David Higham Associates, Inc.

Warner Bros. Music: Excerpt from lyrics to "Mack the Knife" by Kurt Weill. Copyright 1928 (Renewed) Universal Edition assigned to Weill-Brecht-Harms Co., Inc. © 1955 (Renewed) Weill-Brecht-Harms Co., Inc. All rights reserved. Used by permission of Warner Bros. Music.

Library of Congress Cataloging in Publication Data

Ungerer, Miriam.
Country food.

Reprint. Originally published:
New York : Random House, c1983.
Includes index.
1. Cookery. I. Title.
[TX715.U548 1985]   641.5   84-40549
ISBN 0-394-72906-4 (pbk.)

Manufactured in the United States of America

BOOK DESIGN & CONTEMPORARY ILLUSTRATIONS
BY LILLY LANGOTSKY

Foreword

What does cookery mean? It means the knowledge of Medea and
of Circe, and of Calypso, and Sheba. It means the economy of
your great-grandmother and the science of modern chemistry, and
French art, and Arabian hospitality. It means, in fine, that you
are to see imperatively that everyone has something nice to eat.
—John Ruskin

It also means learning to love the drudgery, so that cooking becomes not a task but
a pastime. When you can take pleasure in a perfectly peeled potato or a swiftly
skinned tomato, you will be on the way from mere kitchen mechanic to skilled
artisan. Then, who knows? Even an *artist,* if cookery continues to climb the social
ladder as it has in the past decade or so. (One of the most satisfying changes in
American conversation is that people who can't cook no longer brag about it.)

People born into households where good food is cherished—and discussed—have an
enormous head start toward becoming fine cooks. Any Frenchman or Chinese. And
the major figures in our own food renaissance—Julia Child and M. F. K. Fisher as
well as James Beard and Craig Claiborne—all came from backgrounds where food
played a major role. But this is not an absolute prerequisite. The food writer who
has had the most profound influence on me is Elizabeth David, who read history at
Cambridge but is an entirely self-taught cook. This Englishwoman, besides being
an authority on British cookery, is also a master of French, Italian and Mediterranean
food and history.

My own mother wasn't of much help except genetically. She was a Southern
beauty, a flapper, and although she cooked very well when no one was looking, she
preferred to be taken out. So I learned little from thoroughly modern Marguerite,
but I inherited a sense of good food from her.

Between bouts of rather extravagant food at home I languished in boarding school,
where the food was so awful that semi-starvation whetted my appetite. Then a
sojourn with my father added self-preservation to my motives for puttering around
kitchens (I was planning to be a great painter, but first things first.) Embarrassment
had its uses, too. It stimulated me to cook for my friends, whom I couldn't bear to
invite home to witness the debacle of the paternal table.

Thus began the making of an autodidactic cook. I've never had any formal
culinary training, but I've read and read and read. And there have been few things

I have been unwilling to skirmish with many times over until I got them right. Whether it's French, Italian, Chinese, German or Japanese, I've added the food and the techniques to my own Low-Country Carolina foundation. This is why it is always difficult for me to categorize my kind of cookery—I make stir-fried ratatouille and put Mexican jalapeñas in my spoon bread. But, mind you, I do not go in for wild experimentation—pineapple in the coleslaw or mint in the meat loaf, or any novelty for the sole sake of novelty.

Above all, this is not a book about "country cookin'" . . . it is about the splendid fresh provender my part of the countryside yields up with the changing seasons. Though the eastern tip of Long Island is well known for its rich and famous summer people, the real business most of the year is farming and fishing. This is heaven to a city-bred cook who has, for the last decade, been re-learning to cook as all Americans did a century ago—with whatever the season provides. I do dry a few herbs and put up some favorite chutneys and preserves, but I don't freeze many things. We eat corn when it is young and fresh, tomatoes at their lush, perfect ripeness, then on to something else the new season brings. Anticipation sharpens both appetite and inventiveness.

—Miriam Ungerer
Sag Harbor, L.I.

Acknowledgments

Most of the work here was published in somewhat different form in my column "Long Island Larder," which I write for the East Hampton *Star*, published weekly in East Hampton, Long Island. My thanks to the editor, Helen Rattray, who lets me ramble on and even cooks my food occasionally.

Parts of articles written for the *New York Times* and the *Daily News, Harper's Bazaar, Food & Wine,* and several short-lived magazines are also included. Some special-occasion meals were designed for sports pages edited by my friend and enthusiastic eater, Vic Ziegel.

All the food professionals mentioned in the foreword helped me in various ways. Alice B. Toklas's wonderful book inspired a lot of the recipes, and Jacques Pepin's illustrated manuals helped me figure out how to execute them.

I wish I had a faithful typist to thank, but I don't . . . that would be me, and it wouldn't be right.

—M. U.

Contents

CONTENTS

FALL

WINTER

Pots and Pans

Few aspects of cookery have altered so radically in the past decade as the demand for good, well-made and usually expensive kitchenware. Sleek, professional caliber pots and pans once found only in the kitchens of restaurants and serious amateur chefs are now available across the country in shops catering to every whim—from woks to Swedish waffle irons.

Until quite recently, the best consumer equipment came from Europe, chiefly France and Italy. But American manufacturers have finally awakened (as did Sleeping-Beauty Detroit to the reality of foreign cars) to the fact that strange colors and dubious decorations won't sell their inferior, thin, poorly balanced pots and pans. The increased number of women in the work force—with the attendant increased number of men in the kitchen—have combined to improve the quality of kitchen tools immensely. But then, the national taste level in all aspects of home design has risen quite dramatically in the past ten or twenty years.

And of course, there is the food processor, often generically called a "Cuisinart" after the prototype, which has vastly enlarged the culinary range of many thousands of home cooks. Not since the invention of the rotary egg beater in the nineteenth century has any kitchen machine made such an impact on how people cook. (Having been asked eight thousand times if it's "really worth buying one," I want to say yes, yes, it definitely is. It needn't be a super-expensive model, but do not get stuck with a cheap, underpowered brand—less than a quarter horsepower—which won't perform efficiently.)

Still, wonderful though these bionic handmaids may be, successful cooking depends more crucially on choosing the right size pot of the right material. The material, size and shape can determine whether the rice is gummy, the bottom of the stew burnt or the sauce too thin.

A really efficient *batterie de cuisine* can only be built by firmly establishing the need for each pot according to the personal repertory of each cook. Ergo, never buy "sets" of anything, for there is no single material, or shape for that matter, that could possibly be the "best" for every cooking purpose. For instance, of what possible use is a ¾-quart cast-iron saucepan except to heat baby food? And who needs a set of six graduated soufflé dishes when most soufflé recipes demand essentially the same volume of ingredients?

Size is incredibly important in choosing the right pot for the right amount of food. Beginners invariably choose a vessel much too large for what they are cooking. As a general rule, the food, especially roasts and fowl, should just fit comfortably into its container, otherwise there is too much air surrounding them and the juices evaporate and burn up; this is the chief reason for the failure of any long-simmered dish.

Conversely, it takes most people about two years of scuffling with a make-do pot until they finally break down and buy a really adequate stockpot big enough to cook spaghetti or soup for a crowd. If I could have only three pots, I think I would choose a 12-quart stockpot, a good medium-to-heavy *sautoir* (a straight-sided 10-inch skillet, 3 inches deep) and a steel wok with a wooden side handle and a cover. In the non-commercial kitchen most cookware should certainly serve more than one purpose (although I must admit to a weakness for little hand gadgets such as olive pitters and egg piercers).

Crepes, pancakes, omelets and eggs can all share the same pan if it is properly cared for. A well-seasoned cast-iron skillet with a tight lid can be used either to fry, sauté or braise in the oven, and it's also a great rice cooker. Stews can be oven-braised in a heavy bean pot.

The Dutch oven (a deep, round, cast-iron casserole with a bail-handle and a heavy lid) is the descendant of the pot that conquered the Plains. Before stoves were commonplace, the Dutch oven had three "feet," so that it could stand on hot ashes for baking as well as be suspended over coals in a fireplace or campfire for making stews. It remains an all-round great American cook pot along with its kissin' cousin, the deep iron chicken-fryer with a heavy lid.

The European enameled cast-iron casseroles and saucepans are much prettier (to some people) and easier to keep clean—and about six times as expensive. Still, they're a sound investment, and if you don't drop them (they chip) or burn them out, will last forever with reasonable care.

After you decide what kind of food you cook most often—not everyone really *needs* a brioche pan—and for how many people, you can begin to choose your kitchen companions. As they may be with you for a lifetime, it is wise to consider the various properties and limitations of the many metals and other materials used in cookware.

COPPER: It is the best conductor of heat and the most easily regulated—thus the favorite of many professionals, particularly for sautéing and sauce making. It should be heavy gauge, lined with smooth, shiny tin and unlacquered. This lining must be replaced from time to time, but re-tinning isn't as impossible to get done as it was ten years ago. The disadvantages? Copper is priced out of sight and should come with a resident polisher to keep it gleaming. It is the weightiest cookware made: heft it several times to be certain that you can handle it.

CAST IRON: This is probably the best value and most endurable type of

American-made cookware, but some people dislike it because it's heavy and not the easiest stuff to keep clean and rust-free. It is a good, even conductor and holder of heat and, once well-seasoned, really not too much bother.

Manufacturers insist most cast-iron pots are now "pre-seasoned," but don't you believe it. Wash them well, dry, then fill with about ¼ inch of plain salad oil, brushing it around the inside surfaces. Leave the pot in a lukewarm oven (lowest possible setting) overnight, discard the oil, wipe with paper towels and the pot is ready to use. Never soak cast iron. Wash it quickly with hot, soapy water, rinse very well and dry thoroughly with paper towels. It may need some re-oiling from time to time. It should be stored in an open, airy place, so that rust won't form. Some people recommend scouring cast iron with coarse salt, but that (like sea air) can cause rust, and I think plain sand is a better substance if something gets burnt onto the surface. If your ironware rusts through disuse or excessive humidity, scour it with steel-wool pads and re-season completely.

ENAMELED CAST IRON: Except for its expense, this has all the virtues of plain cast iron and none of the headaches, although it is equally heavy. But it can chip with careless handling, or crack from being allowed to burn dry or having cold water put into the hot vessel. This type of ware is easily cleaned with hot, soapy water and the outsides can be kept free of grungy dark stains by a light rubbing with scouring powder. The enameled interiors can be brightened up with household bleach if necessary. Enameled ware should never be placed empty over an open flame and it certainly should not be dried that way, although plain cast iron often is.

ALUMINUM: For recent generations the commonest type of cookware aluminum has been made in every grade, from thin, treacherous, dime-store quality to heavy-duty institutional stockpots, and in varying alloys with stainless steel. Aluminum pots were first marketed around the turn of the century, and an unfounded rumor—that aluminum causes cancer—has, incredibly, persisted since that time. The evidence, however, is overwhelmingly to the contrary. Aluminum was and is still popular because it is a very fast, even heat conductor if the pot bottoms are smooth and heavy (double-clad). It is reasonably lightweight, easily cleaned and almost impervious to abuse. Although the natural alkalis and acids found in many foods may eventually pit some aluminum after long use, steel wool will keep it clean and bright. Commercial Aluminum, a line once available only to mess halls and asylums, now sells to the general consumer a fine array of heavy-duty pots and pans.

Some of the best all-purpose skillets are heavy-duty aluminum lined with non-stick surfaces, such as the American "Silverstone" and the French "T-Fal." Commercial Aluminum has developed a professional line of aluminum called Calphalon. Its beautiful satiny gray finish is electrochemically integrated and is not marred by normal stirring and whisking. Neither does this finish discolor egg or wine sauces (as plain aluminum can) and although some oil must be used, it is an easy-release surface. It is simply and elegantly designed and in my view the best all-purpose metal cookware there is. Not cheap.

STAINLESS STEEL: The Rolls-Royce of cookware is the glittering Cuisinart line, with their very flat, heavy base of aluminum sandwiched between two layers of stainless steel. This eliminates the hot spots that are the one drawback of pure stainless. However, I have heard owners of these super-expensive pots complain that the indented line around the base of the pots tends to burn food in that crevice. But they have beautifully fitting tight covers and for long-simmered foods the crevice problem could be eliminated by using a simple asbestos pad. Paderno is an equally fine and equally expensive but more commercially designed line from Italy. It is to be found almost entirely in professional kitchens—for a single reason: few women can lift it. If you choose one of these heavy metals, it's important to select pots with a short grip handle on the opposite side of the long handle usually provided, to make lifting easier. Happily, more and more manufacturers are beginning to see the wisdom of this arrangement. Allclad (a most advanced type of pot with stainless steel inside and aluminum outside), Cuisinart and Calphalon all make their large pots with two handles.

Stainless steel without aluminum-clad bottoms really cannot be recommended for anything except boiling because of the "hot spot" problem. And, ironically, the "stainless" gets an unappetizing bluish or brownish caste when it is overheated. As the metal actually turns color, there is no way to return it to its original state. I do thoroughly recommend, however, a high, 6-quart, straight-sided pot with a lid, for use with a separate steaming basket for cooking vegetables.

CARBON STEEL: The usually rather thin, plain steel crepe and frying pans are the workhorses of professional kitchens. They heat and cool with lightning speed, are easily wiped clean but also rust readily. This is a pro's pan; the handles are long, skinny and get very hot; a no-frills, no-nonsense type of cookware meant to stay in constant use. They can take abuse and very high heat, but must be kept moving over the flame. An oval sauté pan is particularly useful for frying fish and other quick jobs. Keep carbon steel well oiled. Most of the best woks are made of this metal because of the intense heat required for stir-frying; all the pan manipulation used by Oriental cooks would be impossible with a weighty metal. With use, this metal gets black—don't worry, that's the way it's supposed to look.

TIN, CLAY, PORCELAIN AND GLASS: Each of these deserves a place in your kitchen, because each has its own superior characteristics.

Tin is used chiefly for molds and as a lining for other metals because food slips from it easily. It is not recommended that you use pure tin over direct heat, as it is inclined to melt. Tinned steel and black sheet steel are preferred for baking. French baking equipment made from these metals are now sold in the fancier cookware shops. (Do not use the black breadpans for pâtés, as they discolor the white fat used to line the pans; the best pâté pans are made of T-Fal, a superslick coating inside an aluminum shell.)

Clay includes terra cotta, glazed and unglazed, and various ceramics, some of which can be used over flame, with caution. The lovely sienna Vallauris earthenware from France is glazed inside but not outside, and can be used over low flame with an asbestos mat. Earthenware retains heat well, maintains temperatures evenly and is my personal favorite for oven-to-table use, especially for buffets.

Mexican clayware ranges from thin and glazed to very thick and unglazed. Sometimes this ware looks very rough and ready, but I like that look and it is also usually very well priced. Most of it seems more brittle in comparison to American and European clayware. Warnings have been issued about some unglazed Mexican clayware, but all I know at firsthand is that it sometimes imparts an all-too-earthy flavor to the food cooked in it. Unglazed interiors should always be cured with a long hot oil bath before use, to seal up the porous material. Bennington Potters in Vermont makes very high quality, beautifully designed earthenware in both high and low glazes.

High-fired porcelain, such as the French Pilyvuyt, can sustain direct heat, but most of it is for oven-to-table use, such as the classic white *gratins* and soufflés. There are imitations of these porcelain dishes, but they are made of ceramic fired at much lower temperatures. They are dangerous to use if one is transferring a cold soufflé dish to a vey hot oven. Also, ceramic chips easily.

Pyrex has been with us for decades, serviceable and cheap albeit unglamorous. Corning Glass has developed a real beauty, though, in its new line called Culinaria, which, although it looks fragile, is not. Heller glass ovenware designed by Massimo Vignelli is pretty dazzling, too.

It must be emphasized that there is no one material that is best for every purpose, and it is important to find out all you can about the properties of everything you buy. For instance, buyers are seldom warned that composition and wood handles on saucepans and lids cannot be put into ovens exceeding 425° F. Most ceramics are not safe above 375° F. So ask a lot of questions and buy from established, knowledgeable merchants who are willing to talk things over with you. The good ones can hardly be silenced, because fine kitchenware is a passion.

S·P·R·I·N·G

Shad Roe and Spring Asparagus

... Some people greet the shad with groans,
Complaining of its countless bones;
I claim the bones teach table poise
And separate the men from boys.
The shad must be dissected subtle-y;
Besides, the roe is boneless, utterly.
—Ogden Nash, "The Shad"

It's spring. And it's all very well for people to go on about crocuses and forsythia, but the mind of The Foodie focuses, not on crocuses, but on shad roe. That peerless delicacy flits in and out of season like the blossoms on a crab-apple tree.

The initiate begin making discreet inquiry at fish stores in early March, leaving phone numbers and pleas for the first pair of shad roe on the premises. And at last the Chesapeake shad with its precious roe arrives. Long Island shad do not arrive until late in the season, when the sea warms up.

The shad itself is one of the finest of fish, so when you see it, snap it up. Shad filleters are in about as short supply as gifted microsurgeons, so of course this bony creature is somewhat costly. Unboned, it's cheap. The price of shad roe is like waterfront property—it *never* goes down. Local shad, when it finally comes along, won't be any cheaper anyway.

In both Southern and French cookbooks one finds recipes for shad stuffed with shad roe, but this seems an atrocious waste to me. The flavor and texture of the delicate roe are completely lost in any such amalgam. But the shad and its roe, sautéed separately then served together with a light, creamy hollandaise or sauce mousseline, luxuriously reveals the qualities of both fish and roe. A squeeze of lemon juice, although egregiously overdone in recent years, is quite appropriate as a simple touch of tartness to this particular fish dish. (I imagine that there exists a whole new generation that can't tell a fish from a lemon, since the "lemon-slice-with-everything" has become as ubiquitous as the pickle with the drugstore sandwich.)

One of the truly regal breakfasts known to man comes from antebellum Charleston: pan-fried shad roe with broiled country bacon and hot biscuits. My mother served this, sometimes with scrambled eggs as well. (One of her more eccentric breakfasts was brains and eggs—not a success with me.)

Cooks of Chesapeake Bay, from whence so many semi-saline delicacies flow, offer,

3

in a book called *Maryland's Way,* a recipe for shad roe stuffed with—what else?—crabmeat! My boundless enthusiasm for every crustacean and mollusk being what it is, I think this sounds wonderful, though I haven't had time to try it out yet.

Another spring passion of mine, and the perfect companion to shad roe, is asparagus. There are some feral patches on the East End—the work of long-ago gardeners. A member of the lily family, this graceful European plant was cultivated by the ancient Greeks and Romans. Most of the asparagus we get comes from California and some of excellent quality from New Jersey. Asparagus will grow almost anywhere not too extreme in climate. It's a generous plant, and once the bed is established, it will keep on producing for more than fifteen years.

But enough digression. Fifteen minutes is enough to produce this superb meal—all undivided attention, however.

SAUTÉED SHAD ROE

One's appetite for this short-season delicacy and the variable size of a pair of roe determine how much is enough. Usually a smallish pair is sufficient for only one, but a large pair (plump and about 7 inches long) will satisfy two diners. This recipe will assume fairly small appetites and large roe.

Serves 1 or 2.

1 large pair shad roe	4 tablespoons melted butter
Butter	Minced parsley (optional)
½ cup milk	Salt and freshly milled pepper
Flour	to taste

Roe that has its membrane ruptured is almost impossible to cook without it exploding all over the kitchen. So be sure yours is intact. Remove the roe from the fridge and let it come to room temperature.

Grease a large non-stick skillet with butter and lay the pair of roe (unsplit) in the pan. Carefully pour lightly salted tepid water around the roe (its covering is extremely fragile) until it is immersed. Turn the heat on low, and slowly bring the water to a bare simmer. Poach the roe, very gently, about 2 minutes. Lift the roe, with two wide spatulas, onto a plate. Separate the roes at the center membrane. Moisten them with a little cold milk and dust them with a film of flour.

Melt 2 tablespoons of the butter in a clean, dry, non-stick skillet, and lay the roes in it. Cook over low heat about 2 minutes on each side—they should be lightly browned and moist inside. Sometimes, no matter what precautions you take, the roe explodes a little—an antispatter screen lid is a great help in making this dish.

Serve the roes on hot plates with the remaining 2 tablespoons of the butter melted and poured over them, and a sprinkle of parsley, if desired. Season at the table.

FIRST SPRING ASPARAGUS

Some of the very simplest dishes—certainly all quickly cooked food—require the most intense attention to detail. Asparagus is a classic example. If any one of the niceties of preparation is omitted, the vegetable is a disaster. Meticulousness, not talent, is all that is required to cook perfect asparagus. Serve it with shad roe, or, in other meals, as a separate first course. It may be served hot with hollandaise or some similar sauce, tepid with homemade mayonnaise or vinaigrette dressing.

Serves 2.

1 pound fresh asparagus	*Salt and freshly milled pepper*
3 to 4 tablespoons melted butter	*to taste*

Choose stalks with unblemished, firmly closed tips and pick out those of approximately the same size. If you are forced to accept a mixed lot, put the fat stalks in the simmering water two minutes before adding the thinner ones.

Cut off the coarse whitish ends of the stalks. Lay each stalk on a cutting board and, using a swivel-blade vegetable peeler, remove the tough, fibrous outer layer all the way up to within a couple of inches of the tip. (If you try holding the stalks in your hand while you peel, a few stalks generally break off short.) Rinse in cold water.

Asparagus cookers are rather superfluous equipment. They were designed for the thick white European asparagus, which must be stood upright because its lower parts take forever to cook. This is totally unnecessary with tender green American asparagus—as long as the stalks are peeled. I use a graniteware roaster to cook asparagus. Any hardware store has them.

Bring a fairly large quantity of salted water to a boil. Quickly lay the asparagus, a few stalks at a time, in the simmering water. Do not cover it. After 3 minutes, lift a spear at the center with a cooking fork. If it barely droops, it is done. Lift the asparagus out onto a folded kitchen towel, then roll it over onto a heated platter. Glisten the whole length of the stalks with plenty of melted butter, sprinkle with a little salt and fresh pepper.

Served with hollandaise, asparagus makes a wonderful lunch all by itself. To back up my own convictions about the serving of wine with asparagus (a lot of dreary stuff has been written on this subject), I quote the eminent French food critic, Robert Courtine: "I once met a thin and gloomy man who claimed to be a gastronomical expert. He lived for edicts and embargoes. He wanted to ban all wine from my table while asparagus was being served. Poor man! Even a *vinaigrette* should not have to drown in tasteless water." Courtine suggests a white or a rosé as a fitting escort.

If it Were Just a Little Nearer...

Late winter and early spring are gray and long on the North Atlantic coast. I escaped to Madeira—where calla lilies grow wild all year round—one early April. Madeira is a Portuguese possession four hundred miles off the west coast of Africa, an island thirty miles long that juts straight up out of the Atlantic but has no beaches. The inhabitants must have the sturdiest legs and hearts in the civilized world, for they trudge up and down miles of steps and paths carved out of the mountainsides to reach the tiny terraces where vegetables grow under the vines that produce the island's most famous export: Madeira wine. Most of the excellent and cheap table wine comes from Portugal, and I wonder why we see so little of it in America.

Shining fresh fruit and flowers, fish and vegetables crowd the stalls on market day in Funchal, the capital city, and while other tourists head for the cathedrals, I make for country markets. Gastronomically speaking, Madeira is almost self-sufficient —there are cattle, dairy cows and sheep in the mountains, and fresh fish and produce all year round. There's even a good local beer. But the generous God that endowed Madeira so handsomely must have decided not to make it perfect: there are no shellfish!

Upon my return to a bountiful but still bleak Long Island, I naturally head for the shellfish, upon which I think I could gratefully live forever. (When Gertrude Stein dieted, she ate only oysters!)

MONK AND MUSSEL STEW

These formerly "second-class citizens" of the deep achieve a Creole grace in this spicy stew without the usual heaviness characteristic of that kind of cookery. The broth is thin, exploding with flavors, and made substantial enough for an entrée by the old Charleston custom of putting a big spoonful of rice in the bottom of the soup plate. Serve good homemade bread or an Italian whole wheat, as there is plenty of sopping up to do.

Serves 6 as a main course.

3 pounds large black mussels
3 pounds monkfish fillets
3 cloves garlic, minced
Mix together: 1 tablespoon
    minced garlic, 1 teaspoon
    ground coriander, 1 tablespoon
    ground cumin, ½ teaspoon
    cayenne
¼ cup cognac
2 cups leeks, finely sliced
¾ cup celery, finely diced
½ cup olive oil (or more)
1 teaspoon dried basil, crushed
    (in summer, use 2 tablespoons
    fresh chopped basil leaves)

1 14-ounce can Italian plum
    tomatoes, finely chopped (or
    use fresh ripe ones when
    in season)
2 cups dry white wine
Thin strip orange peel 3 inches
    long
Salt and pepper to taste
1 cup parsley, minced
4 cups cooked rice

Wash the mussels well in cold running water, then scrub them with a plastic mesh pot cleaner to remove barnacles, limpets, etc. Use a clam knife to pull out the beard, or *byssus* as it is properly known. Put the mussels to soak in fresh cold water.

Remove the thin, grayish membrane, if any, from the monkfish. Cut the fish into 1-inch chunks. Remove one tablespoon of the minced garlic and mix with the coriander, cumin and cayenne. Rub this mixture into the fish, and pour the cognac over it, mixing well. Cover with plastic wrap and let stand, an hour at room temperature or as long as overnight in the fridge.

Wash the leeks, trim the roots and discard most of the green, which is as tough as sugar cane. Leeks are extremely sandy as they are banked up to keep them white (like European asparagus). Cut them four ways, from tops almost to bulb. Open up, rinse under a strong stream of water and dry before slicing. Peel the celery with a vegetable cutter to eliminate the unpalatable stringiness.

Heat the olive oil and gently sauté remaining garlic, the leeks and celery, until tender, adding more oil as necessary. Add the basil and the chopped tomatoes, saving all the juice. Add these things to the sautéed vegetables, along with the orange peel.

Meanwhile, cook the mussels in the basic way: put them in a wide, shallow pan. Pour in the wine and enough water to provide an inch of liquid depth, cover the pot and steam the mussels open, shaking it often so they cook evenly. This will take about 2 minutes. Drain off the juices and reserve; cover mussels, which will be reheated in the stew anyway. Strain the mussel juices into the stewpot. Add the monkfish to the stew and simmer about 10 minutes, stirring a couple of times. Return the mussels to the pot and heat through.

To serve, put a spoonful of cooked rice in the bottom of each bowl and ladle on large helpings of stew. Scatter generously with parsley. (For a buffet, stir the parsley into the stew and demonstrate a "model bowl" of rice first, stew over, for those unfamiliar with this custom.) Provide bowls for empty shells and a large number of napkins. White wine or beer, of course, and a fresh, crisp green salad (romaine and Boston lettuce, mixed) with a dressing of walnut oil and lemon juice and a little goat cheese would end this meal nicely.

Although there are, admittedly, many ingredients—this is after all, a one-dish meal—only the mussel-cleaning is a bit slow, and if you have two people, scrubbing and chatting away, it doesn't seem so onerous.

White Easter Sweets

Loveliest of trees, the cherry now
Is hung with bloom along the bough,
And stands about the woodland ride
Wearing white for Eastertide.
　　　　　　　—A. E. Housman, "A Shropshire Lad"

Besides the stately lily, the priests' vestments, the blossoming fruit trees—all white for Easter—there was the traditional me as a child: white shoes, socks, dress and hair thingummy. Others could prance out looking like a bunch of Easter eggs, but I always insisted on celebrating Easter in a blaze of whiteness.

In Czarist Russia and most European countries, Easter was always a more celebrated holiday than Christmas. Accordingly, there are very special desserts to climax the feast that marks the happiest of Christian holy days. Paskha, undoubtedly the most famous of the Easter desserts (unless one counts chocolate bunnies), is white with cottage cheese and sour cream, rich and sweet with almonds and white raisins. (Oddly, this arch-Russian dessert goes unmentioned in a newly translated Russian cookbook a friend brought me from Moscow—can the Soviets be repressing *paskha*?)

Coeur à la crème is a French dessert that salutes the pure in heart with the "heart of the cheese" shaped into Valentines and usually outlined with the brilliance of strawberries. Although local berries do not arrive until June, there are good ones in the stores, and this is a fine time to have this fresh, springlike dessert.

Then we come to good old New York cheesecake. I know that cheesecake has foreign origins, but, like pizza and pastrami, New York has made it hers. I imagine that if a dessert referendum were held in New York, the hands-down preference would be cheesecake. Department stores sponsor cheesecake contests that draw thousands of entries. All different. And that's confusing—I've never seen two cheesecake recipes that agreed very much about anything. How long to cook it? How long to cool it in the oven? Whether to make it in a springform or a deep cake pan—all are matters of serious disagreement, but somehow they all seem to work. There must be at least thirty excellent ways to make a cheesecake, and mine is one of the easiest. It has been adapted for the food processor.

APRICOT CHEESECAKE

A purée of cooked dried apricots gives this a peach blush, but if you want a pristine white cheesecake, you can omit the apricots and flavor it simply with grated lemon zest. The yellow flecks are almost undiscernible in the finished cake. Start with the finest, freshest unprocessed cream cheese. This may be bought in bulk form at fine specialty food stores.

Serves 10.

⅓ cup graham cracker crumbs
1 tablespoon softened butter
¼ pound fine dried California
    apricots
1 cup sugar

Zest of 1 lemon
1½ pounds fresh cream cheese
4 eggs (Grade A "large")
½ cup sour cream
Apricot glaze (optional)

Pre-heat oven to 350° F.

Either buy the pre-made crumbs or spin a few graham crackers in the food processor to make ⅓ cup of crumbs. Lavishly butter an 8- x 3-inch springform cake pan.

Rinse the apricots and barely cover with cold water. Cover and cook slowly over low heat until fruit is tender and nearly all water has been absorbed, about 15 minutes. Set aside.

Process the sugar and the lemon zest (this is the thin yellow peel only—avoid the bitter white pith that lies just underneath). Add the apricots and purée. Add a third of the cream cheese and one egg. Process about 10 seconds until well combined. Scrape down the container. Repeat this step until all the cheese and eggs are used, then blend in the sour cream, scraping down with a rubber spatula after each addition. Scrape the batter into the prepared springform pan. Gently place on a cookie sheet and bake in the center of the oven about 50 minutes—until a skewer comes out clean. Do not overbake, or the cake will be dry.

Turn off the oven, prop it open a few inches and leave the cake there for 30 minutes. Remove it to a draught-free place and let it get cold. Do not refrigerate unless the weather is hot or the cake made a day ahead. This cheesecake is really best eaten on the day made, served cool, not cold.

Apricot glaze makes the cake look very professional, but it should not be overdone or the cheesecake will seem heavy. Melt a few tablespoonfuls of apricot preserves and thin with a tablespoon of brandy. Cool slightly and pour into the center of the cooled cheesecake. Spread it gently out to the inner rim of the cake. All cheesecakes sink when they cool unless they have had flour and leavening added to them.

PASKHA

(traditional Easter dessert)

This recipe is from an anthology of recipes compiled by the late Peggy Harvey. Long out of print, the book is called *The Horn of Plenty,* not to be confused with a book about Louis Armstrong which *is* in print. Peggy Harvey was a much-admired and respected food writer who always attributed her sources. This recipe was given to her by Kyra Petrovskaya, a White Russian émigré.

Serves 6–10.

"2½ *pounds very dry cottage cheese*
5 *large eggs, separated*
1 *pound sugar*
1 *teaspoon vanilla*
½ *pint sour cream*
½ *pound melted butter (unsalted)*

½ *pound almonds, blanched and shredded*
½ *cup seedless white raisins*
½ *cup candied orange or lemon peel, or a mixture of both*

"The main secret in making really good paskha is to have very dry cottage cheese, the kind that hasn't been creamed. Don't even attempt to make paskha unless you are able to get it. I have tried to make paskha with creamed cottage cheese and each time it was a complete failure.

[Here Peggy Harvey recommends using a food mill as opposed to the sieve in the Petrovskaya recipe. I would use a food processor to cream the cheese smooth.—M. U.]

"Crumble the cheese and force it through a coarse sieve twice.

"Beat egg yolks with sugar until very light. Add vanilla and sour cream. Slowly add melted butter; continue to beat until all the ingredients are completely mixed. Combine the cottage cheese with the egg yolk mixture. Beat the egg whites with a dash of salt until stiff. Fold carefully into cottage cheese and mix thoroughly. Add almonds, raisins and candied orange or lemon peel.

"Cook on a very slow fire until the bubbles form at the edges of the kettle. Remove from fire and chill in the same kettle. When cool, pour the mixture into a colander lined with cheesecloth or a thin napkin, and let it drip for two or three hours.

"Without removing the cheesecloth or the napkin, place the mixture in a conical form. (Peggy Harvey says: A large, unglazed clay flower pot served me beautifully, for like the majority of American women, I don't have the traditional Russian paskha form.)

"Place a small saucepan over the folded ends of the cheesecloth or napkins, put a weight over it and let the excess moisture come out through the draining hole of the flower pot. To make sure that the moisture drips freely, place the flower pot in such a way that its bottom doesn't touch the drippings below it [on a rack set over a pan— M. U.]. Put the whole contraption in the refrigerator for several hours (I usually leave it there overnight).

"Just before serving paskha, remove the weights, unfold the edges of the cheese-cloth or napkin, place a large plate or platter over the flower pot and turn it over very carefully. Remove the cheesecloth with the utmost care, for the paskha might break.

"Decorate the very top with an artificial flower (it looks naïve, but it is traditional). Slice horizontally and serve with koolich (Russian cake—P. H.) Paskha will keep for a long time in the refrigerator, but cover tightly to prevent drying out." [As noted, this recipe serves from 6 to 10 people—I guess it must allow for some real paskha pigs—M. U.]

COEUR À LA CRÈME

The true, classic French recipe for this dessert takes twenty-four hours to make and is, more or less, "the heart of the cream." This is a much lighter, less rich variation. It was developed by the American Dairy Association and altered somewhat by me about fifteen years ago. This smooth, light, summery dessert has been a longtime family favorite.

Serves 12.

2 pints creamed cottage cheese
2 cups commercial sour cream
¼ teaspoon salt
2 envelopes plain unflavored
*   gelatin*

⅓ cup milk
Fresh strawberries or
*   Strawberry–Orange Sauce (see*
*   below)*

In a blender or food processor, purée the cottage cheese, sour cream and salt. Soften the gelatin in the milk and stir it in the top of a double boiler over hot water until completely dissolved. Blend with the cottage cheese. A heart-shaped mold is ideal for this, but any pretty shape will do. Rinse a 1½-quart mold with cold water and pour in the cheese mixture. Refrigerate, covered with plastic wrap, until firm. Unmold and serve with a garnish of fresh strawberries or the following sauce:

STRAWBERRY–ORANGE SAUCE

½ *cup sugar*   ¼ *cup lemon juice*

2 *tablespoons cornstarch*   *Zest of one lemon*

¾ *cup orange juice*   1 *pint fresh strawberries*

Stir the sugar and cornstarch together in a small saucepan. Gradually stir in the orange and lemon juices. When blended, cook over medium low heat, stirring constantly until thickened. Set aside. Stir in lemon zest. Reserve a few whole berries for garnish and slice the rest. Stir them into the sauce. Refrigerate until needed—the sauce will thicken considerably, so should be removed half an hour before serving. The entire recipe may be completed a day ahead of time, but the sauce is better if freshly made.

Jambon Persillé—or Leftover Ham

Breathes there a cook with soul so dead who never to herself has said, "Why did I buy this enormous ham for Easter?" (Forgive the liberty, Sir Walter Scott.) I buy a whole ham because a half ham just doesn't have the proper gala impact. But no matter how many guests there are, the ham remains are usually plentiful enough to become a bore. And if one more person makes the stunning observation that I "can make a lovely pea soup with the bone," they will be hit with it. Sure, there are yet some pea-soup days ahead of us in late spring, but is there anyone beyond the age of reason who hasn't heard that piece of ham-bone wisdom?

Ham sandwiches are good. Once. Then there's ham and eggs. Maybe twice. Although there are lots of nice uses for little bits of ham, this old Burgundian dish, *jambon persillé,* uses up quite a lot of leftover ham while not seeming like a rerun. It's worth buying a good piece of country ham just to make this dish for a cold buffet table.

Although it looks quite elegant, the molded ham is really rather a country dish, along the lines of the headcheese made by farmers everywhere. At any rate, I've never seen it on a restaurant menu, so I presume it falls into the realm of French home cooking or *paysanne* dishes. All the proportions may be altered somewhat according to individual preference. The final effect should be a mosaic of pink and green, set in clear aspic, which should be quite tender and not rubbery.

PARSLEYED JELLIED HAM

Old recipes for *jambon persillé* call for calf's-foot jelly and they do, in fact, make a more tender, delicate aspic. However, I was chastised by a wire service reviewer for suggesting in a previous book of mine that anyone seek out such an outlandish object. While you won't generally find them in a supermarket meat case, most butchers will get you a couple of calves' feet (or pigs' feet) on special request. They freeze perfectly.

For expediency's sake this recipe will assume there are no calves within a hundred miles, and substitute innocent, clean little packets of unflavored Knox gelatin. If possible, use a good piece of richly flavored country ham.

Serves 6 as a first course.

2 packed cups lean cooked ham,
   cut in chunks
2 cups dry white wine
1 bay leaf
1 teaspoon fresh tarragon,
   minced
½ teaspoon dried thyme (use
   fresh if available)

1 envelope unflavored gelatin
2 tablespoons fresh chives,
   minced
¾ cup fresh parsley, minced
2 teaspoons coarsely milled
   fresh black pepper
Salt to taste

Put the ham in a small saucepan and cover with the wine. Tie the bay leaf, tarragon and thyme in a cheesecloth bag and add it. Cover and simmer about half an hour or until the ham is soft. Discard the herb bag and strain the broth through a piece of damp cheesecloth placed in a sieve. Soften the gelatin in ¼ cup cold water about 10 minutes, then stir it into the broth and heat until all the granules are thoroughly dissolved. Cool.

Chop the ham with a sharp knife. Don't turn it to pink dust in a food processor— it should have a few identifiable chunks of ham. Put the ham in a bowl and mix it with the chives, parsley and black pepper. Mix the aspic (it should be cooled to a thick syrupy consistency, otherwise the solids will float to the top) with the ham and taste for seasoning. You may like a bit more salt and perhaps a few drops of white vinegar. Pour the mixture into a chilled 1-quart bowl or mold. Cover with plastic wrap and put in the refrigerator to set. This is a nice simple dish to make ahead.

When ready to serve, lightly oil a pretty round plate—glass, green or white—and place it on top of the mold, face down. (The oil is to facilitate moving the aspic should it fail to drop exactly in the center of the plate.) Dip the mold into fairly hot water to loosen it; if it doesn't fall out easily, run a thin knife around the inner rim of the mold, then invert it, and, holding the plate and mold firmly together, give the whole thing a sharp downward jerk.

Obviously, this makes only a modest amount—but it is simple to double or triple for a large buffet centerpiece.

Note: If you wish to make the *echt jambon persillé*, using a calf's foot, have the butcher cut it in four pieces. Simmer for one hour or more with the wine, herbs and an extra cup of water (to accommodate evaporation), before adding the ham. Discard the pieces of calf's foot before proceeding with the recipe.

Sometimes an unfamiliar dish gets into bad company and is never properly appreciated because it is presented with incompatible foods. First, last and always, anything in aspic should be served on a cold plate with other foods that are also cold, or at least no warmer than room temperature. I've seen people at big summer parties loading their plates with the most incredible assortment of runny cheeses, cold mousses, hot baked beans, drippy salads, barbequed ribs and, Heaven forfend, hot cannelloni! If the same person were served such a mess in a restaurant, he'd stalk out in a rage.

Jambon persillé is at its best with a simple French potato salad, a green salad, perhaps some *céleri rémoulade,* a few cold pickled beets, deviled eggs or a cold bean salad of some kind. As a first course, place a wedge on a perfect leaf of pale Boston lettuce and serve just bread and butter with it. White wine or a dry rosé is the usual drink with ham dishes.

Cheap Chic

To think of all the adorable things there are to eat in the world,
and then to go through life munching sawdust and being proud
of it.

—Saki (H. H. Munro), "The Chronicles of Clovis"

Among the most interesting and neglected of native sea critters are the big blue-black mussels that cling to rocks and pilings from Maine to North Carolina. Until about a dozen years ago, most people around East Hampton regarded mussels merely as bait, and quite possibly actually poisonous. (Their plenitude also made them too cheap and therefore not very profitable for commercial watermen.) But along the Atlantic coastline they are now a popular food.

If you gather your own mussels, make sure you are taking them from clean, non-polluted areas, as the mussel is peculiarly susceptible to certain blights that can cause illness in humans. Most of the mussels sold in fish stores are probably from controlled and cultivated mussel beds that have been started in recent years. The Dutch and Danes have long had "mussel parks" for the cultivation of these little bivalves so treasured by Europeans and so ignored by us. They are a wonderfully cheap and delicious source of protein, and low in calories.

It is said that mussels are good on the half shell, but I have never tried them that way. They are simple to cook, and the only mildly tedious job is scrubbing and de-bearding them (see procedure on page 8). Although it looks nicer, it isn't necessary to scrape off every barnacle. Mussels, after cleaning, are usually soaked for a while in cold salted water, but actually they contain very little sand or other effluvia. The following two recipes begin with *Moules Marinière*, the jumping-off place for most mussel dishes.

MOULES GRIBICHE

Moules is the French word for mussels, and is almost universally employed on menus—probably since "mussels" don't sound so glamorous. *Sauce Gribiche* is a classic French sauce that starts out as plain mayonnaise, then is embellished with capers, herbs, pickles and chopped egg white. But please don't cheat on this sauce by using commercial mayonnaise: it is the wrong texture and too salty for the addition of pickles and capers. Homemade mayonnaise is not difficult to make, especially if one has a food processor or blender (see page 153).

Serves 10 as a first course.

5 pounds large mussels	*2 cloves garlic, minced*
(approximately 12 to a pound)	*2 tablespoons onion or shallots,*
2 tablespoons olive oil	*chopped*
2 bay leaves	*1 cup dry white wine*
Sprig of parsley	*Freshly milled pepper*

Scrub the mussels, de-beard them and soak in cold salted water for about an hour. Lift them out, leaving any grit behind, and put them in a large shallow pot with a cover. A deep pot is difficult because you must keep stirring the mussels down to cook evenly, whereas with a big shallow one just shaking the pot several times will ensure even cooking.

Add the oil, bay leaves, parsley, garlic, chopped onion, white wine and pepper. Shake them around to mix everything up and set the pot over fairly high heat. Cook about 3 to 5 minutes, shaking the pot frequently to redistribute the mussels. They are done when they open; further cooking simply toughens and shrivels them. Lift them out onto a big shallow pan to cool. Reserve a little of the mussel broth to thin the *Sauce Gribiche* (see page 157).

''TAPAS'' MUSSELS

One of the charms of Spain is the custom of serving the delicious little dishes known as "tapas" with drinks in cafés and restaurants. As the fashionable dinner hour is not before ten o'clock, one soon learns that the complimentary "tapas" are not only delicious pastimes but a hedge against starvation and eventual unconsciousness. Try to imagine the sounds of *cante jondo*, the "deep song" of Spanish gypsies, as you eat these cool, plump mussels directly from their shells.

Makes 3 dozen.

36–40 large black mussels

1 cup dry white wine

TOPPING

1 red bell pepper
1 yellow bell pepper
6 scallions (½ cup minced)
1 large clove garlic, minced
1 ripe tomato, peeled, seeded and diced
1 tablespoon white wine vinegar

1 tablespoon olive oil
Salt and freshly milled pepper to taste
Cayenne or hot chili oil (optional)

Insist on uniformly large mussels, as little ones are too tedious to work with in this preparation. Mussels of wildly varying sizes will not cook evenly and are difficult to arrange attractively. Always buy a few extras as some may be broken or mud-filled duds. Scrub them under cool running water; you can skip de-bearding them at this point. Put them in a large shallow pan and pour the wine over them. Cover and cook over a high flame, shaking the pan constantly, until all are open: 5 minutes should do it. Remove at once and drain in a colander. Spread them out to cool rapidly to avoid overcooking them. Remove the top shell from each mussel and snip off the beards. Loosen the mussels from their undershells and arrange on a platter. Cover with plastic wrap after splashing a bit of the cooking broth on each mussel.

Remove seeds and pith from the bell peppers and dice them finely. (All the dicing and mincing can be done in a food processor, but the machine seems to blur the colors and one must be extraordinarily careful not to overprocess to mush.) Combine with all remaining ingredients and taste carefully, seasoning with salt and fresh pepper. If you like spiciness (the Spanish do not, but I do), add a few drops of hot chili oil or some cayenne. Spoon some of this mixture over each mussel and serve at once. The mussels can be cooked, trimmed and refrigerated, then dressed at the last minute. The vegetable topping is best at room temperature.

MUSSEL AND POTATO SALAD

This combination, of which I think I am the sole perpetrator, makes a most felicitous summer luncheon dish. Very good for buffets too, as it requires only a fork. The foregoing *Moules Gribiche* are excellent "finger food" for cocktail parties too, but smaller mussels should be used.

Serves 8.

2 pounds mussels, plus the
   ingredients used for steaming
   them in the preceding recipe
2 to 3 pounds small red or
   brown new potatoes
2 large shallots, minced, or
   4 scallions
1½ cups plain homemade
   mayonnaise
Mussel broth
½ cup vinaigrette dressing:
   olive oil, vinegar, salt and

pepper mixed together—
   4 parts oil and 1 part vinegar
1 large head ruby-leaf lettuce
1 cup fresh parsley, minced
Fresh chervil, tarragon, chives
   (in season), minced together—
   about ½ cup
Salt and coarsely milled pepper
   to taste

Steam the mussels as for basic *Moules Marinière* recipe, page 20. Lift out to cool and reserve about ½ cup of the broth.

Scrub and steam the new potatoes whole. If you have no steamer, boil them in a very small amount of water after sprinkling them with a little salt. Meanwhile detach the whole leaves from the lettuce and wash and dry them very carefully, taking care to leave them whole. Lay them out on a large bath towel, roll it up gently, then shake it, holding the towel by the ends. This is the most efficient way I know to dry whole leaves, as they will not dry in a spinner. Put the whole leaves in a jumbo plastic bag, leaving plenty of air around them; tie it shut and refrigerate until needed.

Put the minced shallots or scallions in a mixing bowl large enough to hold the completed salad. When the potatoes are just tender—15 minutes is often enough time for little new potatoes—remove them and cut in quarters. Do not peel. Put them in the bowl with the shallots, remove the mussels from their shells* and add them, along with the parsley and any of the fresh herbs you wish to use. Add the mayonnaise and turn the salad very gently so that you do not mash or break the potatoes or mussels.

Quickly shake up the vinaigrette. Turn the whole lettuce leaves very gently in this and arrange them as a green-red lining for the salad bowl—a glass one looks best for this salad. The addition of a good vinaigrette dressing makes the leaves shine invitingly as well as making them good to eat . . . not just lining material.

Turn the mixed potato-and-mussel salad—after seasoning to taste with salt and freshly milled black pepper—into the lettuce-lined bowl and scatter with a little more freshly minced parsley.

To make this in advance, put the potato-mussel mixture in a covered dish and refrigerate it, but return it to room temperature before serving. Any concoction of shellfish and mayonnaise should be served and eaten promptly. If a buffet has to stand for any length of time, it is best to serve the mussel-potato salad in several installments.

MUSSELS REVISITED

Two readers wrote to tell me that I am not the sole inventor of mussel and potato salad, and, of course, they are right. They jogged the old cells into remembering a book I have had since 1958, Alexandre Dumas, Junior's, *Dictionary of Cuisine*. I frittered away a pleasant hour in a bootless search through this charming book, which

---

* It is an elegance to trim the mussels of the black rim around them and snip out the little black "foot" inside—especially in large mussels, where the beard is sometimes stubbornly lurking. With small mussels this is not so important.

turns out to be a heavily abridged and edited edition. Then it came to me where I really did first read about the combination of mussels and potatoes in a salad: in one of my most treatured possessions, *The Alice B. Toklas Cook Book*. Here, then, is the absolutely, original, *vrai,* recipe:

"ALEXANDRE DUMAS, JUNIOR'S, FRANÇILLON SALAD

"This is the recipe as he gives it in his play *Françillon,* first produced at the Comédie Française.

ANNETTE: Cook some potatoes in bouillon, cut them in slices as for an ordinary salad, and while they are still warm season them with salt, pepper and a very good fruity olive oil, vinegar . . .

HENRI: Tarragon?

ANNETTE: Orléans is better, but that is not of great importance. What is important is a half glass of white wine, Château Yquem if it is possible. A great deal of herbs finely chopped. At the same time, cook very large mussels in a *court-bouillon* with a stalk of celery; drain them well and add them to the potatoes.

HENRI: Less mussels than potatoes?

ANNETTE: A third less. One should taste the mussels little by little. One should not foretaste them, nor should they obtrude. When the salad is finished, lightly turned, cover it with round slices of truffles; a real *calotte* (or crown) for the connoisseur.

HENRI: And cooked in champagne?

ANNETTE: That goes without saying. All this, two hours before dinner, so that the salad is very cold when it is served.

HENRI: One could surround the salad with ice.

ANNETTE: No, no, no. It must not be roughly treated; it is very delicate and all its flavours need to be quietly combined.

"It is a combination that is exquisitely and typically a French one. Why it is more popularly known as Japanese Salad no one has been able to tell me." Thus endeth Miss Toklas's musing.

Perhaps none will ever know. Even Escoffier is close-mouthed about the matter. I quote: "*Salade Japonaise.* This is another name for *Salade Françillon.*"

Escoffier's *Le Guide Culinaire* was written as a set of instructions for professional chefs, and he did not go in for a lot of long-winded explanations. Here is a typical Escoffier recipe:

"Filet de Boeuf Macédoine

"Lard the fillet and roast it.

"Place it on a long dish and surround with a *Macédoine* of vegetables and small *Pommes Château* arranged in alternate bouquets.

"Serve separately an unthickened gravy made from the juices from the cooking."

In stark contrast to the Mâitre's terse directions, American food writers are required by many editors to write as if their readers were a vast nation of duchesses, unable to select a pan for frying two eggs. I know that the Verbose-School-of-Painstaking-Explication has its admirers, because I get some astounding questions from readers.

There seems to be much bafflement over "season to taste." That means leave out, reduce or increase the amount of spice, herb or salt and pepper until the dish tastes the way you want it to. Likewise "adjust the seasoning" mystifies others; it means the same thing as "season to taste." Cookery has its own lexicon, and it must be learned if one is interested in the subject and would like to follow a recipe with speed and accuracy. After all, you wouldn't venture out sailing alone if you didn't know a spar from a spinnaker. Yet people flounder around daily in a kitchen without bothering to find out even the language of cookery. One inanity that was the mainstay of early cookbook writers and which I have never understood either: "Cook until done."

Mackerel

Sir, I say every nation has some eximious virtue; and your country [England] is pre-eminent in the glory of fish for breakfast. We have much to learn from you in that line at any rate.
—Thomas Love Peacock, *Crotchet Castle*

Fish for breakfast used to be relatively common in America—in the days when people still ate real breakfasts. Fried smelts, codfish balls and especially fried or grilled mackerel were particular favorites. As it happens, local waters are full of beautiful black-patterned blue mackerel, which have returned after wintering in the icy waters of the North Atlantic. Their firm, rather rich, pinkish flesh allows them to be prepared in most of the ways one might treat blues. (Incidentally, the blues adore mackerel even more than I do, and will be coming along very shortly to savage the mackerel population and send them fleeing to God knows where.) Here are some ways to deal with this fish while it lasts.

FOR BREAKFAST

Or lunch or dinner if you fancy it. Buy one small (1½ pounds) mackerel for each person, or a larger one to split for two. Have them cleaned and left whole or filleted, as you prefer. Slash the skin lightly in three diagonal lines. Rub the inside (or flesh side) well with salt, pepper and a touch of Dijon-style mustard. Rub the inside and outside with olive oil. Preheat the broiler for at least 5 minues. Grill the whole fish (or any fillet) according to the Canadian Fishery Council's rule: 10 minutes total cooking time for each inch of thickness, measured with a ruler at the thickest point.

This formula for cooking fish by any method—frying, broiling, baking, poaching—is absolutely foolproof. Well, maybe not literally "fool"-proof; it wouldn't work if you threw the fish onto a raging flame. Grilled fish should be turned only once to avoid breaking it (fish cooked by other means need not be turned at all, except for cosmetic effect).

You can also pan-fry the fish in either olive oil or a mixture of salad oil and butter, turning once to brown both sides. Serve the fish on a hot, hot plate, escorted by a rasher of crisp bacon. Hot corn muffins would round out a nice spring brunch.

COLD MACKEREL AS AN HORS D'OEUVRE

Maquereau à vin blanc appears often on the menus of modest French restaurants, as well as in ordinary households, because it is cheap, delicious and simple to make. You can also buy it in flat tins imported from France, but then it would no longer be cheap and an especially silly buy at a time when our own waters are alive with fresh mackerel. Make this recipe a day in advance of serving it.

Serves 4 as a first course, more as part of a cocktail party hors d'oeuvre.

2 small whole mackerel, about 2 pounds each

COURT-BOUILLON

1 cup water plus *1 cup dry white wine*
2 or 3 onion slices
1 slice lemon peel
Pinch of dried thyme (or fresh)
1 bay leaf
1 slice ginger root, about the size of a quarter (optional)

About 10 thin carrot slices
½ teaspoon salt (or more)
Grind of fresh white pepper
1 teaspoon Dijon-style mustard
Fresh parsley, minced

Have the mackerel filleted, and ask the fishmonger to remove the soft roes, if any, intact *before* he starts cutting. Fish dealers usually throw them away, so you have to be quick in asking for them.

Combine the court-bouillon ingredients and boil gently, covered, for 10 minutes. Add the fish fillets and poach gently for 5 to 7 minutes (depending on the thickness of the fish). Remove them to a cold platter, peel off every trace of skin and pull out any little bones that may be lurking. When cold, cut the fish along its natural dividing lines and then into 2-inch lengths. Lay the pieces in a shallow earthenware or china dish. Strain the court-bouillon.

Mix ½ to ¾ cups (enough to cover) of the strained court-bouillon with the mustard, and pour it over the fish. Decorate with some of the carrot slices removed from the cooking liquid. Cover with plastic wrap and refrigerate. To serve, apportion the mackerel on four small plates and spoon a bit of the juices over before sprinkling with minced parsley. For a buffet, leave your *maquereau* in its dish and provide a pie server for guests to help themselves. Of course, offer crisp crackers or toast in lieu of a plate.

Note: The roes should be poached separately about 2 minutes after removing mackerel from the court-bouillon. Arrange them among the fillets.

SASHIMI

The Japanese revere fresh mackerel as part of a raw fish platter served with wasabi (a stinging hot green horseradish paste made from a powder that can be bought in little tins from Oriental food stores), or you can substitute red pepper flakes mixed with a little soy sauce to make a dipping sauce. The mackerel for any dish should be utterly fresh and of course for *sashimi* it must be "stand-up" fresh (you've heard about "stiff as a mackerel"?). Limp fish are stale. Buy fillets and cut them into small bite-size slices, leaving the skin on.

ESCABÈCHE OF MACKEREL

If raw fish is not your dish, you may like this Mexican hors d'oeuvre, in which the fish is first sautéed, then sauced and chilled. It can also serve as a pleasant lunch dish:

Serves 6.

6 mackerel fillets (about
   ½ pound each)
Juice of 2 limes or lemons
Flour seasoned with salt and
   pepper

1 clove garlic
3 tablespoons olive oil

SAUCE

¼ cup olive oil
2 tablespoons lime or lemon
   juice
½ teaspoon ground coriander
   (or fresh, chopped)

¼ cup scallions, sliced
½ teaspoon red pepper flakes

Marinate the fish for 15 minutes in the lime or lemon juice, then flour it lightly, shaking off all excess. Sauté the garlic and fish in olive oil until golden and just done, then remove fish to a deep platter.

For the sauce, beat the olive oil together with the lemon or lime juice and the coriander. Pour this over the fish, and sprinkle it with the sliced scallions and red pepper flakes. Refrigerate, covered, until half an hour before serving; it should not be icy cold.

Moving Feasts

People really are kind and sympathetic when they know someone is going through the agony of moving house—the pain of withdrawing from a much-loved house, and resisting the impulse to dig up all your tulips and day lilies and take them along. But even with warm hand-patting and "it will soon be overs," the choice is still all yours and seemingly endless. Will I ever see my beautiful Sabatier and Solingen knives again in this lifetime?

Meanwhile, mealtimes among the packing boxes go on 'midst cries and curses. I carefully set out our little baking potatoes—no bother there—our little head of Boston lettuce and two little strip steaks for our first dinner in our new digs. We wound up more dead than alive for a late burger at a saloon after discovering, or rather not discovering: the salt, a knife, anything whatsoever to eat with, or a plate. Movers should carefully assemble a sort of hiker's backpack that will enable them to live in the ruins of a new house.

After four days of depending on the kindness of strangers and paying restaurant after restaurant, we attempted to eat lunch on our sunny deck. Still no knives, still no real kitchen to work in. We did have fire, and rude shells to eat with, so I served up a pure—oh, achingly pure—version of *Moules Marinière*. With bread and wine.

MOVING-TIME MUSSELS

This could be made and eaten around a campfire—but you absolutely must have water and fire. (There are times when these great earth signs can seem like luxuries.) A clam knife and a small stiff brush and maybe a Swiss army knife should be carried by anyone attempting to cook while in the throes of moving.

Serves 2.

2 *pounds large black mussels*	2 *tablespoons fresh parsley,*
2 *tablespoons butter*	*minced*
2 *or* 3 *shallots, minced*	1 *loaf French* or *Italian bread,*
1 *cup dry white wine* or	*heated*
vermouth	*Additional cold butter*

Wash the mussels under cold running water and clean them, following the procedure described on page 8. Soak them several hours, or overnight in the refrigerator. Should you stumble on the dry stores, a little flour thrown into the mussels helps to plump them up and rid them of sand. Cornmeal will also do this.

While you are washing the mussels, discard any that remain open when you hold them under cold running water. Unusually heavy mussels are generally full of mud and will slide apart and ruin your whole mess of mussels, so discard them, too.

Melt the butter in a heavy-bottomed pan at least 3 inches deep. Throw in the minced shallots—you can add a bit of garlic, too, if you can find it in box jungle. (This reminds me: put your pepper mill in your purse, or you may find it when looking for the spare parts to your woodstove, sometime when the leaves begin to turn color.)

Stir the shallots around until tender—there are usually odd bits of clean wood lying around if your cooking spoons still haven't revealed themselves. Put in the mussels and stir them, then add the wine or vermouth, cover the pan and cook over medium high flame, shaking the pan occasionally for about 5 minutes. When all the mussels are open, sprinkle them with parsley. Take the pan out onto the deck, porch or wherever the First Feast is to be eaten.

Bring a bottle of cold white wine (you should pack the corkscrew with the pepper mill in your purse, otherwise you will have to knock the neck off against a tree), some plastic glasses, the warm bread and some fresh cold butter to the eating site. You can use the clam knife to spread the butter, and mussels were cleverly designed as utensils as well as food: simply tear off the top shell and use it to dig out the mussel from the bottom shell. It also serves as a spoon for the juices, so eat the largest mussel first.

CELEBRATORY DINNER

This celebration was in honor of finally uncovering a box of china, glasses and eating utensils. And two knives: both of them divinely special. One, a *meluzza,* is a curved, double-handled blade Italians use to mince vegetables and herbs. The other, a spindly little French tomato knife. But we had a hammer to substitute for claw crackers, and thus I could serve the following menu for two:

Boiled Lobster with Melted Butter

Baked Potatoes

Boston Lettuce with Walnut Oil Dressing

Champagne

I presume nearly everyone knows how to boil a lobster, melt butter and bake potatoes—and wash and dry lettuce. Having packed my own refrigerator stuff, I had a bottle of French walnut oil and some homemade basil wine vinegar, which I used to make the dressing. The lobsters weighed only about 1¼ pounds, so were easy to dismember with my hands protected by kitchen towels. I smashed the claws lightly with a hammer.

This is one of the simplest and best meals I can think of. Salt was our only condiment, and I really longed for my pepper mill as I gazed at that relentlessly white baked potato. But the deprivation was softened by a bottle of champagne presented as a "new house" gift by our loyal liquor dealer, Christy.

I guess we've survived—but this is definitely it. The deer and the dogwood will just have to get used to me, because I never intend to move again as far as the two miles we traversed from bustling downtown Sag Harbor.

The Flowers Low, Low, Low

> In the year 1929, I used two rock-crystal vases in which were branches of white orchids, but those days are gone, I fear, forever, and a few white carnations have to suffice now. *Enfin*, perhaps the orchids will bloom again.
>
> —Elsie de Wolfe

It was my enormous good fortune to have found Elsie's *Recipes for Successful Dining* at a book fair here many years ago. Although some beastly person had actually *cut* some of the recipes from the little persimmon-and-black-bound book, I paid twenty cents for it anyway. I am greatly relieved to see Lady Mendl, as she later became, back in the news where she belongs, the subject of a biography written some thirty years after her death by Jane S. Smith, and high time too.

She was reputed to be the First Lady Decorator ever. There are those who dispute this, but so it goes. Somewhat sexually undifferentiated, Elsie lived a rather spectacular life with her good friend Bessie Marbury during the earlier part of this century. Her late marriage to Sir Charles Mendl was to provide both of them with a firm social base in Paris in the twenties, where she gave sublime little dinners and continued to "do" villas and apartments for a few carefully selected clients.

Elsie's career as a decorator began at thirty-nine after an amazing career as an actress—she had no talent whatsoever. But she dressed with taste and daring and people bought tickets to see her clothes. Although "outrageous" was the word most often used to describe her, the divine Miss de Wolfe's most unshakeable tenet was that one must never wear, serve or sit in anything "inappropriate." I cannot think of any better guide to "taste." What further endeared this marvelous woman to me were her exhortations to "keep the flowers low, low, low" and "the plates hot, hot, hot." You will remember that, won't you, all through any social season?

PANCAKES BARBARA

(Restaurant Walterspeil, Munich, Germany)

Lady Mendl believed that every dinner party should yield at least one "surprise." She early-on pruned her menus to only four courses, which shocked the late Victorians right off their antimacassars. Elsie wrote: "These [pancakes], to be properly served, take the *maître d'hôtel* and four other servants following in order with the different ingredients:

> First, French pancakes
> Second, vanilla ice-cream
> Third, whipped cream
> Fourth, blanched walnuts
> Fifth, hot chocolate sauce
> (This is not a joke.)

"Make thin, round pancakes (see recipe) about five inches in diameter. Serve on very hot plates. Then put on top of the pancake a tablespoonful of vanilla ice-cream; then a tablespoonful of whipped cream; then a tablespoonful of hot chocolate sauce in a trellis design and sprinkle on top blanched white walnuts which have been skinned and soaked overnight in milk to render them a pure white.

"When one is serving this dish it is absolutely necessary to keep a *réchaud,* or dishwarmer, in the dining room so that the pancakes and sauce . . ." (Here the vandal snipped out the half page for the recipe on the reverse side! But we can infer the rest: Keep your plates and pancakes, hot, hot, hot!)

The following recipes are mine—not because Lady Mendl's are unusable, they are perfectly clear—but because chunks of the original recipes were missing.

FRENCH PANCAKES

(now called crepes from Fisher's Island to Waycross, Ga.)

Makes 16 to 20 crepes.

3 eggs (U.S. grade A "jumbo")
1 cup milk
3 tablespoons melted butter
1 tablespoon sugar

2 tablespoons cognac
Pinch of salt
1 cup flour (plain or "instant")

Put eggs, milk, butter, sugar, cognac and salt into a blender (or processor) and whirl briefly. Or beat the ingredients together with a wire whisk. Add flour and blend quickly but thoroughly. Pour approximately ½ cup water in a stream through top opening until batter approximates the consistency of heavy cream. Refrigerate the batter for two hours if using plain flour or for 30 minutes if using "instant," or Wondra, flour. The granulated flour absorbs liquid and air more readily than ordinary flour, but there's no difference in the finished crepe.

Heat a small (6-inch) crepe pan or skillet to medium hot and smear it with peanut oil. Clarified butter is even better, but one must strain it carefully and remove every trace of whey or the batter will burn at the high heat required. Pour about two tablespoonfuls of batter into the center of the pan with a small ladle and quickly roll it around to coat the bottom. Pour out any excess batter as the crepes should be as thin as possible—you can trim any ragged edges.

As soon as the edges begin to curl, turn it over to brown the other side briefly. My method of doing this is to slide the crepe slightly out of the pan and turn it with my fingers. The first couple of pancakes may have to be discarded until you and the pan heat get in tune. Lay the finished crepes out on kitchen towels, then stack them between layers of wax paper. Later you can wrap them in a series of foil bundles and reheat them in the oven. Then transfer them to a hot platter and keep them on your *réchaud*—or, 'ow we say in zis countree? Salton Hotray.

Buy or make the best vanilla ice cream you possibly can, put it in a large glass bowl when it has softened enough in the refrigerator, and stir it around to look creamy.

Have a bowl of whipped cream ready.

You can buy chocolate sauce and heat it in a heavy pitcher set into a pot of simmering water or you can make this sauce:

HOT CHOCOLATE SAUCE

8 ounces semisweet chocolate   *2 tablespoons boiling water*
2 tablespoons white corn syrup   *¼ cup heavy cream*

Melt the chocolate in the top of the double boiler with the corn syrup. Add the boiling water and stir until smooth, then stir in the cream. Serve hot. Keep the sauce liquid over a candle warmer or on an electric tray.

If your *maître d'* and other servants are off for the evening, set up a dessert bar and let the guests scuffle for themselves.

Monkfish, a.k.a Anglerfish

Undoubtedly the mythologically ugly monkfish must have been one of the fabulous beasties of the deep so often sighted by medieval sailors. Its loose dark skin and huge, cowl-like flapping fins probably account for the name "monkfish." These days, however, the customer at the fish market is spared all this unloveliness: underneath that Quasimodo exterior there lie fillets of pristine, snowy flesh.

The French, who call it *"lotte,"* caught on to this delicacy a long time ago, and it is a prized (and expensive) fish in France. But here it was unloved, and our fishermen have been throwing it back as a "trash" fish until just recently. (The law of "supply and demand" means that no matter how plentiful a thing is, if anyone shows any interest in it whatsoever, the price goes up—so the price will undoubtedly not be as attractive now that monkfish is gaining respectability.)

British food writer Jane Grigson praises the monkfish's "sweet flavor and succulent firmness of flesh [which has] led some writers to compare it with lobster." Me, for one. And I find it an excellent way of extending the more costly crustaceans in a mixed seafood salad. It shares another quality with lobster, too—it easily becomes dry and rubbery if cooked too long or too violently. But monkfish, treated gently, has a firm-tender texture and a non-assertive flavor that makes it an amiable companion for a wide variety of sauces and herbs. It's sort of the veal of fishdom, except that it's fairly cheap and not raised in inhumane conditions.

MONKFISH SALAD WITH CRUSTACEANS

Assisted by a few bits of lobster and some diced shrimp, the humble monkfish turns into a princess on the buffet table. Homemade mayonnaise, now within the grasp of almost anyone able to push a button, is essential to the suavity of this dish.

Serves 8 to 10 as a main course, many more for a party buffet.

3 pounds monkfish fillet, skinned

1 small lobster (female if possible)

⅓ pound small raw shrimp, in the shell

COURT-BOUILLON

2 cups dry white wine

2 cups broth from the lobster and shrimp

½ small carrot, sliced

½ cup onions, sliced

1 bay leaf

Dash cayenne pepper

Salt to taste

½ cup celery, chopped fine (optional)

2 tablespoons chives or scallions, minced

2 cups homemade mayonnaise made with olive oil and salad oil in equal proportions (see page 150)

Steam or boil the lobster in plain salted water for 8 to 10 minutes (for a 1¼-pound lobster). Remove the lobster and let it cool. Reduce the water to a slow simmer and cook the shrimp in their shells for 1 or 2 minutes. Drain, but reserve the liquid so that it can flavor the monkfish. Shell the shrimp, put the shells back in the lobster water. Remove the sac near the head of the lobster and discard. Carefully scrape all the tomalley (green stuff) and roe or coral (red stuff), if any, into a small container. Also keep all the white, curdy stuff which are the lobster's precious bodily fluids after they've cooked. Add this to the roe and tomalley. Remove all the lobster meat, taking care to get the nuggets out where the legs join the body. Then crack all the lobster shells and legs and throw them back into the pot with the shrimp detritus. Simmer the shells, uncovered, about 20 minutes, until you have a fairly strong and reduced broth. Strain the broth.

Make the court-bouillon: Simmer the wine, broth, carrot, onions, bay leaf, pepper and salt for 10 minutes. Taste for seasoning, and let cool.

Monkfish fillets tend to be thick, so divide them along their center seam and cut each fillet into three pieces, so that it will cook evenly. Lay the pieces in a buttered non-aluminum pan (aluminum sometimes discolors wine-based stock) and strain the cool stock over the fish. Bring slowly to the simmer and poach in barely simmering stock, 10 minutes for each 1 inch of thickness. Remove to a cold plate; save the broth in case you need some to thin out your mayonnaise.

Cut the lobster into about ½-inch dice, reserving the claw tips for garnish. Dice the cooled monkfish and cut the shrimp into ¼-inch dice. If you like it, add ½ cup of finely chopped celery for a bit of crunch. Stir the chives or scallions into 1 cup of the mayonnaise, thinning it out a bit with some of the lobster broth so the salad will not be too rich and heavy. Fold it into the cooked fish and chill.

Pass the remaining plain mayonnaise in a small bowl. Arrange the salad on a bed of pale Boston lettuce mixed with some dark heads of baby Bibb, if you can get it. Sliced cucumbers, hard-cooked eggs and Greek olives are traditional and very sound choices as garnishes.

SIMPLIFIED VERSIONS

1. Omit the lobster, and proceed with just the shrimp and monkfish.

2. Omit both the lobster and the shrimp, and you still have a splendid Monkfish Mayonnaise. In this case, add 3 tablespoons of fresh chopped chives and tarragon leaves. Or you might add a touch of fresh curry powder to the homemade mayonnaise.

3. Marinate the poached, cubed monkfish in a vinaigrette made with good olive oil and a very little vinegar and serve it cold, mixed lavishly with chopped fresh dillweed.

Some Fish with Unlovely Names

A couple of hundred people rimmed the shoreline at Long Beach about sundown, all standing and staring out over the water. My first thought, as I drove past, was that someone must have drowned. But Long Beach is Sag Harbor's local beach and local people don't go swimming in May. Then I made out the fishing gear in the gloaming. I found out what was running the next day, when my electrician's wife told me that he couldn't possibly be reached until the weakfishing was over. Every year when weakfish fever strikes, East Enders can forget about home repairs for a while.

The weakfish arrive in June and they're big and handsome—running from 5 to 8 pounds on average, and even if you can't catch 'em yourself, they're cheap. The name "weakfish" puts some people off, but it connotes only their tender mouths and is in no way a slander on their character or bodies. The other official name for this delicious troutlike critter is not much of an improvement: the spotted squeteague. Croaker, drum, sea trout and grey trout are some other monikers for the same fish, but on Long Island it's best to stick with "weakfish."

Weaks have lean white flesh and can be cooked in any of the ways one might prepare striped bass. They can also be filleted and cut into pieces for frying or sautéing in butter. Well soaked in oil, they could be broiled whole over a slow charcoal fire. Weakfish is a most suitable fish for soups and chowder, as striped bass really isn't. Besides, the vogue for striped bass having run its price into the stratosphere, it would be idiotic to use such an expensive fish in a stew. The excellent, cheap and plentiful weakfish would be perfect if it didn't, like a lot of great beauties, have one fatal flaw: if it isn't superfresh—out of the cold sea and into the hot pan within twenty-four hours—the flesh becomes very soft and, to me, unappetizing. Because it runs in large schools, a lot of it must get frozen. And it must be just awful, since freezing turns far sturdier fish to flab. Freshly caught weakfish isn't just preferable, it's the *only* kind to eat.

Another common fish that has returned to Long Island waters after an unfortunate hiatus of several years is the blowfish. Possibly the least expensive fish on the Northeast coast and probably the ugliest, it is nevertheless delicious. (Although the blowfish must have heard about "The Hamptons" becoming an international resort area—I saw a basket of them at our poshest food store priced at a very posh $8.50 a pound.)

I've always been on the prowl for unfashionable or unpopular foods that are neglected by the basically conservative American eater. In the summer of 1963 I worked out the following recipe for blowfish, which was then used for fertilizer.

SEA SQUAB PROVENÇALE

Serves 4.

Sea squab is the euphemism created by sensitive fish dealers for the lowly blowfish. It is always sold cleaned, skinned and beheaded so that it resembles a very large shrimp with a backbone. Overcooking these morsels turns them into little rubber balls. I use certain elements typical of southern French cooking, hence the name for my purely Long Island invention.

1½ pounds blowfish
Salt and pepper

Flour
⅓ cup olive oil

TOMATO SAUCE

1 pound peeled, seeded and
  chopped ripe red tomatoes, or
  1 can whole Italian plum
  tomatoes, chopped
1 onion, chopped
2 cloves garlic, minced

½ cup dry white wine
½ bay leaf
Sprig of fresh thyme, or pinch
  of dried parsley
Dried red pepper flakes
  (optional)

Season the blowfish with salt and pepper and dredge lightly with flour. Sauté them in the olive oil in a heavy skillet until golden. Remove fish and set aside while you make the sauce: Chop the fresh tomatoes in a bowl so as not to lose the juice. In the same skillet, cook the onion and garlic until soft, adding a bit more olive oil if necessary.

Add the tomatoes, white wine and herbs and simmer, uncovered, for 30 minutes. (Recipe may be prepared in advance up to this point.) Return the blowfish to the skillet and let them simmer in the sauce for 5 minutes to heat through. Serve sprinkled with parsley and red pepper flakes if you like. Rice is good with this.

FRICASSEED WEAKFISH

Fish puddings and fricassees were popular in early New England cookery—a direct heritage from the old country. They have been largely forgotten, and it's too bad, because there has to be more to fish cookery than cold poached fish with green mayonnaise, the latest fad to become a royal bore. Buy a fresh weakfish and have it gutted but left whole. Best of all, try to cadge one from a fishing friend or catch one yourself.

Serves 6.

*1 5- to 6-pound weakfish,
    left whole*
2 cups dry white wine
2 whole bay leaves
2 or 3 sprigs parsley
1 carrot, sliced thin
1 onion, sliced thin
*½ pound fresh white button
    mushrooms*

¼ pound sweet butter
4 tablespoons flour
1 cup heavy cream
2 cups fish broth (from above)
2 tablespoons minced chives
1 tablespoon minced parsley
Cayenne to taste

Wash the fish in cold running water. Remove the head if necessary, but put it into the pan with the fish. Cover the fish with cold water and throw in a little salt. Add the white wine, bay leaves, parsley, carrot and onion. Bring slowly to the simmer and skim if necessary. Cover and barely simmer (let "tremble," as the French say) for approximately 10 minutes per inch of thickness. Slashing the body in the thickest part at three or four intervals will help the fish to cook more evenly. It is imperative not to overcook weakfish. If you have time, it is best to boil the fish head and the other ingredients in advance, so that the flavors are more intense.

When the fish is done, remove it to a platter, skin and bone it, cut in large chunks and set aside. Strain the fish broth and measure out two cups. Reserve the remainder for a soup or stew—it will keep in the freezer for a few weeks.

Wash, trim and dry the button mushrooms. Sauté them in half the butter and set aside. Melt the remaining butter in a heavy saucepan and stir in the flour to make a roux. Cook, stirring, over low heat a couple of minutes. Heat the cream and fish broth to boiling, then, off heat, beat the roux into it quickly with a wire whisk. Place the saucepan on an asbestos pad and let it simmer over very low heat about 10 minutes, stirring often.

Add the herbs (*fresh* only) and cayenne, and taste for salt. Add the mushrooms and their juices and the fish chunks. Heat thoroughly but do not boil. Serve this over rice or short biscuits, or in puff-pastry shells.

A fresh, crunchy green salad made from a selection of spring lettuce—no cucumbers or foreign matter—is the best and only accompaniment this dish needs. Keep the dressing simple: use a good olive oil flavored with a few drops of lemon juice, and skip the garlic, which would overpower the delicate fish dish.

A Diety Dinner in Spring

Part of the secret of success in life is to eat what you like and let the food fight it out inside.

—Mark Twain

A food philosophy much to be admired in this age of crank fads, diet madness, compulsive eating and anorexia. Unfortunately, however, few of us keep the splendid metabolism we had at eighteen and the food begins to fight a losing battle with the fat at some point. Regular exercise, such as pushing away from the table, becomes necessary.

Since I know that I cannot stick with anyone else's prefabricated diet, I simply devise meals of as few high-calorie foods as possible and cook them simply. I don't enjoy this at all. Very plain cookery is boring, but if the basic ingredients are exceptional (I treat myself to luxuries like lobster and expensive embryonic green beans), the whole process can be made tolerable. No one can convince me that food cooked without salt or salads served naked are anything but a penance, but one can cook with *less* salt and pass the dressings and sauces separately. My meals, diet and other, are always shared with anywhere from one to seven people, who may or may not wish to share my strictures. Here's a dinner designed for this time and this place and guests who may or may not be overweight.

Menu

Spring Greens with Chèvre
Charcoal-roasted Chicken Tarragon
Stir-fried Snow Peas, Scallions and Mushrooms
Chive Cornbread
Fresh Pineapple with Kirsch

SPRING GREENS WITH CHÈVRE

Lettuces are at their peak, and the selection is diverse at the better roadside vegetable stands. Buy a mixture of Bibb, ruby leaf, oak leaf, lambs' tongues or young spinach or any of the soft leaf lettuces. Serve this salad first so that it gets the attention it deserves, and also curbs the appetite. Important salads should always be served first and plain little green salads last, as *digestifs* in the French manner.

Serves 8.

Large bowl of mixed lettuces,
washed, dried and chilled
in plastic bags
⅓ cup French olive oil
(such as Plaignol)
2 tablespoons fresh lemon juice
Salt and freshly milled pepper
to taste

¼ pound soft, fresh chèvre
(such as Bucheron—the tart
flavor and somewhat dry
texture of goat cheeses make
them ideal with salads)

Just before serving, mix the olive oil with the lemon juice and seasonings. Carefully blend it with the greens, using your hands to avoid crushing the tender soft lettuces. Crumble the goat cheese over the top and serve at once.

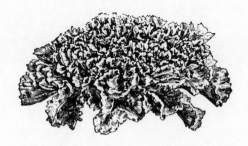

CHARCOAL-ROASTED CHICKEN TARRAGON

You will need the kettledrum-type charcoal grill, such as a Weber or a Smoke 'n Pit, which have covers. Both have drip pans and are equipped to maintain a slow fire for several hours. It is best to follow the directions that come with your particular grill (but not the recipes, which are generally just awful).

Hot-smoking with apple or cherrywood chips is a super-succulent method of cookery, but takes much longer than the Weber grill method. Both are effortless; they just take time—about three hours to charcoal roast and about eight hours of smoke cookery for this size bird.

Serves 8.

1 *fresh-killed roaster, about*	*Handful of tarragon sprigs*
6 *pounds, drawn weight*	*Salt*
¼ *pound sweet butter*	*Pepper*
(1 *stick*)	2 *cups dry white wine*

There aren't many small chicken farmers left, but if you can find one, buy your chicken from a local farm. Do not use frozen chicken. This simple preparation really requires a fine, fresh, well-flavored chicken. If you have the time, put the bird down in a plain cold brine and refrigerate it for five or six hours. Then dry it well and proceed.

Rub the inside of the chicken with some of the butter, stuff it with the tarragon and sprinkle inside and out with salt and pepper. Truss the bird and snap its wings behind it. Rub in the remaining butter.

When your coals have burned to a fine white ash cover, put in the drip pan with the wine and enough water to fill it. Put the rack over the pan, lay the chicken on it, cover and roast for about 20 minutes to the pound. You may have to add live coals after an hour or two.

Take a 1-quart juice can and punch four or five holes around the base with a beer-can opener. Put charcoal in this, drench it with starter jelly or whatever you use, and let it burn until coals are red hot. Using tongs, pick up the can and add the coals to your existing fire. You should use lots of coals to begin with because of the length of time the fire needs to burn. (Most people don't realize it, but their fires are at their best for cooking for a couple of hours *after* they have removed their food from the grill!)

Remove the chicken when it reaches an interior temperature of around 170° F. (Most books advise 185° F., but I think this is excessive and very drying.) If you have no meat thermometer, use the old reliable—puncture with a sharp fork at the thickest part of the thigh. If the juices run yellow, the chicken is done.

If you want a slight smoky flavor without the whole smoking process, soak a big handful of hardwood chips and throw them on the fire just before laying the chicken on the grill.

The bird may also be roasted in the oven, but if you use this method be sure to baste frequently with melted butter. Spit-roasting, either in the oven or on an electric rotisserie, produces a moist, juicy bird, effortlessly. If you have a spit for your charcoal grill, you can achieve a truly spectacular result.

Let the chicken rest for at least one hour before attempting to carve it. Hot chicken will simply shred and the juices run out instead of retreating into the chicken flesh where they belong. There's no point in trying to keep a large roast bird really hot, because it will be tepid by the time it is carved anyway. If you wish to serve hot roast chicken, it is best to cook a number of small birds and split them at the last minute.

STIR-FRIED SNOW PEAS, SCALLIONS AND MUSHROOMS

Snow peas are raised locally now, and the early ones I've had are among the best things I've tasted all spring. Stir-frying is done in a twinkling, so everything else must be in readiness and the vegetables cut up in advance.

Serves 8.

1½ pounds baby snow peas
2 bunches scallions
½ pound fresh white
* mushrooms*

½ cup plain vegetable oil
1 clove garlic, peeled
Salt and pepper to taste

Wash and dry the snow peas; put them in a plastic bag. Wash, trim and cut the scallions into diagonal ½-inch pieces, including half the green tops. Quicky rinse the mushrooms, pat dry, trim and slice rather thickly. Put them and the scallions in a plastic bag and refrigerate along with the snow peas.

After the salad is served and the chicken carved, heat the wok, pour a necklace of oil around the interior rim and roll it around to coat the surface. Sauté the garlic over medium heat until golden, then discard it. Toss in all three vegetables and turn the heat up to high. Stir and toss the vegeables about 3 minutes. Season with salt and pepper. Turn them into a colander set over a bowl to drain off all the oil. Put them in a warm serving dish and serve at once.

CHIVE CORNBREAD

Make your favorite cornbread recipe. Before baking—either in a square pan or in muffin tins—stir in a large handful of fresh snipped chives. The pungent herb serves to distract the palate a bit and make the lack of butter less grievous. Serve butter to the lucky non-dieters, because cornbread is at its best dripping with butter (you can see why the diet became necessary in the first place).

PINEAPPLE WITH KIRSCH

Obviously there is never any pineapple in a "Long Island Larder"* unless it comes from far Hawaii or Mexico. It is never as sweet or deeply flavored when we get it here as in its native habitat; still, it is a very good thing. Buy it a day or two in advance to ripen.

Split the fruit lengthwise, then slash it in opposite diagonals. Finally slide a sharp thin knife between the flesh and the skin to release the diagonal cuts. Leave the slices in place, wrap the halves tightly in plastic wrap and refrigerate until serving time. Serve on a platter and pass a bottle of chilled Kirsch for each diner to douse on as he sees fit.

* "Long Island Larder" is Ms. Ungerer's regular column in the East Hampton *Star*.

Berrying

Strawberry fields are definitely not Forever. In fact, the blushing *Fragaria* demands rather intensive care, and even with that, bears only two crops in three years before it's ploughed under and the farmer starts all over again. So all you nice, considerate berry pickers will understand the farmer's testiness when *those other people* stomp all over the little plants. A single plant provides about 1 pint of fruit per season.

During about two and a half weeks in June, the South Fork's annual abundance of America's most popular berry is in the fields. Some growers welcome pickers with children in tow. Others, adults only, and most definitely nobody wants your wonderful, friendly dog to tag along. Many farmers would just as lief pick their own crops—mainly because of plant damage and the tension that mounts when an occasional Greedy-Gus tries to pile 2 pounds of berries in a 1-quart basket. Quart baskets are designed to hold about 1½ pounds of strawberries.

How to Pick Berries
To pick fully ripe average-sized berries without bruising them, slip your index and second fingers behind a berry with its stem between your fingers, twist the stem a bit and pull with a sharp jerk; the stem will snap off about ½-inch from the berry. If the berries are large and thick-stemmed, cradle each one in your hand and pinch off the stem between your thumbnail and index finger.
—From the Time-Life *Encyclopedia of Gardening*

Note: Don't waste time hunting behemoths; your labor becomes uneconomical and size doesn't really matter—only ripeness. Also, just as in clamming, if you see that someone else has found a mother lode, don't traipse over to his turf.

Once you've bought or picked them, get your strawberries out of the sun and home to a cool place. Ideally, they should be eaten the day they're picked. Failing this, refrigerate them unwashed and well covered with plastic wrap, as these luscious, dimpled beauties deteriorate quickly. If you're going to freeze some or make jam, pick early and get on with the job before day is done.

CHILLED STRAWBERRY SOUP
WITH CANTALOUPE

Bob Wilford, chef-owner of a well-run little Wainscott restaurant* with the discreet
charm of the bourgeoisie, gave me this invention of his.

Serves 6.

1 quart fresh strawberries, washed and hulled	1 teaspoon grated lemon rind
1 cup orange juice	1 tablespoon lemon juice
1 tablespoon instant tapioca	1 cup buttermilk
⅛ teaspoon allspice	4 to 6 ounces ripe cantaloupe (small, thin pieces)
⅛ teaspoon cinnamon	Grand Marnier to taste (Don't overdo this.—M.U.)
½ cup sugar	

Reserve six fine berries for garnish and purée the remainder in a blender. Combine
the purée and orange juice in a 4-quart saucepan. Dissolve the tapioca in a bit of
cold purée and stir it into the rest of the purée. Heat the mixture slowly, stirring
constantly, until it comes to a boil and thickens. Remove from heat and add sugar,
spices, lemon zest and juice, mixing well with a wooden spoon. Let cool thoroughly
before stirring in the cold buttermilk. Chill for eight hours or overnight. Do not
add the cantaloupe and Grand Marnier until just before serving as the melon will
get mushy and the liqueur just disappear. Garnish each bowl with a reserved berry.

Iced fruit soups are Scandinavian in concept and are usually served as a first
course. However, there's nothing to stop you from having strawberry soup for
dessert.

---

* Mr. Wilford, to my regret, closed his restaurant to devote his time to catering for the carriage
trade.

S·U·M·M·E·R

Fourth of July Picnic

The Glorious Fourth is traditionally the most rollicking holiday on the American calendar. Marching bands, fireworks, picnics and beach parties—how awful if the Founding Fathers had decided to make their Declaration of Independence on, say, the Fourth of February! I can think of no other holiday that is, almost by national decree, a picnic.

Besides food, glorious food, fireworks—the most thrilling display seen by eighteenth-century eyes—still dazzle. The East Hampton Fire Department sets off its wonderful annual show at Main Beach every Fourth when darkness falls, and George Plimpton, our town's best-known pyromaniac, touches off another spectacle at the Duke estate that goes to benefit Boy's Harbour.

For these outings, a blanket, a basket of good things and something to drink must be brought. It's safest to assume that there won't be any barbeque grills available at public events, but private picnics usually feature some outdoor cooking.

One of my favorite "bring-your-own-grub" July 4th festivities used to be the artists' picnic at Georgica Beach. Syd Solomon, the Abstract Expressionist painter, would find a bedspring from somewhere every year and build a great roaring bonfire under it. You could see everything roasting on that bedspring—from kielbasa to dainty little lamb chops. Alas, that is no more.

Beach food really should be simple to eat and require as little temperature control as possible. Beer, wine and soft drinks should be all one has to fuss with cooling. Watermelon coexists with beer in a big icy tub and is, of course, *the* classic dessert for the day. Most kids, as well as adults, adore the big rosy melons. I, to my regret, developed a childhood indifference to this handsome all-American, because it appeared incessantly on the family board, bench or back porch. (Watermelon makes a nifty fruit ice, however.) Rich, melting, messy fried pies filled with fresh strawberries are my favorite picnic sweet.

Tradition rules with a tyrannical hand wielded by my daughters when it comes to national holidays. I would like to order a huge box of *sushi* for my picnic, but I'm usually stuck with frying eight zillion pieces of chicken and stuffing dozens of very unsophisticated deviled eggs. Over the years I have managed to edge in baby green beans vinaigrette (which can be easily eaten with the fingers), and my own version of pipérade.

PIPÉRADE

A sort of egg pie, this Basque dish may be served hot, warm or at room temperature. It is primarily a melange of sautéed vegetables held together with beaten egg, cooked slowly in a skillet then browned under the broiler. It can be made in advance, although I don't think it profits from refrigeration.

Serves 6.

¼ cup olive oil
6 scallions, peeled and sliced fine
⅓ cup cooked potato
(a left-over baked one is
excellent), finely diced
½ cup zucchini, shredded and
squeezed dry
2 mildly hot long Italian
peppers, seeded and julienned

1 ripe tomato, peeled, seeded
and diced
3 slices prosciutto, julienned
¼ cup fresh parsley, minced
8 "jumbo" eggs
Salt and pepper to taste
¾ cup Parmesan or Romano
cheese, grated

Heat the oil in a large (10-inch) non-stick skillet. Add all the vegetables and cook gently over low heat a few minutes, then add the prosciutto. Beat the parsley into the eggs, add salt and pepper and pour over the vegetables. Amalgamate the mixture gently and let cook over very low heat for about 10 minutes, or until the top is still a bit runny. Sprinkle with cheese and brown under the broiler for a very few minutes, just until it puffs up and takes on a little color. Slide it out (do not fold) onto a foil-covered paper plate to take on a picnic. Let it cool, uncovered, then slice it in wedges, and wrap it up until needed.

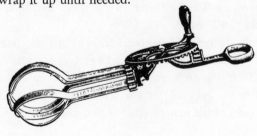

SMOKED GAME HENS

This was another of my efforts to escape the Great Fried Chicken Tyranny. If you haven't a smoker, you can roast the little darlings in the oven or on a covered barbeque grill. But smoking is best. The Lil'Chief electric smoker will accommodate eight of these at once and many people will be content with just a half of the plump little hens.

Wash them well in cold water, discarding the neck and giblets. Then put them, untrussed, into a cold brine made thus: Boil 1 quart of water with ½ cup of coarse salt and 2 tablespoons of Mixed Pickling Spice (it comes, already mixed, in a little white box). Add this to enough cold water to submerge the birds. The brine must be cold—add ice cubes if it isn't. Put in the birds, weight them down so they will not float above the brine and put them in the refrigerator overnight.

Next day, dry them lightly, put them on the smoker rack and set them in front of an electric fan for about an hour. This gives them their beautiful shiny look. Lower the rack into the smoker, which has been pre-heated, put in your pan of hardwood chips and let the birds hot-smoke about five or six hours. You can add another pan of wood chips after a few hours if you prefer a heavily smoky flavor. These are really delicious served with a homemade herb mayonnaise, but are quite fine plain and they pull apart easily and require no utensils.

If there's going to be a grill available, take along some sweet and hot Italian sausages, pre-poached in wine, some bratwurst or kielbasa, or some chicken wings marinated in olive oil, herbs and lemon juice. The wings cook quickly to a crisp succulence, and you do not have to hang around the grill taking up all the space. No one should bring anything to a communal grill that requires more than 5 or 10 minutes cooking time.

Mount Ararat Menus

... And summer's lease hath all too short a date ...
—William Shakespeare, Sonnet XVIII

Have faith, summer folk, we're bound to have a spate of hot, sunny weather before summer's lease, and yours, ends.* Rain or shine, summery food makes every aspect pleasanter, and mousses, soufflés and sherbets are just the airy concoctions to brighten up victims of cabin fever. What's more, most can be made ahead at some quiet moment before all the hilarity breaks out.

The food processor, bless it, has taken most of the drudgery out of the puréeing and pounding and mincing that used to make this type of food so delightful for the guests, so onerous for the cook. If there's one appliance a summer house needs, it is certainly the food processor, since a whole year's worth of entertaining is frequently crammed into these three short months. The following recipes require either a processor, an Oriental chef or an accomplished chopper and pounder willing to sacrifice a piece of his summer to the greater culinary good of his fellows.

CUCUMBER MOUSSE

Fresh crabmeat in mayonnaise or shrimp boiled in beer are lovely with this pale, delicate vegetable mousse. It is also good with any cold sliced leftover roasts or cold fish and shellfish salads. The cucumber mousse is the very essence of summer, a wonderful adjunct to other food, but too insubstantial to be served alone. All the herbs must be fresh, not dried. The mousse will keep one or two days in the refrigerator, tightly covered, without coming to harm.

* The rain poured almost ceaselessly during June of 1982, and much of the northeastern U.S. was flooded.

Makes approximately 1 quart.

1 long (about 14-inch)
   English-type cucumber or the
   equivalent in regular
   cucumbers to produce 1½ cups
   cucumber purée
Salt
2 envelopes plain unflavored
   gelatin
¼ cup cool water
1 cup watercress leaves, loosely
   packed

¼ cup scallions, minced
1 tablespoon tarragon, minced
2 tablespoons parsley, minced
1 tablespoon chives, minced
¼ teaspoon freshly milled white
   pepper
1 cup sour cream
4 tablespoons mayonnaise
Salt to taste
2 tablespoons boiling water

The long, thin-skinned "English" cucumbers, if grown in greenhouses, are seedless and "burpless." As a rule they need not be peeled, but in this mousse the skin would be obtrusive. So, peel them, halve them lengthwise and scoop out seeds, if any. (Field grown, they may have some seeds.) If you must use regular cucumbers, pick out long, thin, firm young specimens with no yellowing places. Peel and seed them, cut them in chunks and salt them lightly. This is to rid them of any possible bitterness —which should be minimal in really fresh cucumbers. After 30 minutes, rinse, drain and dry them. Purée in the food processor and measure out 1½ cups.

Meanwhile, sprinkle two envelopes gelatin over the ¼ cup of cool water. Put the watercress leaves, scallions, tarragon, parsley and chives in a small bowl, and pour a little boiling water on them. After 2 minutes, drain and refresh with cold water. They will be a brilliant green. Drain and pat dry. Add the herbs and all remaining ingredients (except the gelatin and boiling water) to the processor, including the cucumber purée. Process until smooth and well combined. Pour the boiling water into the gelatin and stir until liquefied. Pour this into the processor and turn it off and on a few times to distribute the gelatin thoroughly. Taste for seasoning. Pour mixture into an oiled 1-quart mold and cover it tightly with plastic wrap. Set it in the refrigerator for about six hours or, better still, overnight. Invert on a platter and ring with watercress branches and sliced cucumbers and whatever seafood or sliced meat you have chosen. Smoked chicken breast is fine with the cucumber mousse, especially if you have made a good fruity mayonnaise to go with it.

DOUBLE PEACH SHERBET

The amber taste of peaches sparkles in this simple dessert. In addition it has a crunchy texture, though not so icy as a *granita,* which is made with water. This is a basic recipe and requires no ice-cream machine. It may be used with any puréed fruit or berry and a change of liqueur to suit each flavor. I find bourbon to be particularly good with peaches, but if you don't care for it, a few drops of almond extract also complements peaches. Two pounds of ripe peaches yields approximately two cups of purée. The first cup is to make the sherbet and the second to make the sauce, thus making it doubly "peachy."

Makes approximately 2 quarts.

2 cups peach purée
Juice of half a lemon (or more)
1 cup sugar
3 cups milk

¼ teaspoon vanilla extract
¼ bourbon
2 egg whites

Buy the peaches several days before you need them, as they invariably require this long to ripen. Lay them in a single layer in a warmish dark place, NOT on the windowsill. Drop them into a pot of boiling water for a count of 20, then immediately drain them and plunge them into a basin of ice water. The skins will slip off easily when you cut around the natural division of the peach.

Squeeze the lemon juice into a glass mixing bowl, then skin the peaches one by one and remove the pits. As you do so, turn the halves immediately in the lemon juice to prevent discoloration. (If you can find it, an ascorbic acid powder called "Fruit Fresh" can be dissolved in water to prevent the discoloration of any fruit you might be working with.) Add more lemon juice if necessary, to coat the peaches well. Chop them roughly and purée them in a food processor. Remove one cup for sauce.

Blend all the other ingredients in the contents of the processor except for the egg whites. Whip these to a soft meringue, then fold the contents of the processor into the whites. Cover with plastic wrap and set the mixture in the freezer. Stir after an hour. After two hours, transfer the sherbet and spin it smooth in the processor. Unless you have a large-bowl processor, this will have to be done in halves. Put it all back in the same bowl, cover tightly and freeze two more hours. Finally, about an hour before serving, put it through the food processor one more time, pack it back into a container, cover and let freeze again.

The peach sauce is made by simply sweetening the remaining cup of purée to your taste, adding a splash of bourbon or brandy and mixing it well. The sauce will be a dark amber, but very attractive on the paler sherbet. Temper the sherbet in the refrigerator for half an hour before serving it in small frozen glasses. It tends to melt extremely quickly.

Herbs, Fresh and Preserved

> There's rosemary, that's for remembrance ...
> —William Shakespeare, *Hamlet*

It's also for pork and lamb, and, according to medieval herbalists, a sure-fire complexion aid when infused in white wine. For centuries, women, in their traditional role of guardians of the family's health and bellies, were generally conversant in the uses of herbs, both medicinally and in cookery. But the Industrial Revolution reduced herb cookery to the addition of a lonely sprig of parsley lolling on the plate, for decoration only.

Fortunately, this sad trend has reversed dramatically in recent years, especially among a younger generation interested in fresh foods, herbal remedies and cosmetics.

And where, you may well ask, are these splendid herbs available? In Suffolk's East End fields, (and on everyone's windowsills) where once the most exotic herb findable was basil. What's more, many of them are at their peak now and should be dried or frozen for winter use. (Actually, I am not much in favor of frozen herbs, because they tend to go limp and blackish upon thawing.)

The Green Thumb, greengrocer to the stars in nearby Water Mill, does a brisk business in herbs now. "Five years ago I had never even *heard* of coriander," said the owner, "but a good customer asked us to grow it and we did." They didn't sell

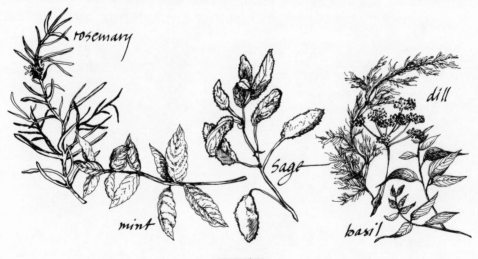

much of it; but that pre-dated the Chinese cookery craze (it is also much used in Indian and Mexican food) but now it is in popular demand. The Green Thumb also plants purple and green basil, tarragon, thyme, upland cress, orange and plain mint and spearmint, dill, oregano, sage and marjoram.

Over on the un-chic Noyac Road near Sag Harbor, The Other Stand offers the most amazing display of ancient herbs I've seen locally except in a hobbyist's garden. Lemon balm, lavender, hyssop, comfrey, rue and pennyroyal are now pushing up where beans and potatoes used to grow. Fred Sands is the young farmer whose produce fills The Other Stand and I asked him why all these uncommon herbs. "I think herbs are sort of fun," he replied. And he must mean it, because he grows a fine array of kitchen herbs too: oregano, sage, marjoram, winter and summer savory, sweet fennel, chervil, coriander, dill, chives and several kinds of mint for tisanes and garnishes. And there is fresh catnip for fussy felines.

Home-dried or preserved herbs are so much superior to any you will ever be able to buy that I strongly urge everyone to put by at least a few personal favorites. Dried herbs can never, of course, compare with the flavor of fresh herbs, but they are certainly indispensable in winter. Herbs that don't dry well can be beautifully preserved in either light olive oil or mild white wine vinegar (harsh, cheap vinegars are quite pointless as they assassinate the herb flavor).

Herbs dried or preserved on the stalk have a much more intense flavor than if the leaves are stripped (dried leaves should never be crushed or ground until you are ready to cook them). Tie them in bunches—wash and dry them only if they really need it—soon after cutting, and hang them upside down in a cool, dim, airy place. To keep off dust and light—and the depredations of my cats—I dry herbs, stalk end up, in thin brown-paper bags punched full of pencil holes. After the herbs are dry—in one to two weeks—store them as whole as possible (on the stalks if you have room) in air-tight plastic containers or Mason jars. Before filling the jars, slide a piece of typing paper inside the circumference to block the light. Label and date your herbs. Some last better than others, but none will survive more than a year.

Large olive jars are good, because of their long thin shape, to pack with tarragon, dillweed, basil or other branch herbs you wish to preserve whole in oil or vinegar. Put the stalks stem end down so that the leaves float upward, realistically. These should also be stored in a cool, dim place. (What we all really need is an old-fashioned larder—a small, cold, well-ventilated pantry to keep food cool without refrigerating it. Although I'll admit it is often necessary, refrigerating fruits and vegetables, especially herbs, seems to radically deaden their flavors.)

But to get back to the summer's herbs in all their aromatic fresh glory, here's a simple dish that glorifies them.

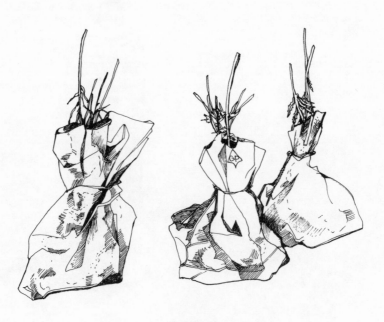

HERBED POTATO SALAD

This salad uses all the four culinary horsemen—parsley, tarragon, chives and chervil —that compose the classic *fines herbes* in a French omelet. Chervil is hard to find, and if you can't get it, put in another herb that appeals to you and is compatible, such as coriander or marjoram.

Serves 6–8.

3 pounds small new potatoes,
  red or brown
¼ cup dry vermouth
1 tablespoon fresh tarragon
  leaves, chopped
1 tablespoon fresh parsley leaves,
  finely chopped
1 tablespoon fresh chive,
  finely snipped (or, if you
  must, substitute scallions with
  their green)

1 tablespoon fresh chervil,
  minced (omit if not available
  fresh)
2 tablespoons wine vinegar
1 teaspoon Dijon-style mustard
1 teaspoon salt
½ cup good olive oil
  (not *tasteless salad oil*)
Freshly ground pepper

FOR GARNISH

Mediterranean black olives and
  hard-boiled eggs

Some spotless leaves of soft
  lettuce

Scrub the potatoes well with a soft brush under cold running water. Start them in cold salted water to cover and cook until just done (or steam them)—usually no more than 15 minutes depending on size. They should not exceed 1½ inches in diameter. Drain them and turn out onto a towel. When cool enough to handle, quarter them *without peeling* and sprinkle the pieces with the vermouth, which should be warmed first.

Sprinkle the potatoes with all the herbs. Shake together in a small jar the vinegar, mustard, salt and olive oil and pour it over the potatoes while they are still a bit warm. Grind on fresh pepper to taste. Gently turn the salad with your hands to avoid breaking the delicate potatoes. This salad should be served tepid—or at least at room temperature—arranged on lettuce leaves and garnished with black olives and a few hard-boiled eggs cut in quarters.

A platter of thinly sliced Westphalian ham or domestic smoked beef, and a dish of transparently thin sliced cucumber marinated in a mild vinaigrette would make a fairly effortless and lovely Sunday lunch.

HERB BUTTERS

These can be made and frozen for future use. A little pat does miracles for a steak or broiled chicken or fish. As soon as possible after it is picked, chop the leaves of your favorite fresh herb and mash 2 tablespoons of it into ¼ pound of sweet butter, along with a few drops of lemon juice. Scrape it onto a piece of plastic wrap, roll it tightly into a little sausage shape, seal it with freezer tape and store in the freezer.

Illusions and Transformations

If you aren't up to a little magic occasionally, you shouldn't waste time trying to cook.

—Colette. *Prisons et Paradise*

Those exponents of plain cooking who insist that, for instance, a good piece of fish "doesn't need anything" are only half right. The cooking of almost anything needs touch, control and that quirk of imagination that makes an ordinary dish special and memorable. Even the greatest fish, sparkling fresh from the sea, cannot be just hurled onto the broiler time after time after time. If man did not forever hare after variety, the art of cookery as well as some other pursuits would have ended in stasis some centuries ago.

Specifically, I've been thinking about what is done with swordfish (broiled), scallops (fried) and squid (squinted at distrustfully). As these three things are in good supply at this time of year—not *bay* scallops, which are absolutely out of season, but the much larger scallops, which are in season all year—and the weather is hot, what better moment for a rather unusual *seviche*. At the American Hotel in Sag Harbor they make it with bluefish, which is similar to the original mackerel version and it's very good. But I prefer it made with a variety of white, non-oily fish "cooked" in lots of fresh lime juice. The lime's citric acid turns a raw, translucent piece of fish an opaque white. Thus it *appears* to be cooked, which generally satisfies, at least esthetically, those who flinch at the thought of raw fish. Although it probably really wouldn't need it, when I introduced squid into this Mexican fandango, I sautéed it gently first, because squid has a way of going very "fishy" indeed, very quickly. But it has a lovely texture and absorbs other flavors gorgeously. I must admit that squid rings, unadorned, look, and I suppose taste, like wide rubber bands. But, as I said, there are an awful lot of them around in midsummer and a little imagination transforms them into a nifty summer dish.

SEVICHE

This is one of the most refreshing of summer appetizers, and is quite simple to make. The flavoring of the hot chilie peppers is extremely important, and so is the use of lime, rather than lemon juice. So please do not play with these two aspects of the recipe. Other kinds of fish may be substituted once you are acquainted with the basics of seviche.

Serves 4 to 6.

3 or 4 medium-sized squid
4 chunks of swordfish (about ½ pound)
½ pound sea scallops
3 fresh, plump limes (about ½ cup juice)
1 tablespoons olive oil
1 clove garlic, peeled
2 medium-sized small, ripe tomatoes, skinned, seeded and chopped into ½-inch dice

3 canned chilies serranos, seeded and chopped, or 2 pickled jalapeños, or chopped fresh hot chilies to taste
1 small red onion, sliced into thin rings
¼ cup olive oil
Salt and freshly milled pepper to taste

GARNISH

1 ripe avocado, sliced
Lemon juice

1 tablespoon fresh coriander, minced, or parsley

Note: It is not enough to "make do" with a sprinkle of cayenne. These chilies, as well as being quite piquant, have a flavor and texture that are necessary. Fresh raw jalapeños are the most fierce of the chilies you are likely to come by at farm stands or in some of the open-air markets in New York—Koreans and Thais have a taste for them. (When handling fresh chilies, wear rubber gloves and be sure to wash both them and your hands with soap and water after you have finished seeding and chopping the hot chilies.)

Clean the squid by pulling out and discarding the soft insides, head, tentacles and the transparent triangle—a sort of spine—that looks like some plastic gadget left there accidentally. Rinse off its filmy veil of skin with cold water, or rub it off with a paper towel. Dry the squid and cut it into rings across its pocket-like body. Set them aside.

Swordfish chunks are a bit cheaper than the steaks and are recommended because the fish is to be cut into ½-inch bits anyway. Rinse and cut the scallops into pieces the same size. Put these in a deep narrow, non-metallic bowl—a Pyrex soufflé dish is ideal.

Squeeze the limes and pour their juices over the swordfish and scallops. Warm the olive oil in a small skillet and sauté the garlic until golden. Discard it. Add the squid rings and sauté quickly over medium heat for a couple of minutes only. Turn them out on a plate to cool, then add to the other seafood and lime juice. Cover tightly and refrigerate for about four hours. Stir the seviche occasionally; do not marinate too long, or the lime juice will toughen the fish. If the seviche seems too watery, discard some of the lime juice. About an hour before serving, add the chopped tomatoes and chilies, onion rings, olive oil, salt and pepper to taste to the fish and mix well. Cover.

When ready to serve, peel the avocado, slice it and roll the slices in lemon juice to prevent their darkening. Portion out the seviche on small plates, and decorate it with slices of avocado and the minced coriander. Coriander (also known as cilantro and Chinese parsley) is used widely in both Mexican and Chinese food. It isn't always easily obtainable in fresh leaf form, so when plentiful, chop some in a food processor and freeze it, mixed with a little water, in ice-cube trays. Then pop the cubes out and store them in a plastic bag in the freezer.

FISH *RILLETTES*

Rillettes are normally made with pork or game, furred or feathered, and sometimes with tame ducks and geese. It is slowly cooked, pounded to shreds and put up in a nice crockery jar to be brought out for guests to spread on hard toast. Since there seems to be such latitude in both the ingredients and the making of *rillettes,* I decided to try the technique on leftover fish. I had some baked weakfish, too good and too much to give the cats, and one smoked porgy and a little homemade mayonnaise in the fridge. I liked the result of this expedient hors d'oeuvre so much I made it again deliberately. It's nice to cook a little extra fish at one meal so that you can look forward to another lovely and quite different dish the next day.

Makes about 3 cups.

*10 ounces (approximately 2 cups)
    leftover fish, loosely packed
1 average-sized whole smoked
    porgy (about 1 pound)
2 small cloves garlic, peeled
¼ cup scallions, minced*

*2 tablespoons olive oil
2 teaspoons white wine vinegar
¼ cup mayonnaise
Salt and white pepper to taste
2 tablespoons minced parsley*

Discard all skin and bones and flake the leftover fish and the porgy. This is quickest done with the fingers. Mince the garlic in a food processor. Add the fish and all remaining ingredients except the parsley and turn the machine off and on a few times until you have a well-mixed but fairly rough, light-textured fish pâté. Taste and adjust salt and pepper, then add the parsley to the bowl of the processor and barely blend it in.

Serve the *rillettes* with some dry toast or crackers and some good, strong, oily black olives.

Variation: The East End abounds with smoked bluefish much of the year. It makes spectacular *rillettes*, but because of its sometimes soft texture, smoked bluefish is more safely shredded by using two table forks or one's fingers before adding it to the remaining ingredients.

Midsummer Berries

Doubtless God could have made a better berry [strawberry], but
doubtless God never did.

—Izaak Walton, *The Compleat Angler*

There are many who would take issue with that opinion—chiefly raspberry lovers.
As they often do, our strawberries came and went with such dizzying speed, it's
reminded me to keep a close watch on the raspberry interval. Raspberries in the
Northeast are only in season a very few weeks, and they do not travel well. Their
scarcity and value are as emeralds almost everywhere except on the North Fork of
Long Island, which is two ferry rides away from me. It's well worth the trip, because farmers there will let you pick your own for about $2 a quart. Apparently all
raspberries ripen within the same few weeks, so there is a glut that must be picked.

This part of the world used to be covered with wild berries; there are still plenty
of beach plums for jelly making, but I have not seen any wild blackberries recently,
or blueberries. Some of our farmers keep patches, mostly for their own use, and
will occasionally let a few friends in to pick their own. But real estate development
has wiped out most of the old berrying haunts—many of them forty or fifty years
old and still producing fine berries. To know a luscious secret patch is one of the
satisfactions lost to me, but we can still buy excellent berries for preserving from
many of the North Fork farmers. I have put in a few raspberry canes of my own;
the birds love them.

Jams and jellies are very simple to make, as are plain preserves, and all are worth
their weight in sugar nowadays. When sugar was cheap (before our troubles with
Fidel), commercial jams and jellies were so inexpensive it was hardly worthwhile
to make your own. Except that somehow the homemade product always tasted
better. Even now, you probably won't save any money by making these lovely things
yourself, but the satisfaction is immeasurable. *The Ball Blue Book of Caninng and
Freezing* (published by The Ball Corporation, Muncie, Indiana) gives the best
instructions I know of for these processes. The booklet can be bought in hardware
stores and other places that carry canning supplies.

It's particularly nice to be able to make up your own combinations, such as
raspberry jam with kirsch. Use the bottled pectin given in *Blue Book* recipes. It is
not an artificial additive, but a natural substance found in ripe fruits and berries.

Some, such as apples, have lots of it, and others need help if the jam or jelly is ever to set. The alternative is endlessly cooking the lovely fresh berries to a brown sludge in order to make them stiff.

The French preserving jars with rubber gaskets and wire bails are extremely pretty, but also extremely hard to seal properly. You cannot process them in a boiling water bath as is recommended for safekeeping over a long period of time. If you do wish to use them (they make splendid house gifts), seal the preserves, jellies, whatever, with melted paraffin as per instructions in the *Blue Book,* and rely on the glass tops only to keep out dust. You cannot sterilize paraffin-sealed preserves after they are bottled.

The most convenient jars are the Ball or Mason jars, specifically, the wide-mouth type with metal dome lids and screw-on bands. These can be sterilized after filling, or they can be frozen. You may, of course, use any thick, boilable glasses for jams and jellies, but they must be sterilized *before* filling, the hot preserves ladled into them at once and, after cooling, must be sealed with two very thin layers of melted paraffin. Home-made preserves need no refrigeration until they are opened. However, ideally, they should be stored in a cool, dark, well-ventilated place.

It's not necessary to make three dozen jars of any one item—my maternal grandmother never thought in terms of less than three dozen—because modern recipes are for smaller, nuclear family quantities. Freezing, if one just wants the fruits and berries for desserts, is even easier than canning. But staring into a freezer doesn't have quite the thrill of looking at pantry shelves lined with Mason jars of summer-bright fruits and vegetable relishes.

The first blueberries usually arrive in July, whether the High Bush berries from Maine, local wild berries or commercial cultivated ones. The jumbo commercial ones, though they are attractive in a fruit compote, have almost as little taste as raw zucchini (which is successful only as a conveyor of highly seasoned dips). Blueberries, briefly cooked with a little sugar—no water—make a queenly sauce for vanilla ice cream.

BLUEBERRY DUMPLINGS

These dumplings are from a collection of Carolina "receipts" contributed by the ladies of Beaufort, S.C. Don't be condescending; some of their other recipes are for Perigord Pie and Quail Soissons.

Serves 6.

"½ cup butter
1 cup flour
1 teaspoon baking powder
1 tablespoon sugar
Pinch of salt

4 tablespoons milk
   (approximately)
1 quart blueberries
¾ cup sugar
2 cups water

"Cut butter into flour, baking powder, sugar and salt. Add enough milk to form a stiff dough. Mix berries, sugar and water and bring to a boil. Drop dumplings [use a wet teaspoon—not a measuring spoon—to scoop out the dough and push it off with your finger—M.U.] into hot berries, cover and cook slowly for 30 minutes. Do not remove lid [until time has elapsed—M.U.]. Serve with cream." [This means plain, unwhipped heavy cream—M.U.]

RASPBERRY CREAM TART

An evaluation of your net worth is what determines how many raspberries you may use in this recipe. I used a modest pint: a quart would be both more *and* better.

Serves 8.

1 pastry shell made with
   almonds
4 eggs (grade A, "extra large")
2½ cups milk
⅔ cup sugar

2 tablespoons bourbon
Grating of nutmeg
1 pint raspberries
¾ cup sugar
Few drops lemon juice

Add ½ cup ground almonds to any standard pie-crust recipe for a single 9-inch shell. Bake this in a pre-heated 375° F. oven for 15 minutes, remove and cool.

Beat the eggs, milk, sugar, bourbon and nutmeg together in a heavy saucepan. Cook, whisking over low heat until the custard begins to thicken. Cool slightly, pour into the half-baked pie shell and bake on the center rack of a 350° F. oven for about 20 minutes, or until firm. Remove and cool.

Mix the raspberries and sugar lightly, sprinkle with lemon juice and cook them in a heavy saucepan *with no added water* over low heat for 2 or 3 minutes. Cool and spread gently over the surface of the cooled pie. Chill well and serve with whipped cream.

RASPBERRY VINEGAR

If you've wondered why this elixir sells for such an outrageous price, the following recipe should explain all. When this was written, though, it is clear that raspberries were commonplace on American tables. Emma Paddock Telford was the food editor of the New York *Herald* in 1908, and this is from her book, *The Good House-keeper's Cook Book*.

"Put two quarts raspberries in a stone jar and cover with one quart good cider vinegar. Cover closely and stand aside for two days. At the end of that time mash the berries and drain off the liquid. Pour this over a third quart of fresh berries and set away for another two days. Strain and allow to each pint of juice one pound sugar. Cook gently for five or ten minutes. Skim, strain and bottle. Vinegar prepared in this way will keep indefinitely, and a teaspoonful added to a glass of water makes a most refreshing and healthful drink."

Back to Basics

Bad cooks sin against food in two conspicuous ways: carelessness and overdoing things. One is too slapdash to really read a recipe, the other too hellbent on improving on it without a trial run. In the case of lamb and fresh green beans, both plentiful now, something terrible has happened in the way of a pendulum effect.

Where once cookbooks instructed people to immolate these two lovely foods, now they're served barely transformed by their brief skirmish with fire. Lamb is not supposed to be blood-red and mushy, nor are green beans supposed to be served hard and starchy. Pink, tender, juicy lamb with a pleasantly browned exterior, and succulent deep-green beans with a crisp-tender texture are the ideals. There is an exact point at which both these simply cooked foods are precisely right, and they demand close and constant scrutiny by the cook. That, of course, is the kicker about all quickly cooked foods.

GRILLED BUTTERFLIED LAMB

Fifteen years ago this was a novelty on the charcoal grill. It became wildly popular, if not particularly well executed. Most butchers nowadays know how to "butterfly" a leg expertly. It should be opened for boning on the thin side of the leg, so that it will be of a fairly uniform thickness and not too ragged. Have the butcher remove the fell (tough membranous covering) and most of the fat. Be sure you buy fresh American spring lamb, as I cannot vouch for the success of this recipe using that flavorless frozen lamb from New Zealand.

Serves 6 to 8.

1 whole "butterflied" leg of
   lamb (6 to 7 pounds)
2 cups dry red or white wine
   (white wine alters the lamb
   flavor less, so I prefer it)

2 cloves garlic, crushed
Salt and freshly milled pepper
Olive oil

Marinate the lamb in the wine and garlic for a couple of hours at room temperature, turning it several times. (This tenderizes it, but young lamb should be tender anyway, so unless you have a large leg from an older animal don't fret if you haven't time for marinating.)

Build a rather large charcoal fire about an hour before you think it's necessary. Flaming coals are responsible for a burnt exterior and raw meat. When the coals have burned for at least half an hour, spread them out in an area large enough to match the area of the spread-out lamb. In another 5 or 10 minutes, when the coals are red through and covered with white ash, they are ready for cooking. The grill should be shielded from the wind. Have a pitcher of water and a bulb baster or plant atomizer at hand to extinguish any flames that flare from the dripping fat, which should be minimal. Be sure the water hits only the coals, not the meat.

Dry the meat, rub it well with coarse salt, pepper and oil. Some cooks rub the lamb with rosemary or thyme as well, but I have come to treasure the pure flavor of the lamb. The grill should be scrubbed clean with a wire brush, dried and oiled before each use. All that burnt residue contributes nothing but evil to the flavor of grilled food. Lay the lamb, fat side down, on the grill and cook it for about 20 minutes. You must keep constant watch and put out any flames with a tiny squirt of water. Turn the meat and grill it another 10 to 15 minutes.

Remove lamb to a cutting board and take its temperature with a thin, instant-read food thermometer, which should read 140° F. (Those big clumsy thermometers that are inserted in the meat before cooking have never given me satisfactory results, and they make an enormous hole in the meat from which the juices flow.) If you lack a thermometer, make a tiny incision at the thickest part. It should be a dark pink—medium rare. If it is not, put the lamb back on the grill for an additional few minutes.

Let the lamb, still on the cutting board, rest in an oven that has been turned on and then off, so that it is just a bit warm. In about 10 minutes the juices will withdraw into the tissues instead of rushing out into the gravy well of the board when you slice the meat, fairly thinly, across the grain. Use a long, thin, very sharp knife and work as quickly as you can, laying the slices in an overlapping pattern on a warmed platter, or onto individual warmed plates. Pour the *jus* over the meat.

Cold grilled pink lamb is superb. But as there is almost never any left over, it is usually necessary to grill expressly for a cold service and conceal it in the back of the fridge until serving time.

BASIC FRESH GREEN BEANS

Also known as French beans (in England), snap beans (in the South) and string beans (a lot of places). One of the difficulties of cooking fresh beans properly is 1) the way they are picked—helter-skelter, big ones and little ones mixed together, and 2) when they are left on the vines to grow too old, too big and too tough. Ideally, green beans should be no larger than ¼ inch in diameter and about 3 inches long. At least a few of the local farm stands are beginning to pick beans smaller and offer them, at an understandably premium price, presorted from their overgrown brothers (I guess *somebody* must think that big is better; they sell). Anyway, once you get your beans home, wash them promptly and drain them well on a towel. Put them into a large plastic bag with a lot of air around them and close the top with a twist-tie. This creates a mini-climate for the beans, and they will stay fresh and crisp for four or five days in the refrigerator. (The reason I know this is because I always buy more than I need for one meal.) I regard fresh baby green beans as a delicacy almost on a par with early asparagus.

Serves 4.

1 pound fresh small green beans	*A basin of ice water*
3 to 4 quarts boiling salted	*3 tablespoons butter*
water	*Salt and pepper to taste*

Top and tail the beans, and rinse them. Bring 3 to 4 quarts salted water to a full rolling boil and start adding the beans, a handful at a time. They should be moving in the water like pasta. This is entirely contrary to the home-ec. school of food writing, which stresses waterless cooking and vitamin conservation no matter how badly the food turns out. My method produces beans of an intense flavor and color, and I'm certain the quick cooking traps all those precious vitamins and minerals. If you are cooking only a small amount you can steam the beans, but this is tricky and you must test them after 3 minutes and every minute thereafter.

When the beans turn deep green and have a slight translucence, take a test bite of one. It should be crisp-tender, not hard and crunchy. Insufficiently cooked beans remain too pale a color and have a raw, starchy taste. Young fresh beans should be cooked just *à point* after about 4 or 5 minutes—but your tooth is the test.

Pour the cooked beans into a colander, then dump them into a waiting basin of ice water with plenty of cubes in it to set their color. After 1 minute, lift out the beans and spread out on a kitchen towel to dry. Now you can toss them in butter just long enough to heat through. Or you can store them in a closed plastic bag for later use, either hot or as a cold salad with vinaigrette dressing. This becomes Green Beans Mimosa when you decorate the top with alternating circles of white and yolk of egg, minced. For hot beans, an airy Beurre Blanc (see page 138) flecked with parsley makes a festive dish worthy of serving as a separate course.

Pasta Thoughts

> Futurist cooking will be liberated from the ancient obsession of weight and volume, and one of its principal aims will be the abolition of *pastasciutta*.
>
> —Filippo Marinetti, Italian Futurist poet, 1930

Signor Marinetti got no further with his campaign to wean the Italian people from pasta than his friend Mussolini did in regimenting them. And I, doubtless, will go down ignominiously before the onslaught of cold pasta salads plunked down on every buffet table from Westhampton to Montauk.

Does anybody here remember when pasta was served *hot?* In *hot* soup plates. In fact, does anyone remember when pasta was called spaghetti, or fettucine, or linguine, and not "*paw*hsta?" There are no cold, gluey, farinaceous salads in any of my Italian cookbooks.*

This whole beastly fad was foisted on us by a caterer who existed in Amagansett about ten years ago. His famous ziti salad! How the other caterers latched on to it! And then private hostesses. Why, it was so *cheap,* so *easy*—and so incredibly *boring*.

I'll admit that the wish simply to fill up the ravening crowd feeding like piranha at the cocktail party becomes overpowering. But how can anyone think that his or her guests wish to go on gnawing away night after night on an everlasting parade of spirals, tubes, screws, shells, strings or elbows of *pastasciutta?* Give them bowls of boiled new potatoes and some homemade *aïoli*. This would be even cheaper and, at least, a change.

There are several summer pasta dishes I admire—none of them cold. Instead, the

---

* Exception. Marcella Hazan, a conservative cook if ever there was one, included in her second book, *More Classic Italian Cooking,* a recipe for *Insalata di Spaghetti*. It combines some conventional elements of Italian cookery and it is served not cold, but at room temperature. Ms. Hazan says, on being introduced to the notion of cold noodles in a Japanese restaurant: "Up to then I had always been convinced that eating cold pasta was an unnatural act, but at that moment I knew there had to be dishes with cold pasta that would be very good." Indeed there are—it's just the monotony of these mayonnaise and sour cream concoctions that really seem more Pennsylvania Dutch than Italian. *Attenzione,* a newish magazine that celebrates the Italian heritage, had a recipe for a pasta salad that very much resembles *Spaghettini Puttanesca* ("Harlot style") served tepid. It would probably be even better served hot.

Waverly Root's encyclopedic *The Food of Italy* does not acknowledge the existence of cold pasta in any form.

fresh vegetables of the season are used to enhance freshly made, quickly cooked *tagliatelle*. Fortunately, there is no need to slave away at making your own pasta during hot days because excellent fresh egg pasta is shipped out to the hinterlands from Greenwich Village almost every day. Both thin *tagliatelle*, sometimes erroneously called fettucine, and the thinner noodle, which is properly called *tagliarini*, are usually obtainable. Both noodles come in either green (spinach) or yellow (plain)—the spinach has no effect on the taste and it is very pretty mixed with the other, as in the well-known *Paglia e Fieno*.

PASTA DI VERDURE

Fresh pasta cooks almost instantly—2 or 3 minutes for most shapes. *Tagliarini* is done by the time the water reboils after adding the pasta. Therefore, simple and quickly made though it is, this sauce must be completely ready before the pasta is committed to the water. Warm flat soup plates containing a little melted sweet butter should be at hand.

Serves 6 as a main course,
12 as a first course.

THE SAUCE

¼ cup olive oil
2 cloves garlic, minced
1½ cups diced, unpeeled
   eggplant
1 large, pale-green Italian
   pepper, seeded and julienned
2 tablespoons fresh thyme leaves
1 tablespoon fresh marjoram
   leaves

4 pounds red ripe tomatoes,
   skinned*, seeded and chopped
6 to 8 scallions, sliced, with
   some green remaining
Salt
Red pepper flakes

* To skin tomatoes quickly: Drop them in a large pan of boiling water and count to twenty at about the rate water leaks from a tap. Drain the tomatoes and plunge into cold water. Core them with a small knife and the skins will slip off easily.

THE PASTA

¼ pound sweet butter (1 stick)   *Freshly grated Asiago or*
1 pound fresh green tagliarini   *Romano cheese*
1 pound fresh yellow tagliarini

Put a large stockpot containing at least 8 quarts of salted water on to boil. Add a splash of oil.

Heat the olive oil in a large deep *sauteuse* (a high-sided skillet) and slowly sauté the garlic along with the eggplant and Italian pepper. Do not brown. Turn off the heat and throw in the herbs. Stir. Add the tomatoes and scallions. Stir everything together and season to taste with salt and the red pepper flakes (these are quite potent, so have a care). When you toss the pasta into the boiling water, turn on the heat under the sauté pan just enough to warm the sauce but not cook it any further.

Variations: You might like to change the sauce a bit with the addition of some black olives, capers and/or anchovies *à la Puttanesca.* As all of these things are salty, withhold salt from the basic sauce.

Divide the butter among the pasta bowls and set them in a warmed oven for the butter to melt.

Cook the pasta. (You can, of course make this dish successfully with any decent store-bought thin spaghettini or fettucine, though it will not be so light and digestible a dish.) You must begin testing fresh pasta for doneness the instant the water re-boils. Do not overcook it, or you will have irretrievable mush. Do not rinse it in cold water. Drain it in a large wide colander (any colander less than 12 inches in diameter is useless) and divide it among the warm soup plates immediately.

Spoon the sauce evenly in the center of each plate of pasta and serve at once. Pass the grated cheese at table.

VEAL MEDALLIONS WITH MUSHROOMS

Occasionally *Plume de Veau* veal can be found in supermarkets at less than the usual stratospheric price. However, it is generally cut so maladroitly as to be almost unusable. If you are going to have veal at all, it is best to have it custom cut. (A butcher at a supermarket once explained his veal's raggedness to me by saying that of course the loin chops *had* to be cut by machine! Which is a little like cutting diamonds with a sledge hammer.) I managed to salvage four not-too-dissimilar chops out of the carnage in order to make this dish. They were served with the *Pasta di Verdure*. As all these dishes are made rapidly at the last minute, it would probably be unwise to attempt the combination unless you are quite experienced or have a good Second Chef in the house. If not, you could serve the medallions with something easily prepared ahead of time, such as a pilaf.

Serves 6.

6 veal loin chops, about ½ pound each	Salt and pepper
Milk	½ pound fresh whole button mushrooms, cleaned
Flour	⅓ cup Madeira
¼ pound sweet butter (1 stick)	Fresh parsley, minced
2 tablespoons salad oil	

Even if you do not manage to get the finest white veal, *Plume de Veau,* this can still be made quite successfully with "bob" veal, which is overaged calf and more on the pink side, but still very tender. Trim away all the bone, fat and sinew and freeze the trimmings to add to your stockpot. You should have six lovely round medallions of veal, each about a ½-inch thick. Flatten them lightly with the flat of a cleaver. Soak them in milk for half an hour. Dry the veal and dredge it lightly in flour, shaking off excess.

Melt half the butter with all the oil in a heavy skillet. Over a medium flame, sauté the veal gently until just cooked through, about 5 minutes on each side at most. Turn with tongs and do not puncture the meat. Salt and pepper the medallions as they cook. Remove them to a warm platter and keep warm.

Add the remaining butter to the skillet and when it melts, add the mushrooms all at once and cook them quickly, bouncing them around the pan about 3 minutes, so that they brown but remain firm and crunchy. Add the Madeira and scrape up the pan juices. Put a spoonful of the mushroom sauce on each serving and sprinkle with a little fresh parsley.

Mako Shark

O, the shark has pretty teeth dear, and he keeps them pearly
white—
> —Bertolt Brecht, translated by
> Marc Blitzstein, *The Threepenny Opera*

The mako shark, whose rosy-fleshed steaks can be enjoyed from midsummer until September, hones his ferocious pearly whites on schools of fast-swimming fish such as mackerel and herring. Unless you are fool enough to jump into the sea forty miles offshore and strike a pugnacious attitude, you have little to fear from the mako. He preys on the highly prized swordfish (perhaps out of sheer spite) for which the mako is often substituted in public eating places. This would be dandy with me, as I much prefer the finer-grained, juicier flesh of the mako.

Restaurateurs used to defend their subterfuge by saying that people will not eat shark if they know what it is. The real reason, of course, is that swordfish costs twice as much (at least) in the wholesale fish market as mako. But mako is gaining respectability, and is not quite the bargain it once was. It is a mild-flavored, firm, meaty fish of boundless versatility, which can and should be treated more like veal than swordfish. As it is not oily, mako is not at its best charcoal-broiled except in small quickly cooked chunks *en brochette*. It is excellent baked in cream or sautéed in plenty of butter or olive oil. Served with a voluptuous, lemony hollandaise, the mako can outswank the costly swordfish any day. The lovely orange-flavored version of hollandaise known as Sauce Maltaise is an unexpected, but delicious, alternative (Grate the entire rind of an orange into the hollandaise.)

The shark is wonderful cut in skinny sticks, dipped in beer batter and deep-fried to make crisp little morsels acceptable even to fish-haters. Serve these as an hors d'oeuvre with the garlicky mayonnaise known as *aïoli,* or just with lemon wedges.

One of my favorite ways to eat this firm, close-textured fish is as *sashimi,* the Japanese raw fish hors d'oeuvre. Mako is not amenable to poaching. And whatever you're going to do to it, avoid buying mako steaks from Pleistocene giants that can weigh up to 1,000 pounds. In my opinion, the best market weight for this fish is from 75 to 120 pounds. Sport fishermen bring in most of the mako, as commercial fishermen ignore it in favor of the highly marketable and more expensive swordfish. Thus the supply may be a little uncertain, but keep asking and the demand will be met.

MAKO BAKED IN CREAM

The steaks are generally cut about 1¼ inches thick, sometimes a bit thicker. There is almost no waste and the center bone is easy to remove. I always remove the skin too; it's tough and adds nothing to the flavor of the fish.

Serves 4.

1 mako steak, about 1¼ pounds
2 tablespoons butter
½ cup shallots or white onions, minced
1 sprig fresh parsley, 1 sprig fresh thyme, 1 bay leaf

Salt and pepper
2 cups light cream, heated
2 egg yolks
Scraping of nutmeg
1 tablespoon fresh parsley, minced

Preheat the oven to 400° F.

Remove the center bone from the fish steak. Cut the fish into pieces along its natural seams, then divide the two larger pieces again, making four thick pieces and two small "belly" pieces. Take a small, very sharp knife and, pressing the blade against the skin, begin pulling it away from the flesh—as if you were skinning a slice of liver. Butter a baking dish that just holds the fish pieces together in one tightly packed layer.

Sauté the shallots (or white onions) in a bit of butter and put these and the parsley, thyme and bay leaf in the baking dish. Salt and pepper the mako and lay it over the herbs. Heat the cream and pour it over the fish, which it should cover by about ¼ inch. Dot with a little more butter, cover with a double thickness of foil and put in a preheated oven. Check after 20 minutes, and remove the mako the minute the thickest pieces are no longer translucent. Do not overcook this fish or it will be dry and tasteless. Cover and keep it warm while you quickly make the sauce.

Strain off the liquids into a small heavy saucepan and discard the herbs. Beat the egg yolks and whisk in some of the hot cream. Then whisk the egg yolks back into the saucepan and cook over very low heat until it thickens—a few minutes. Off heat, grate in a sprinkling of nutmeg and correct the seasonings. Pour over the fish, strew it with fresh parsley and serve hot.

MAKO *EN BROCHETTE* (SKEWERED)

Although I don't regard mako as a good candidate for broiling, here it is cut into tiny chunks that cook too fast to dry out. The inspiration for this is *yakitori,* bits of chicken broiled on thin bamboo skewers. This Japanese technique is very successful for mako. The bamboo skewers are superior to metal for fish because food doesn't slip around on them. They come in cheap little bundles in Oriental food stores.

Serves 4.

1 pound boneless, skinless mako
8 slices bacon, slightly cooked
10 large scallions (approximately)
⅓ cup Japanese soy sauce
  (or Kikkoman teriyaki sauce)
1 piece green ginger root,
  size of a quarter, grated

2 tablespoons rice wine or
  dry sherry
1 tablespoon toasted sesame
  seeds (optional)

Soak the bamboo skewers for an hour in cold water. Cut the mako into cubes about 1 inch square. Cut the bacon to match. Skin the scallions and cut into 1-inch lengths, using a little of the green part. Push a hole through the thick part of the scallion with a thin metal skewer, as the bamboo isn't sharp enough to do this.

Thread the mako, bacon and scallions on the skewers, using about three pieces of fish to each, with bacon and scallions in between. Make a sauce of the remaining ingredients mixed together. Put the skewers in a shallow bowl and pour the sauce over them to marinate for about 15 minutes. Turn the skewers in plain cooking oil, then broil the brochettes on a hibachi or other gentle charcoal fire for about 8 to 10 minutes, turning them often. The marinade makes a nice dipping sauce or it may be poured over the fish when it is taken from the grill. Although this is usually a first course, it could serve as a meal if the brochettes were laid across steamed rice and served with a few little side dishes.

SASHIMI

Mako has a splendid texture that makes it perfect for eating raw. A reliable fish dealer will tell you if the fish is fresh enough (which should be *very* fresh indeed) to serve raw if you just tell him that's what you plan to do. The mako eats only other fish, lives in deep, cold water, and has a more sophisticated elimination system than many other sharks, which pass their wastes through their skin. The mako has a conventional system, and is a very clean machine.

Skin and bone the mako steak and divide it into convenient pieces as described in the recipe for Mako Baked in Cream, page 82. Slice the chilled fish across the grain, either ¼ inch thick or transparently thin, as you prefer. Arrange on a chilled plate and cover with plastic wrap; serve within the hour.

You may serve it in the French style, "*nu et cru,*" with lemons and freshly milled pepper, or with a Japanese sauce.

The commonest dipping sauce is made of soy sauce, a little wasabi (green horse-radish powder mixed with cold water to a stiff paste), rice wine and a few table-spoons of dried bonito. If you can't get the bonito, the sauce will still be good, but the wasabi is essential. I often ask weekend guests to bring me some Oriental supplies from the many Japanese, Indonesian and Chinese groceries in New York, but I find many of the things even way out here in the country. A growing number of supermarkets, nationwide, have "exotic" food departments in which most of these ingredients can be found.

August Laments and Cures

I have dined too long off delicate food:
I am now in far too coarse a mood:
Bring me . . .
Garlic soup and a smoking mess
Of fish unknown to bouillabaisse!
—George Slocombe, "Plaint of a Perverse Palate"

I am certainly not one to knock the fruits of ambitious cooking, but there comes a time—usually on Mondays and Tuesdays—when I crave something hot and straightforward. A dish of good, simple pasta with an uncomplicated sauce is just the thing to comfort the beleaguered weekend stomach. Or a soothing fish gumbo to be spooned up with no thought of other courses—a satisfaction in itself.

There is fresh okra to be had—those unique green pods from Africa that were introduced through the West Indies and now are a treasured ingredient in the cookery of the American South, where they were once known as "lady fingers." (Okra is actually a member of the hibiscus family, and produces gorgeous, red-centered yellow flowers.)

After a shambling start to this summer, local field tomatoes, rich, luscious, inimitable, will be with us for a couple of months. Both of the following dishes take advantage of this wonderful season. As I only eat and cook with fresh tomatoes in their season, I risk becoming a tomato bore during August and September. I even make tomato jam—this has not been received with wild enthusiasm except by the most adventuresome palates.

TAGLIATELLE WITH SALSA CRUDA
(Pasta with Uncooked Tomato Sauce)

As the sauce is prepared in advance and left to mature at room temperature, there is no jarring effect of cold, raw tomatoes on hot pasta. The sauce is warmed by the hot, hot pasta in the hot, hot soup plates. If the kitchen is on the cool side, it is wise to warm the sauce very slightly to tepid. The uncooked sauce is particularly fine with flavor-absorbing fresh yellow *tagliatelle*. This is easy to make in a pasta machine and, moreover, can be bought in a number of specialty food shops.

Serves 4.

THE SAUCE

4 pounds ripe, meaty tomatoes, skinned, seeded and chopped into ½-inch dice (for procedure, see page 78)

2 tablespoons shallots, finely minced

1 tablespoon fresh marjoram, minced

1 tablespoon fresh parsley, minced

1 or 2 bottled jalapeña chilies (optional)

Freshly milled pepper

10 imported black olives, pitted*

Salt to taste

* Either Italian, Greek or French cured olives—California producers stand pat with their watery, canned giant orbs, apparently oblivious to what olives are supposed to taste like.

THE PASTA

1 pound fresh egg pasta (tagliatelle or tagliarini) or ¾ pound dry pasta such as spaghettini

1 gallon boiling salted water

4 tablespoons olive oil

½ cup freshly grated Parmesan or Romano cheese

Put the diced tomatoes in a china bowl and stir in the shallots, marjoram and parsley. If using the jalapeñas, which are very hot, mince them as finely as possible or put them in a food processor, then scrape into the tomatoes. Grind in some pepper, and add the olives. Do not add salt at this point; it extracts too much juice from the tomato pulp. Set the sauce aside, loosely covered, for up to two hours before it will be served.

When ready to cook the pasta, remember that fresh *tagliatelle* and *tagliarini* are done in just moments—you cannot turn your back on it or it congeals into a hopeless mush. Keep it moving briskly in the boiling water. About 1½ to 3 minutes, depending on thickness, usually does it. Spaghettini should be *al dente,* but this matter is up to you. Some imported brands cook in about 5 or 6 minutes after the water returns to the boil—other brands take a bit longer. Keep testing until it is barely tender "to the tooth."

The pasta should at once be drained and divided among four hot pasta plates, each containing a tablespoon of good olive oil. Warm the *Salsa Cruda* slightly, salt to taste and put a generous serving in the center of each mound of pasta. Serve with the freshly grated cheese on the side.

FISH GUMBO SOUP

A true gumbo is generally conceived of as a thick brownish stew of a number of ingredients plus okra, cooked to a sludge. This dish is my own invention and spots me as a renegade Southerner because I cook the okra for only 5 minutes! People have been burned at the stake for less egregious heresies. This recipe makes excellent use of leftover baked or poached fish. As it is a one-dish meal, rather a large quantity is allotted for each person.

Serves 4.

1½ pounds cooked white fish
2 quarts fish fumet
3 tablespoons olive oil
1 large onion, thinly sliced
2 cloves garlic, minced
1 tablespoon hot Vindaloo
   curry powder

2 pounds red ripe tomatoes,
   peeled and finely chopped
1 pound fresh young okra
3 cups cooked white rice
Salt to taste
Minced fresh parsley

Skin and bone the fish if necessary and pull it into small chunks. If you have no *fumet* on hand, buy a large fish head (from a white-fleshed fish) and put it into cold water with a small carrot, sliced, a few sprigs of parsley, a small onion, sliced, a bay leaf, a teaspoonful of "crab boil" seasonings and a bit of salt and pepper. Simmer it all together about 20 minutes. Fish *fumets* are not improved by long cooking; it makes them bitter. Strain the *fumet,* salvage what flesh you can from the fish head and discard the debris.

Heat the olive oil in a large heavy pot, such as an iron dutch oven. Stir in the onion and garlic, and cook over gentle heat until tender, but do not brown. Add the curry powder and stir over low heat several minutes to cook the spices.

Add the tomatoes to the *fumet*. Add the fish, and simmer all together about 10 minutes. Slice the stem end off the okra pods, then slice the pods into rounds about ¼ inch thick. Throw these into the soup and simmer another 5 minutes, or until the okra is just crisp-tender. Stir in the cooked white rice, add salt to taste and serve in big bowls sprinkled with parsley.

As you have fish, a starch and vegetable all in one dish, there really isn't much else needed. Some good bread and cheese with chilled grapes, or a light fruit dessert or sherbet could be a satisfying conclusion to this summer stew. I realize that not everyone shares my view that an interesting soup or stew is a fine meal unto itself.

Invasion of the Pods

Burpee Hybrid Zucchini. 50 days. Excellent flavor, astounding hybrid vigor and exceptionally heavy yields make this one of our most popular vegetable varieties . . . best eaten when 6 to 8 in. long, when texture is most tender.
—*The Burpee Seed Catalogue*, 1980

The Burpee prose style often runs to lush hyperbole, but this particular entry is an example of masterful restraint. Zucchini, a cucurbit scarcely known outside of Italian kitchens a mere decade ago, is on the verge of becoming a culinary pest. (Restaurants adore its cheapness and availability.) Their vigor is truly astounding: I think it has even astounded some farmers.

Once when I was buying corn at a farm stand I was offered free zucchini as a bonus. They were the size of calabashes, so I took just two of the smallest I could find. Vegetable marrows, as the English call them, have to be picked often and small —from 6 to 8 inches long is the optimum size. At this point they are tender and crisp, have only tiny seeds and skins so thin they needn't be peeled. But as every home gardener knows, your zucchini patch can look like an invasion of the Pods almost overnight.

Since my monster zucchini were a well-meant gift, I decided to see if they could be pounded or pummeled into something not only tolerable but delicious. I did a lot of zucchini research several years ago when I was the sharecropper of the novelist Jean Stafford, and we were up to our snoods in this prolific squash. In the course of that zucchini infestation I developed and published a recipe for a delicate, pale-green cold soup, which was made of whole baby squash. This one, which has been worked out to take advantage of the all-too-plentiful overgrown specimens, is entirely different in flavor. I doubt that many people could detect the jolly green giant that is the basic ingredient of this creamy pale beige soup. Victims of zucchini rampant will welcome this anonymous quality.

BOMBAYSSOISE

This is an intriguing cold soup tingling with the spices of India. I make my own garam masala from a recipe given me by a cooking friend from Bombay. The recipe follows (see page 92), but it is rather expensive to make because of its multitudinous ingredients.

A masala—garam just means "hot"—is a mixture of various sweet and pungent spices; they are ground, then toasted or fried before being added to a great many Indian dishes. Indian cooks grind a different mixture for every dish they make. I am not quite that industrious, and make up an all-purpose masala that lasts several months in a tightly closed container kept in a dark place. It is a scintillating blend of flavors that prepared curry powder from the supermarket has very little in common with. In the absence of a homemade masala, buy a good brand of curry powder that is stamped "made in India." Sun Brand Madras, for example. There are other good brands of course (they must be made for the British market, since Indians don't use them). The hottest spice mixes come from the southern states. Those marked "Vindaloo" are always quite fiery.

Makes approximately 2½ quarts.

4 tablespoons unsalted butter
2 fat cloves garlic, minced
2 medium onions, sliced (about
  1 cup)
4 cups zucchini, peeled, seeded
  and sliced
1¼ cups raw potato, peeled
  and diced
1 teaspoon salt
2 teaspoons very hot curry
  powder (or homemade masala)

⅛th teaspoon ground allspice
⅛th teaspoon ground cloves
3 cups thin chicken broth
  (see Note)
2 teaspoons fresh lemon juice
1½ cups light cream or
  half-and-half
Salt to taste

Melt butter in a heavy 4- or 5-quart pot. Add the garlic, onions, zucchini and potatoes, turning them well in the butter. Add salt, cover the soup pot and "sweat" the vegetables over very low heat for about 10 minutes, or until they are soft. Stir them from time to time and do not allow them to brown in the least or you will have a mud-colored soup.

Push the vegetables to the sides of the pot and put the spices in the center. Stir them a little until they form a paste. Simmer for a couple of minutes. Pour in the chicken broth, add the lemon juice and simmer all together for about 20 minutes.

Strain the broth into a pitcher and purée the vegetables in a processor or food mill after they cool off a bit. Do the vegetables in two batches if using a processor, using the light cream to thin and cool the purée. Re-combine and purée with the broth, stirring well. This should be a smooth, rather thin soup, not in the least like those ersatz vichyssoise made puddingy with massive doses of sour cream. Taste for salt and chill the soup four or five hours or overnight. When it is quite cold, taste again, add more salt if necessary. I also add a dash of cayenne as I prefer the soup highly spiced. This is not for the faint-hearted if you are using strong, fresh curry powder or a homemade masala.

Note: Using homemade chicken broth in soups that will be served cold can be tricky, as homemade broth is generally quite gelatinous. Ergo, one might wind up with an unpleasant texture when the soup is chilled. Always thin out your broth with cold water, so that you can gauge the proper consistency, *before* you add it to the hot soup base. Canned chicken broth or that made with cubes or packets of powder answer fairly well in this rather highly flavored soup. If you are not a fan of spicy food, you may omit the cayenne and lessen the amount of curry powder. But if you dull it down too much, the soup will be refreshing but unexciting.

HOMEMADE GARAM MASALA

For the Indian cook this is somewhat the same basic spice mixture as the French *quatre épices*. This masala is an infinitely more complex arrangement of flavors than that found in commercially prepared "curry powder." Stored in an airtight bottle in the refrigerator, the masala keeps its pungency for at least six months. Spices bought from Middle Eastern or Indian grocers are immensely cheaper than the bottled ones in the supermarket.

Makes approximately ¼ cup.

¼ teaspoon grated nutmeg

1½ teaspoon cumin seeds

1 teaspoon whole cloves

2 teaspoons cinnamon (crushed stick)

2 teaspoons black cardamom*

2 teaspoons white cardamom

2 teaspoons black peppercorns

Toast the spices in a heavy iron skillet over very low flame, stirring often, for about 20 minutes. Crack the cardamom pods and discard the outer husks, retaining the tiny black seeds. Put these and the remaining spices in the blender jar and grind to a fine powder—well, as fine as the blender will get it. The final pounding can be done with a mortar and pestle. The ideal tool for grinding the spices would be an electric coffee-bean grinder, but I don't see how the machine could ever again be used for coffee. I have a *tava,* a sort of thin black iron plate given me by a friend who travels India often, which I use only to toast spices because my old iron skillets seem to absorb the flavors. Another way of toasting the spices is to put them on a jelly-roll pan lined with aluminum foil and roast them in a 400° F. oven for about 20 minutes, stirring often. Then there are no intractable odors in pans.

A touch of this masala can add a little mystery to a lot of ordinary foods: it can be mixed with the butter or oil and spread on broiled fish, stirred into a mayonnaise, mixed with the yolk of stuffed eggs, and used in all sorts of other egg and vegetable as well as chicken dishes. I don't find this terribly *garam* myself, and usually add some pounded dried red chilies and green ginger to any dish that I use the masala for. As I said, this is only a rudimentary mixture, and Indian cooks add four or five more spices according to what dish is being prepared.

* Black cardamom is difficult to come by; use twice as many white cardamom pods if it is not available. The pods are discarded and only the inside seeds used.

SESAME ZUCCHINI STICKS

Although this smacks of "health food," this notion is mitigated by frying the vegetable in garlicky olive oil. The inside of the zucchini is creamy and more intensely flavored than you might dream the bland little squash could ever be. The outside is crisp and brown. The vegetables must be well drained and consumed at once—never a problem.

As one of several hors d'oeuvre,
the following amount will serve about 6.

3 small, fresh, shiny zucchini
  (about 1 pound)
½ cup flour
¼ cup white sesame seeds

1 large clove garlic, peeled
  and lightly crushed
Olive oil
Salt

Scrub but do not peel the zucchini. They must be young, firm and fresh (old ones will be soggy and seedy). Trim off the ends and cut the zucchini into 3-inch sticks about ⅓-inch thick. Dry well. Shake them about in a bag containing the flour, then turn into a dry colander and shake off excess flour. Put the sesame seeds on a tray and roll each stick in them, coating them as well as you can—the seeds won't stick on the unpeeled surface. Sauté the garlic in about ¼ inch of olive oil in a heavy 10-inch skillet. Discard the garlic.

Fry the zucchini sticks, in several uncrowded batches, for about 2 minutes on each side over fairly high flame. Use a slotted spatula to remove them to paper towels. Transfer them to a paper-napkin–lined basket, salt them lightly and serve at once.

Birthday Mousses

Bring on the dessert—I think I am about to die.
—Pierrette, sister of Brillat-Savarin

The lady died at table shortly before her hundredth birthday. If she could celebrate that many I suppose I can too—but not all within one or two months.

Why half my friends and relations chose to be born in July and August I can't imagine—something to do with the Christmas holidays I guess. Birthday cake is not my dish. They started boring me after my tenth one, chiefly I think, because they came in such horrific colors and only one flavor—dull. (In protest I once made a black chocolate birthday cake with blue frosting for one of my daughters. She loved it!)

Birthday cake is not a hot-weather food—unless someone else makes it. Unfortunately, my friends and relations with all these humid birthdays would be shocked and hurt if I commissioned a nice gaudy birthday cake with their name on it. So I have taken to making birthday mousses—lovely, cool, silky things that don't require ovens. A few sparklers held aloft during lusty renderings of "Happy Birthday, dear Poo-Bah" seem to satisfy the requirements of the occasion.

PEACH MOUSSE

This birthday mousse is particularly appealing for late July and August, when luxurious peaches are so gorgeous and plentiful here. Peaches have always been considered an opulent fruit, chiefly because in chilly climates only the rich had the hothouses necessary to grow them in. They are delicate and contrary: peaches must be picked just a little green to survive shipping even a few miles. Buy them two or three days before they will be needed, and make certain they have a healthy pink blush—this indicates that they were not picked *too* green. Ideally, buy from a local farmer for the deepest "tree-ripened" flavor.

Makes approximately 1½ quarts.

2 envelopes plain unflavored
  gelatin
½ cup cold milk
¼ pint heavy cream
2 tablespoons cognac

¾ cup sugar
2½ pounds fresh ripe peaches,
  prepared as indicated on
  page 58

Soften the gelatin in the cold milk in a small saucepan. Stir it over very low heat just long enough to dissolve the granules. Cool. Beat the cream stiff, add the cognac and sugar. Purée the peaches and stir the gelatin into them, then fold in the whipped cream. Rinse a 1½-quart mold with cold water, turn the mixture into it, cover with plastic wrap and refrigerate overnight.

MOUSSE CAFÉ

A seasonless dessert, but especially nice in hot weather, this coffee mousse appears to be light as a cloud. It is, however, sinfully rich and just right for special celebrations —like birthdays.

Serves 10–12.

6 egg yolks
½ cup sugar
1½ cups espresso coffee

2 envelopes unflavored gelatin,
  softened in ½ cup cold water
1½ pints heavy cream

Beat the egg yolks with the sugar. Beat in the coffee and cook, stirring, over very low heat until the mixture forms a thin custard. Off heat, stir in the softened gelatin and blend thoroughly. Cool the custard. Whip the cream and fold it into the cooled custard. Rinse a 2-quart mold with cold water, scrape the mousse into it and chill overnight covered with plastic wrap. Unmold and serve with the following sauce:

SAUCE

The sauce is really a thin, dark glaze for the pale mousse, and does not appreciably alter its flavor.

⅔ cup sugar	*1 tablespoon arrowroot*
1 cup espresso, heated	*1 tablespoon cognac*

Dissolve the sugar in the hot coffee. Mix the arrowroot to a thin paste with cold water and stir into the espresso. Cook, stirring constantly, until clear and thickened. Add cognac. Chill, covered with plastic wrap.

Mussels Elaborated

Moules Marinières has a depressing effect on me. Not because there's anything at all wrong with them; it's just that usually the people I see eating them in restaurants are near anorectic. And that makes me think of Audrey Hepburn, who, like me, wanted to be a ballet dancer, and there the resemblance ends. Then I force myself to think of Lillian Russell, adored by millions and weighing in at well over two hundred pounds.

Her Billowiness passed many evenings dining with Diamond Jim Brady, who would never have ordered *Moules Marinières* except as a snack for "elevenses." (He ate six meals a day and customarily downed three or four dozen shellfish to tide him over until lunch.) And in truth, this simple dish of mussels stewed in white wine and shallots really never was meant to be a meal. It is a snack, a bistro preparation quickly made.

Moules Marinières is but the foundation recipe for quite a number of other, more interesting dishes. These are not so well-suited to the taste of the spartan dieter. However, the mussel itself is so low in calories that the addition of sauces or cream or a few breadcrumbs still leaves them in a relatively low-calorie state.

MOULES, FAÇON LUCIEN
(Mussels Lucien's Style)

Alexander Watt, author of a unique guide to the bistros of Paris, contributed this recipe to his friend the late Peggy Harvey's previously mentioned *The Horn of Plenty*. The recipe is given exactly as it appeared in the book.

"[To devotees of Moules Marinières, this recipe may seem like gilding the lily but, if one is lucky enough to live in a locality in which these marvelous shellfish are available, it is notably worth trying for a change. It is a specialty of Chez Lucien, a bistro near the Eiffel Tower.—P.H.]

Serves 2–4.

"*4 pints mussels*
1 shallot, finely chopped
6 parsley stalks [sprigs], finely
* chopped*
1 tablespoon fresh cream
Juice of 1 lemon
Pinch pepper

1 dessertspoon finely chopped
* parsley, chives, chervil,*
* tarragon*
3 tomatoes, peeled, seeded and
* finely chopped*
½ cup dry white wine
Sauce hollandaise

"Scrape and brush the mussels well in several waters. Place them in a stewpan. Add shallots, parsley and wine. Cover the pan tightly and put it on a fast flame. After two minutes, shake the pan vigorously. Do this three times more during the cooking of the mussels, which should take only 5 or 6 minutes in all. The mussels should then be cooked and their shells wide open. Remove the mussels and keep hot. Leave the juices in the pan and prepare the

SAUCE HOLLANDAISE

"*3 egg yolks*
1 teaspoon water
1 cup butter (unsalted)

Salt
1 teaspoon lemon juice

"Place the egg yolks and water in the top of a double boiler over hot but not boiling water. [I find it a safer practice to use a heavy china bowl set over a saucepan of very hot water; the china does not become overheated as easily as a metal pan does.—M.U.] Whisk until creamy. Add the butter, bit by bit, wisking gently all the time. Season with a pinch of salt, add the lemon juice and strain through cheesecloth. Keep warm." [I have never in my life seen the need to strain hollandaise through cheesecloth—if it's curdled, you have ruined it and must begin again with a fresh egg yolk.—M.U.]

"Pass the juice in the pan in which the mussels cooked through a fine sieve. Return to the rinsed pan, heat and pour in the cream. Bring to a boil, gently whisk, and allow to reduce by half. Heat the tomatoes in a small pan—to evaporate the water— and add to the stewpan. Remove from the fire and pour in the hollandaise. Reheat, but be careful the sauce does not approach the boiling point; otherwise it will turn. Add the lemon juice and pepper but no salt.

"Remove the upper shell from each of the mussels and place the mussels on the bottom of four hot plates. Pour the sauce over the mussels and sprinkle with herbs. Serve at once."

For all its seeming endlessness, this is really a quite simple recipe. You stew the mussels, make a hollandaise (by blender or processor if you choose), then combine with a couple of other ingredients and pour it over the mussels. There is one caution: you must have fairly large mussels—say 3 inches long—because removing the top shells from a zillion tiny mussels, combined with the impossibility of keeping them warm, would make this a very tedious dish to prepare.

MUSSELS VINAIGRETTE

Try to find fairly large mussels for this dish, which is lovely for luncheon or, in smaller helpings, makes an interesting hors d'oeuvre. For lunch it is good with French potato salad, a hard-boiled egg and a few slices of cucumber. As a first course it should be served simply on a leaf of lettuce.

Serves 4.

3 pounds large mussels
½ cup dry white wine
½ cup white onions, sliced
2 bay leaves

1 clove garlic, crushed
3 sprigs parsley
1 sprig fresh tarragon

THE DRESSING

Pinch of salt
½ teaspoon Dijon-style mustard
1 clove garlic, crushed
2 tablespoons wine vinegar

½ cup good olive oil
Freshly ground pepper to taste
½ cup parsley and ½ cup
scallions, minced

Wash the mussels in cold water and let them soak in fresh cold water while you de-beard them. When they are all cleaned, put them in a large shallow stewpan into which you have previously put all the ingredients down through the tarragon. Cover and bring to a boil over high heat, shaking the pan from time to time. Stir the top layer of mussels down to the bottom after about three minutes, re-cover and cook until all mussels are well opened. Cool, then shell the mussels. If the mollusks are quite large, it is a good idea to examine the insides to remove the little baby crabs that may lurk there. This also gives you an opportunity to snip out any beard you may have left, along with the rather tough black neck to which it was attached. Cover the shelled mussels with some of their liquor, carefully strained from the pot to avoid sand. Refrigerate.

Put the salt, mustard, garlic and vinegar into a small bowl and whisk in the olive oil in a thin stream. Add pepper to taste and stir in the parsley and scallions. Drain the mussels, pour the dressing over them, mix well and wait 15 minutes before serving.

Peaches Down Home and Up North

If you don't like my peaches,
Daddy don't you shake my tree.
—Bessie Smith (blues)

Peaches, peach cobbler, homemade peach ice cream, peach brandy—in fact, just about anything made of this luscious fruit sets off food ecstasies in all Southerners. But peach cobbler, the quintessential Southern dessert, is considered soul food by blacks and down-home cookin' by whites.

Muhammad Ali, an irrepressible dessert man, had technicolor dreams of gigantic peach cobblers when he was in training. Several years ago I hit the Ali trail with my husband, who was writing a book about The Champion. We had occasion to listen to "The Prettiest" recite endless lists of dessert he planned to gorge on when the fight was over.

Peach cobbler led all the rest in Ali's litany. Possibly one of the reasons he wasn't exactly "floating like a butterfly." But who cares about calories! Fresh August peaches, the food of the gods, are in season.

PEACH COBBLER

An authentic peach cobbler does not have a bottom crust and is at least 2 inches deep in sweet, tender peaches. I'd choose a wide earthenware casserole about 2½ inches deep and about 10 inches in diameter in which to cook it. Often, a lattice of pastry is used for the top crust, but the *echt* country version is made with a rich biscuit cover.

Serves 8.

8 or 9 large "firm-ripe" peaches, prepared as indicated on page 58
Juice of half a lemon
1 cup sugar (or to taste)
Pinch salt
Freshly grated nutmeg
1 tablespoon cornstarch mixed to a thin paste with cold water

6 tablespoons butter (approximately ¾ of a stick), diced fine
½ pint heavy cream
2 tablespoons Wild Turkey bourbon (optional; you can use another fine bourbon)

Slice the prepared peaches into the lemon juice to prevent their discoloring. Mix them with the sugar, salt and nutmeg, cover and let steep. Meanwhile, prepare the

RICH BISCUIT DOUGH

2 cups unbleached flour
½ teaspoon salt
3 teaspoons baking powder

3 ounces (about ⅓ cup) unsalted butter
¾ cup milk

Preheat the oven to 450° F.

Sift the flour, salt and baking powder together. Cut the butter in with a pastry blender or two table knives until it resembles coarse meal. (You may also do this with your fingers if the weather and your hands are cool.) Stir in enough of the cold milk to make a soft dough. Gather it together and turn it out on a lightly floured pastry cloth. Knead it gently for about half a minute, then pat it or roll the dough out to ½-inch thickness. With a small (1½-inch) glass or cutter, cut out the biscuits. You will have more than you need for the cobbler, but you can bake the remainders separately in a pie tin and someone will manage to eat them.

Put the peaches into a saucepan with the cornstarch paste and simmer them for about 5 minutes. Cool them a little. Butter a deep oven-proof glass or earthenware dish that is presentable at table. Pour the peaches into it and dot the surface with the butter.

Lay the little biscuits over the surface of the peaches, leaving about ¼-inch space between them. Set the cobbler in the middle of the preheated oven, close the door and in two minutes reduce the heat to 425° F. Bake 10 minutes and check. If the biscuits are browning too rapidly, cover them loosely with a piece of foil and continue baking another 5 minutes. Cool the cobbler for about 20 minutes so that no mouths will be seared.

Whip the cream just enough to thicken it—it should not be stiff—and blend in the bourbon. Pass it in a bowl to be spooned over the hot cobbler, which should be served in small glass berry dishes.

At the other end of the sophisticated scale there are:

PÊCHES FLAMBÉES

This produces a quite spectacular result without too much work. Also it gives you an opportunity to use the chafing dish or fancy warmer whose storage space you've been wondering how to ever justify.

Serves 8.

8 fine large "firm-ripe" peaches
Juice of half a lemon
1½ quarts thin simple syrup
  (1 quart water and 2 cups
  sugar)

½ cup good French brandy
1 tablespoon cornstarch mixed
  to a thin paste with cold
  water

You will need some kind of chafing dish or warmer to do your table dazzle with—an electric frying pan will do. You will also need a large metal ladle. In restaurants the peaches are served, still flaming, to each guest, but unless you have several footmen, this is not a possibility for the home cook.

Skin the peaches, but leave whole. Drop them into cold water acidulated with the lemon juice.

Make a simple syrup by boiling together the water and the 2 cups of sugar, stirring constantly until the sugar crystals dissolve, about 5 minutes.

Arange the peaches in a saucepan into which they will just fit in one layer. Pour the simple syrup over them and poach, covered, over gentle heat until tender but still shapely. The poaching time will depend on the size and ripeness of the peaches. Test after about 10 minutes with a trussing needle, and keep testing until they are just done. The recipe can be made ahead up to this point.

Remove the peaches to the chafing dish. Pour about 1 cup of the syrup into a small saucepan, add the cornstarch-and-water paste and cook gently until the syrup thickens and clears. Pour this mixture over the peaches and take the whole business to the dinner table, where you have waiting a bottle of brandy, a ladle, a candle warmer or some kind of heat source, and a small votive candle to heat the brandy. When the brandy is quite hot (be careful or it will catch fire even without a match), pour it over the peaches and instantly set it alight. With tongs or a long spoon, serve each guest his *pêche flambée.* Some kind of light, delicate cookies are nice to serve with the peaches. So is champagne, if you're feeling generous.

Food thought for the day: "People who indulge in private colloquies at table are heart-scalds. So are talkers of politics."   —Robert Courtine, French gastronome

Before the Fall

It is a flaw
In happiness, to see beyond our bourn,—
It forces us in summer skies to mourn,

—John Keats, "Epistle to J. H. Reynolds"

August *angst* causes me to buy too much of everything—stopping at roadside stands, helplessly filling baskets with produce I will barely have time to use. Among the temptations—small shining eggplants, softly ruffled lettuces I won't see again for a year. But the most seductive for me are the tomatoes and peaches. I want to gaze at opulent pounds of them arranged in my kitchen baskets.

Something leaves the life of a tomato or a peach when it goes into the icebox—their flavors and textures are never the same. So I don't refrigerate them. Consequently I lose a few. But my lack of restraint at farm stands does pay off, because despite my extravagance I am also pained by waste. All this leads to a good deal of forced improvisation (is there any *un*forced improvisation?) that I think I must be rather deliberately inflicting on myself.

The smart thing, of course, would be to freeze a lot of all this wonderful stuff. But a fanatic for fresh produce like me does not do the smart thing. No, I have all these bins and baskets of perishables demanding immediate attention. And I must think of how best to preserve the much-cherished herbs. I have found no satisfactory way of wintering them over—even in our greenhouse—because herbs grown indoors are nearly tasteless, and not all herbs dry well—basil for instance. One good way to preserve fresh herbs, for a few months anyway, is to make them up into herb butters.

But let us revel in the here and now of ripe fruits and vegetables. Peaches are luscious and fairly cheap in late summer. And so is just about everything else, so here are some recipes to cope with the plenitude.

PEACH DESSERT

My abandon at the peach stand precipitated this dessert for a rather impromptu dinner. Peaches must be bought at least a day or two in advance, spread out in a single layer cushioned by crumpled paper towels and left to ripen in a dim, airy place.

Serves 8.

5 to 6 medium-large ripe
    peaches, prepared as indicated
    on page 58
1 *frozen loaf pound cake,*
    thawed, or your own
    homemade

1 *cup brown sugar*
3 *tablespoons sweet butter*
2 *tablespoons sliced almonds*
½ *pint whipping cream*
1 *to 2 tablespoons light rum*

Preheat the oven to 375° F.

Prepare the peaches: Peel, halve and drop into a bowl with the juice of 1 lemon mixed with water. Set aside.

Slice the pound cake a bit less than ½ an inch thick, and fit these slices into a buttered shallow oblong baking dish, covering the bottom entirely. Slice the peach halves, holding them together. With a spatula transfer the sliced peach halves onto the cake slices, arranging them in neat rows, accordion fashion. Sprinkle the brown sugar over the peaches, dot with the butter and sprinkle with almonds. Bake in a preheated oven until peaches are tender—about 30 minutes. Serve warm, topped with whipped cream to which you have added rum to taste. (If the dessert must be made early in the afternoon, it can be reheated in the evening. However, it is quick to assemble and much better made as near serving time as possible.)

CHILLED CREAM OF TOMATO SOUP

Hot cream of tomato soup *à la* Campbell's blighted the days of my childhood. It was years before I could risk a taste of any tomato soup—hot, cold, thick or thin. Cold soups were almost never served in Southern homes (nor anywhere else in America, for that matter) until a decade or so ago. Jellied madrilène, vichyssoise and various debaucheries of gazpacho one encountered in restaurants occasionally, but not private houses. Finally I have found a tomato soup I can love, and it is both easy to make and freezeable.

Serves 8.

3 pounds red ripe tomatoes,
skinned, seeded and chopped
(see page 78)
3 tablespoons olive oil
½ cup sliced scallions
(white only)
¼ cup celery, peeled and
chopped
1 clove garlic, minced

1 quart water or thin, defatted
chicken broth
1 tablespoon fresh thyme leaves
1 tablespoon fresh basil, minced
1 pint half-and-half, scalded
Salt and freshly milled white
pepper to taste
Sour cream (optional)
Minced chives (optional)

Prepare the tomatoes and set aside.

Heat the olive oil in a heavy saucepan of about 4-quart capacity (not cast iron). Over low heat, stir in the scallions and the celery. Add the garlic, and sauté all together, stirring often, until the vegetables are transparent and tender but not browned. Add the tomatoes and the water or broth and simmer all together about 15 minutes. Stir in the herbs and simmer 2 minutes longer.

Remove the soup from the heat, and let it cool at least 10 minutes before puréeing it in a processor or blender. Never fill these machines more than half full—and never try to purée very hot mixtures, as the heat blows the lids off the machines. The half-and-half (or light cream) is scalded to prevent the acid in the tomatoes from curdling it. Blend the tomato soup and cream well, and season to taste with the salt and pepper. Chill thoroughly. Taste the soup again before serving, as chilled soups need more salt than hot ones. This is a rather thin soup, so you may add a small dollop of sour cream to each serving, or, if you prefer, some finely cut chives. Or both, for that matter.

ZUCCHINI SOUP VINDALOO

Easily grown in ungovernable quantities, this vegetable is the werewolf of the South Fork in late summer and needs every recipe it can get. Its taste is rich and the soup is filling even though it is extremely low in calories—about 12 calories an ounce. In its original version I made it with heavy cream and lemon juice, which is also delectable but no boon to the over-fed.

Makes about 2 quarts.

2 pounds young, slender zucchini
6 tablespoons butter
1 large clove garlic, minced
1 cup scallions, minced (or
  plain onions)
1 tablespoon cumin
1 tablespoon fresh Vindaloo
(hot) curry powder

2 cups clear chicken broth,
  undiluted
1/4 cup parsley leaves
Handful of watercress leaves
3 cups fresh buttermilk
Salt and white pepper to taste

Wash, dry and slice the zucchini. Melt the butter in a heavy soup kettle. Add the zucchini, garlic and scallions and stir, then cover and "sweat" them slowly for 15 minutes over very low heat. Stir in cumin and curry powder, cook over low heat, stirring, for about 5 minutes. Stir in the chicken broth and bring to the simmer for 10 minutes. Add parsley and watercress, simmer 1 minute and cool quickly. Purée the zucchini mixture, stir in the cold buttermilk and adjust seasonings. Chill well. Garnish each serving with a bit of minced chive or parsley.

Note: the curry powder must be fairly strong; if you can't find any Vindaloo, use a bit more of a blander type. Or add a very little cayenne.

Atlantic Blue Crabs

Callinectes is Greek for beautiful swimmer. *Sapidus,* of course,
means tasty or savory in Latin.
—William W. Warner, *Beautiful Swimmers—Watermen,*
Crabs & the Chesapeake Bay

All summer long I pester John Haessler at his seafood shop in Wainscott to find
me some big, beautiful Atlantic blue crabs. Some years there are none at all and
other years they are too small. Any smaller then 7 inches from point to point are
hardly worth picking (though good for gumbo). Sometimes John comes up with a
mess of "Jimmies" weighing in at about a pound each.

A "Jimmy" is a mature male crab. The female is called a "sook" as well as some
other colorful names coined by the Chesapeake Bay watermen. Berried females are
known by several names: lemon bellies, busted sooks, punks and sponges. It is
illegal to take them. A crab of either sex that is about to moult (i.e., throw his too-
tight shell) is called a "peeler." This true-blue American crustacean is indescribably
delicious whether male, female, soft or hard, and infinitely more delicate and tender
than lobster. The reason may be found, perhaps, in William Warner's enchanting
account of two old-time watermen discussing the crab's courting habits:

"My friend, you never seen crabs making love?"

"Act real horny, they do. Males get way up on their tippy toes."

"Do I think so? I don't think so, I *know* so!"

"That's right, the Jimmies on their toes and the females rocking side to side,
contented like."

Jimmies, despite thier tenderness in love, are fierce defenders of their personal
safety. Crabs are not pegged, banded or otherwise made safe for the uninitiate to
handle. You can, of course, pick them up with long tongs, but then they cling to
each other in an unwieldy daisy chain and you find yourself trying to put about a
yard of crabs into a pot of boiling water. A crab cannot harm you if, with one
hand, you grab the two back fins (called "paddlers") firmly and use them as a
handle. If you let go of either of the fins you are doomed, because the crab can then
flip over and nab you with his big front claws. Out of the water, crabs are about
twenty times faster and more active than lobsters.

As a child in South Carolina, I used to go crabbing at low tide armed with nothing but a sawed-off broomstick and a bucket. This is the highly refined technique: Hold the crab down with the broomstick; pick it up by its back fins and throw it in the bucket. The crabs were emptied into seaweed-lined bushel baskets, covered with more seaweed and taken home to be boiled instantly in a vat of heavily salted water laced with a mixture of herbs and spices known as "crab boil." This is still easy to find but is often stale. Be sure what you buy is in fresh and aromatic condition. To this mixture I add several dried red-hot chilies.

Crabs, whether bought or caught, must be kept cool, wet and alive until they can be put into the cooking pot. To do this as humanely as possible—and also to prevent them tearing off one another's claws—I put them in a big sink of cold fresh running water for about five minutes. This seems to anaesthetize them. I then lift them out by the hind fins, one by one, and add them to the pot.

A crab weighing about a pound will be cooked in 10 minutes with the water gently simmering. Add 5 minutes for each additional 8 ounces of body weight. Off heat, let the crabs rest in their cooking water for 10 minutes to absorb the flavor of the spices. Spread out on newspapers to cool.

Now comes the hard part. When the crabs are cool, pick the meat out in the following manner: Break off the large claws and all the legs. A nutcracker, a pair of heavy kitchen shears and a clam knife are my chosen weapons in this battle for the sweet, succulent crabmeat. Crack the claws gently and extract the meat leaving the clawmeat as intact as possible. Snip off the pointed joint of each leg with the shears—the meat from the middle, large joint will fall out or can be coaxed out with the clam knife.

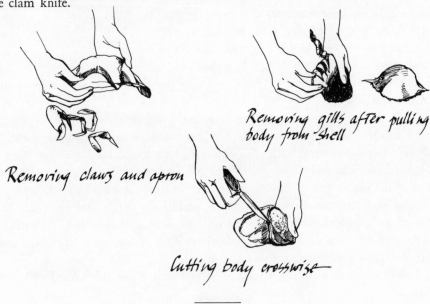

Removing gills after pulling body from shell

Removing claws and apron

Cutting body crosswise

Turn the crab over so that it is lying on its top shell. Pull off the apron and discard it. Then pull the crab's body from its shell and reserve the shell if you wish to use it as a container for Deviled Crabs (page 112) or crab mayonnaise or a *gratin*. Remove and discard the pointed white spongy gills which are called "the dead man's fingers." Snap out the mouth of the crab and remove the attached sac, which contains the stomach and other inedible parts. This sounds just awful, but it really is all so peculiar looking that unfortunate connections between the crustacean's body and the humanoid would not occur except to the most quiveringly sensitive.

There is roe in the female and tomalley—a greenish yellow substance that is a great delicacy—in both sexes. Put this tomalley, and roe, if any, in a small bowl to mix with whatever sauce you will serve with the crab.

Using the clam knife, cut the body crosswise, then again, so that you have four equal pieces with the snowy white meat exposed. Using your fingers and the clam knife, extract all of the meat assiduously.

Champions at the Crisfield (Maryland) annual National Hard Crab Derby can pick a crab in about 40 seconds. I can do it in about 5 *minutes*—but even a rank beginner should be able to pick his own crab in about 10 minutes. If you eat while you pick, a good-sized crab can occupy you for up to 45 minutes. My policy on serious crab eating is to give a single demonstration, then it's everyone for himself.

When large crabs are available—this is unpredictable because crabs settle down and then suddenly decamp from an area for no known reasons—they are well worth the trouble it is to pick them. First of all, no manner of pasteurized, refrigerated tinned crabmeat can compare with the matchless flavor and texture of freshly cooked crab. Secondly, crabmeat by the pound has become wildly expensive—which is why so many restaurant "crab" dishes are padded out with white fish flakes. The following two recipes are pure and basic crab.

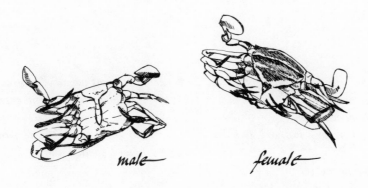

male   female

COLD DRESSED CRAB

Allow one large (1 pound) crab or two smaller ones for each person. Cook and cool as described above. Wash and scrub them with a brush in cool running water, drain. Some people like their crab ice cold, but I think it's better just cool. Make a good rich homemade mayonnaise (see page 150) using half olive oil and half peanut oil. Flavor it with the roe and tomalley of one or two crabs. Stir in some chopped chives or scallions and minced parsley and, if desired, a little minced hard-boiled egg. Pass this at table.

DEVILED CRABS

Food writers have a greater opportunity than other people to bore the public with reminiscences of their childhood foods. (Although almost any kind of writer will do it if you let him.) But freshly made deviled crabs eaten at the beach in South Carolina remains one of my fondest memories, and I see no reason why this pleasure should not spread to northern or even western beaches. My recipe is adapted from an old cookbook, *The Picayune Creole Cook Book* published in New Orleans in 1901.

Serves 6–12.

1 dozen fine large crabs
2 tablespoons butter
2 tablespoons flour
2 teaspoons dry mustard powder
2 teaspoons salt
½ pint heavy cream
Yolks of 4 hard-boiled eggs
2 tablespoons scallions, minced

2 tablespoons parsley, minced
½ teaspoon cayenne (or more, to taste)
2 cups fresh white breadcrumbs
¼ pound melted butter
Tabasco sauce
Lemon wedges

Boil the crabs and pick them. Cover and set aside the crabmeat. Scrub the top shells with a brush and hot water, dry them and lightly oil the red surface. Set aside.

Melt the two tablespoons of butter in a small heavy saucepan and stir in the flour over low heat. Blend in mustard powder and salt. Beat in cream with a wire whisk until sauce is smooth. Mash the yolks to a paste and add them to the sauce, blending thoroughly. Stir in the scallions, parsley and cayenne. Taste. The mixture should be biting hot, as it is still to be mixed with the crab. Blend the crab with the sauce and taste again for salt and cayenne. (Some Southern cooks add a scraping of nutmeg and some put in minced green sweet peppers, but I think this interferes with the crab flavor.)

Pack the crabmeat mixture lightly into the reserved shells—you will probably have several shells left over. Sprinkle the breadcrumbs over the top of the crab mixture, patting it down lightly. Drizzle the melted butter over the breadcrumbs.

Preheat the oven to 400° F., put the crabs on a cookie sheet and bake in the center of the oven until the crabs are hot through and the tops ligthly browned, about 10 minutes. Serve with Tabasco sauce on the side and lemon wedges. These are also good tepid, but at their best hot.

Late Summer Lushness

O, who can hold a fire in his hand
By thinking on the frosty Caucasus?
Or cloy the hungry edge of appetite
By bare imagination of a feast?
Or wallow naked in December snow
By thinking on fantastic summer's heat?
—W. Shakespeare, *King Richard III*

And who can hold the memory of a ripe field tomato when in his hand he holds a winter tomato, gassed pink on its way here from California? With fall coming in unseemly haste, we still have a lot of summer left and, best of all, lots of summer vegetables to enjoy from now 'til frost.

It's definitely the season to make dishes that can be made at no other time of year without dismal substitutions of canned or shipped produce. The luxury of cooking with fresh tomatoes should be particularly exploited, since there is no known method of preserving the texture and taste of a real vine-ripened field tomato.

In late summer, a mushroom-basketful, holding about 7 pounds of tomatoes, can be bought cheaply at farm stands. Similar bargains are also to be had in green and yellow squashes, eggplant, both hot and sweet peppers, late plantings of green beans and still-abundant herbs (except for dill). There's still plenty of healthy basil for those who want to freeze up a stock of pesto base for winter use: it's not so pretty, but the taste is there.

LATE SUMMERTIME PASTA SAUCE

Most summers I have a glut of the ingredients in my garden for this unusually light but spicy sauce. Which is why this rather odd miscellany came about. If you happen to have a lot of zucchini and crookneck squash on hand, you could add that and omit the shrimp. It then becomes a delicious, cheap vegetarian dish.

*Serves 4 as a main course or
8 as a first course.*

4 or 5 pounds red ripe
   tomatoes, skinned and chopped
¼ cup olive oil
2 large cloves garlic, minced
2 medium onions, chopped
2 or 3 yellow "Hungarian
   banana" peppers or any other
   fresh hot chili pepper,
   seeded and minced
1 small eggplant (about
   1 pound), unpeeled, diced
1 pound medium-size raw
   shrimp, shelled

3 or 4 fresh basil leaves,
   shredded
2 tablespoons fresh thyme leaves
Salt to taste
2 tablespoons cornstarch mixed
   to a thin paste with cold
   water
1 pound thin spaghetti (#9)
⅛ pound softened butter
2 tablespoons fresh parsley,
   chopped
1 cup freshly grated Parmesan
   cheese (optional)

Prepare all the raw ingredients first, as this dish is made very quickly, stir-fried in a wok. (If you haven't a wok use an iron dutch oven or a chicken fryer.) Skin the tomatoes by dropping them into boiling water for 30 seconds, then dumping them into cold water. Core them and the skins will slip off. Chop coarsely and set aside.

When working with hot chili peppers, wear rubber gloves to avoid burning your skin, and wash the gloves with soap and hot water before you take them off. The juices and oils of some chilies are so hot they raise little blisters, but the Hungarian banana peppers I have suggested aren't all that fiery. Chilies—even the same species —can vary wildly in hotness, so it is wise to taste a bit before adding them to any dish.

Organize the ingredients, in order used, on a tray. Have the pasta boiling and plates heated before you start the sauce—the pasta can wait a few minutes, tossed in hot butter, if necessary, but the vegetables can't. If you can get someone else to boil the pasta, drain it, butter it, and apportion it on the plates, your job will be less harried, and the dish true perfection.

Put the oil in the wok and heat it up to near smoking, rolling it around to coat up the sides. Put the garlic, onions, peppers and eggplant in the wok and stir-fry about 4 minutes over medium high heat. Add the shrimp and stir-fry one or two minutes. Add the tomatoes, herbs and about 1 tablespoon of salt and stir-fry about half a minute, just enough to heat the tomatoes. Stir in the cornstarch paste, stirring vigorously to thicken and bind the sauce. Taste and add salt if needed.

Apportion the sauce on top of four waiting dishes of hot buttered pasta. Sprinkle the parsley over each and serve at once. This kind of sauce really shines, with all its distinct flavors and textures, when served on a good homemade egg pasta such as *tagliatelle* (also called fettucine) which can now be bought fresh in fancy food stores.

Pass the grated cheese separately at the table if you wish. However, it seems rather pointless to me, after having painstakingly preserved the integrity of the separate ingredients, to blur the whole in cheesy flavor. There are many devotees of Italian food who firmly believe that all pasta must wear a shawl of cheese. Understandable I suppose, if one has never tasted anything but those acrid thick sauces and the pre-cooked spaghetti of the endless "Luigi's," with their checkered tablecloths and Chianti-bottle decor. That sort of food needs all the help it can get.

SIMPLE HERB SAUCE FOR PASTA

Freshly made *tagliatelle,* a mixture of both the yellow and green spinach noodles (called *paglia e fieno*), shows its special airy qualities under this plain dressing. There is not very much of it because it is meant to be used sparingly. This is most suitably served as a small first course for four:

¾ cup fine cold-pressed olive oil
2 cloves garlic, peeled and flattened slightly
2 tablespoons fresh thyme leaves
2 tablespoons fresh parsley, minced

2 tablespoons fresh basil, minced
Salt and pepper to taste
1 cup freshly grated Parmesan or Romano cheese (or Sbrinz, a hard grating cheese from Switzerland)

Warm the oil in a small heavy saucepan and put in the garlic. Cook it gently for a minute or two until golden and discard the garlic. Off heat and with the oil just warm, add the thyme, parsley, basil and salt and fresh pepper to taste. Mix with the hot pasta and serve in very hot soup plates. The Sbrinz is quite untraditional, but then so is my recipe. Sbrinz dates from Roman times and can only be found in rather ambitious stores.

Summer's End Parties

One half of the world cannot understand the pleasures of the other.

—Jane Austen, *Emma*

Only four more weekends until the crescendo of parties on Labor Day. For every wind-surfer there are a thousand "lawn people" eating and drinking on the East End of Long Island. Except for Imperial China, no culture has ever placed more emphasis on food than South Fork party goers.

There are two approaches to the "Annual Bash." Lovers of tradition go in for repetition—some people do meatballs, others do chili . . . or stuffed turkey . . . or, Lord spare us, pasta salad! Something new and startling for every party is the other tack. I try to steer a course between the two, and scatter new and unusual things among old favorites. This is partly because mass cooking bores me and I prefer to make a larger variety of smaller dishes to fill out the buffet table. This used to be easier when people came to cocktail parties to talk and drink. Now they seem to come to eat. So my subject here is food specifically designed for parties.

Do you ever wonder whatever happened to *canapés?* Those little widgets of bread or toast spread with anchovy paste or shrimp butter and rushed from broiler to guest demanded cooks and waitresses on constant alert. Along with household help, the canapé faded from American life about 1947. Now we have a massive array of things prepared in advance by the host or hostess—*les hors d'oeuvre.* (*Les hors d'oeuvre* is like *les* sheep and *les* deer—the same whether one or many.)

Although we Americans invented the cocktail party, nearly every other cuisine seems to have food better suited to this form of entertaining. The French, the Chinese, the East Indians, and, of course, the Scandinavians have an infinite variety of small tasty things to serve with wine or drinks. The splendors of smorgasbord were revealed to me some years ago when I worked (anonymously) on a Scandinavian cookbook.

A diverting, if somewhat expensive, way of making a party a food smash hit could be an assortment of *dim sum* ordered from a good Chinese restaurant. All play and no work. Then there are the beautiful Japanese appetizers, *sushi,* that have captivated New York in recent years.

A visiting Japanese chef made my family a most amazingly wonderful *sushi* lunch one dazzling summer Sunday. (He has a standing open invitation for any weekend he chooses—chefs on holiday cook to relax.) Alas, we have no Japanese restaurant at all on the East End amid all these fresh fish and vegetables. It takes years of practice and considerable culinary talent to make *sushi* properly. (My Japanese friend discreetly removed the *sushi* I had made—he was teaching me—from the platter containing *his* magnificent creations.)

However, anybody with a reasonably sure carving hand can make *sashimi,* which are cubes and slices of extremely fresh fish. Fish to be served raw must come from a source you know and trust (if you catch the fish yourself, gut it and ice it immediately). Platters of *sashimi* should be chilled, served and replenished promptly.

One of my cardinal rules for party food is that each kind be served in relatively small amounts and the platters washed and replenished frequently. There are few things more hideous than a table of decimated food. Another revolting practice to be avoided is using the same ice for drinks that is also employed to keep the wine and beer cold. Those big, cheap Styrofoam chests keep ice well and, most importantly, clean, for quite a long time. Galvanized tin tubs do very well for beer and wine coolers. Another rule: never run out of ice. Or club soda.

GRAVLAX

Fresh salmon, cured in salt, sugar and fresh dillweed, is one of Sweden's great gifts to the culinary art. Only it isn't cooked. *Gravlax* is quite simple to make; all you have to do that is critical is to turn it every twelve hours.

*2 matching center-cut fillets of
 salmon, about 3 to 4 pounds*
¼ cup coarse salt
2 tablespoons white sugar

*2 tablespoons coarsely ground
 white pepper*
2 big bunches fresh dill

THE SAUCE

*1½ cups thin homemade
 mayonnaise* (see page 150)*

¼ cup Dijon-style mustard
½ cup fresh dill, minced

* *Note:* Made without salt, as mustard is salty enough.

Wash the salmon fillets in cold water and dry them well. It is easy to remove the twenty to thirty bones embedded in the flesh with a small pair of needle-nosed pliers. You can feel these with your fingers quite easily and they *must* be removed to facilitate carving. It is easiest to do before curing the salmon.

Mix together the salt, sugar and pepper and rub it into the flesh side of the fish. Lay one piece of fish on a double thickness of aluminum foil, flesh side up. Cover it thickly with fresh dill which has been carefully washed and dried (a salad spinner makes quick work of this). *There must be abundant dill*—enough to form a thick, shaggy mattress between the two fish fillets. Cover the dill with the other piece of salmon, flesh side down on the dill.

Cover the fish with another piece of foil and fold the edges together all around to make a firm package. Put the package in a glass or ceramic dish and refrigerate it for three days. Weight it with something flat—a board or another platter—on which you can balance three cans weighing about 10 ounces each. Turn the *gravlax* over once every twelve hours and replace the weights.

After three days, unwrap the salmon and dry it well with paper towels, discarding the dill. (It can be carved for up to five days ahead if desired.)

The firm, sweet flesh is carved in the same manner as smoked salmon, though not quite so thinly. If you can carve a flank steak, you can carve *gravlax*. The knife should be long, thin and razor sharp. Do not saw at the fish, but rather use a quick, decisive diagonal slicing motion right down to, but not through, the skin. Release each slice from the skin as you carve it and lay it on a chilled platter in overlapping slices. Discard the brown flesh, if any, in the center and separate each slice into two halves.* This is both more economical and easier. The brilliant red-orange salmon should be decorated with a few wisps of fresh dill. Serve it with whole-grain or brown bread, buttered and cut into crustless fingers.

Commercial mayonnaise is so strongly flavored and thick it is really not suitable for saucing this delicate fish. Blender or food processor mayonnaise is delicious and effortless, and you can control its thickness by simply diluting it was a little hot water. This also stabilizes it. (You can, of course, make mayonnaise using a soup plate and an ordinary table fork.) Stir the mustard and dill into the mayonnaise and serve. It should be quite mild and used sparingly to avoid masking the flavor of the *gravlax*.

* When serving *gravlax* on a plate as a first course, the slices are left whole.

SMOKED EEL WITH HORSERADISH SAUCE

Buy a couple of large smoked eels, neither too greasy nor too dry. The very soft ones are disagreeably fatty and the hard ones are much too dry. Cut off the heads and skin them. The fillets lift off very easily and should be cut into small oblongs.

For the sauce, mix some bottled, drained horseradish with ¼ pint whipping cream, not too stiffly beaten. Add salt to taste. Pumpernickel, cut in slender fingers, is good with this.

CHICKEN LIVER MOUSSE

If you have a food processor, this is simplicity itself to make. It's a bit more trouble if you must use a food mill and sieve. It has an opulent flavor and an airy texture and is not expensive unless you decide to add some minced truffles. The mousse can be made two or three days in advance.

*1½ pounds fresh pale chicken
  livers (frozen ones are dark)*
½ cup chopped onion
1 cup clear chicken broth
½ pound sweet butter, softened

1 teaspoon salt
1 teaspoon freshly milled pepper
½ cup heavy cream
1 tablespoon cognac

Wash, dry and trim the livers of all fat and membrane. Put them in a small non-aluminum (this metal discolors livers) saucepan with the onions and the chicken broth. Bring slowly to a simmer, cover and poach for 10 minutes with the water just below the simmer. Do not boil. Remove from burner and let the livers cool, uncovered, in the broth for 15 minutes. Drain them, reserving the liquid for another use. Cool the livers to tepid in the refrigerator.

In the blender or food processor, mix together the liver, onions, butter, salt and pepper—in two batches if necessary. Scrape into bowl. Whip the cream until stiff and blend it with a spatula into the liver paste, which should be perfectly smooth and creamy. Season with cognac and add more salt or pepper if necessary. If you have a truffle or two, here's the place to add them, finely minced, along with their juice.

Turn the liver mousse into a small terrine just large enough to hold it and cover it loosely with plastic wrap. When the surface of the mousse firms up in the refrigerator, push the plastic wrap down to meet the surface so that no air can spoil the flavor or color of the mousse. Cover the terrine with its own top or one made of foil and refrigerate at least twenty-four hours. Serve with dry, crisp toast.

F·A·L·L

Summer in a Jar

The way to ensure summer in England is to have it framed and
glazed in a comfortable room.
—Horace Walpole. *Letters*

A great deal of grumbling about 1983's less than spectacular summer has been
heard, but here we are in mid-October, still having summer. One way to preserve
it tangibly is in Mason jars.

Tomatoes and ever more tomatoes are heavy on the vine. Zucchini never gives
up under lesser circumstances than a death-dealing frost—though by this time of
year even the most ardent zucchini lover will not take unusual steps to prolong the
life of this wildly prolific plant. Tomato fanciers, though, begin to get a little hys-
terical in late summer: they know they will not taste the rich, deep flavor of a real
field tomato until next July. Those handsome bores from California and points south
will be all there is to tempt, and disappoint, us in midwinter.

At this season, Long Island tomatoes are at their best—and cheapest. It's a wise
time to make up a store of tomato-based sauces, either canned or frozen. Green
tomatoes that may never get the chance to mature are in abundance. Most farmers
will be glad, if you offer to pick your own, to sell them for almost nothing. Usually
I have my own private glut of green tomatoes and begin mulling over their possi-
bilities. Fried green tomatoes aren't a thing you can get people to go along with every
day. The supreme sacrifice a green tomato can make is to become chutney.

My readers will think I'm obsessed with tomatoes and their uses, but this is only
partly true. Year before last I ran a green tomato and pear chutney recipe similar to
this one that follows, but every fall I pursue the Perfect Chutney, so rarely make the
same one twice. However, this year's batch is so good I really think I'm going to
leave the recipe alone. It contains a rather grand amount of fresh green ginger root
and fresh hot chilies, and is a brilliant companion for roast chicken, pork chops and
many other things besides curries.

Canning supplies and booklets may be bought at most good hardware stores . . .
though their stocks are probably a little thin this late in the canning season. I consider *The Ball Blue Book* (mentioned elsewhere) an essential in every culinary
library. However, I do wish the Ball people would list all the primary ingredients
in pounds rather than quarts—it is beyond the ken of most of us to fix a beady eye

on a basket of pears and decide how many quarts or cups of prepared fruit they will yield. This peculiarity in many cook books (stating volume rather than weight) is in deference to the average American kitchen, which rarely contains a scale. But kitchen scales are essential to anyone even halfway serious about cooking, and indispensable when canning and freezing food.

A wide-mouthed funnel for transferring the preserves from kettle to jar and a large ladle of at least 8-ounce capacity are necessities for preserving. A graniteware canner large enough to process seven pint jars is also very convenient for boiling corn, lobsters and spaghetti. An old-fashioned heavy-gauge enameled dishpan makes a very good preserving pan if used with an asbestos pad under it. Preserving pans should be wide and shallow, with heavy bottoms, so that liquids evaporate quickly. A blanching pot is a convenience useful for cooking vegetables all year round, as well as being invaluable for canning.

High-acid fruits and vegetables do not require pressure steam canning. In fact, this particular chutney is such a high-acid fruit product that only we super-fussy Americans would bother to process it at all. In old recipes, chutneys were simply put into clean, scalded jars, sealed and stored in a cool, dark cellar. However, the "hot-water bath" process is so simple, and compounds confidence in home-canned food, that it is well worth the extra step.

SPICY TOMATO AND PEAR CHUTNEY

Although there seem to be an endless list of ingredients here, they are necessary to achieve the complex flavors and textures of the chutney. A food processor takes the grief out of all the mincing and slicing, etc., anyway. Choose the cheaper, small brown Seckel or russet Bosc pears (or any firm variety of pears in large supply), which are best for cooking and should be slightly underripe. The tomatoes should be hard, green and blemishless. I have used white sugar and unsulphured molasses in an effort to duplicate the *jaggery* (crude brown raw sugar) commonly used in India. (Our domestic brown sugar is not raw—it is merely colored brown with a little molasses or syrup.)

Makes 10 pints.

6 pounds green tomatoes, sliced thinly

2 teaspoons kosher or pickling salt

3 pounds pears, peeled, cored and chopped

1 box (10 ounces) dried currants

1 quart brown cider vinegar

6 large cloves garlic, peeled and minced

8 ounces green ginger root, peeled and minced

2 pounds yellow onions, chopped finely

4 to 5 fresh hot chilies (Anaheims or jalapeñas for instance) minced, or the equivalent canned

Rinds of 3 oranges, shredded

2 lemons, with their juice, rinds shredded

3 pounds white sugar

1 bottle (12 ounces) Mott's "Grandma's Molasses" (unsulphured)

1 tablespoon ground dried red chilies or cayenne to taste

2 teaspoons arrowroot mixed with ½ cup cold water

Large tomatoes should be cut in half before slicing so that the slices are all approximately the same size. Sprinkle them with salt and set aside. Prepare the pears, and put them into the preserving pan with the currants and vinegar and add all the remaining ingredients (except the dried red chilies, arrowroot and water) in the order listed. Finally, drain the tomatoes of whatever juices they have accumulated and add them to the kettle.

Bring to the simmer, stirring often, and place an asbestos pad under the preserving pan. This type of thing scorches easily and it must cook about two hours, perhaps more, to a thick glossy jam with dark translucent fruits and vegetables suspended in it. It should bubble along rather slowly and be stirred at least every 15 minutes with a long wooden spoon. Add ground red chilies or cayenne to taste. Tighten the texture of the chutney by stirring in the arrowroot mixed with water. Stir and cook 2 or 3 minutes.

Meanwhile, wash and scald the jars and leave them in a pot of hot water until you need them. Boil the dome lids and screw bands in a small separate saucepan for a few minutes. Place a folded teatowel on a tray and invert several jars on it. Leave the other jars in the hot water. Turn the jars right side up and, working as quickly as you can, insert the wide-mouth funnel into the jars one by one and fill them with the hot chutney (using the ladle) up to ¼ inch of the rim of the jar—this is called "headroom," and allows for a little expansion when the jars are processed.

When all the jars are filled, wipe their rims with a clean damp towel to ensure that the dome lids form an airtight seal. Place the dome lids on each jar and fasten them in place with the screw bands. These are to keep the flat lids in place while they are forming a seal; the screw bands may be removed after processing, although most people leave them on for extra safety. Put the jars in a canner on a rack and pour hot water over them to cover the tops of the jars by a depth of one inch. Cover and bring to a boil. Boil slowly 10 minutes.

Remove jars to trays padded with tea towels and let them stand, not touching and out of drafts, overnight. Test the seals, but do not screw the bands down further. Label, date and store in a cupboard away from light.

Hot-Water Bath

Set the jars on a rack in a large deep pot (this will probably have to be done either in two operations or two pots). If you have no rack that fits, use a folded towel to prevent the jars from striking the metal pot as they simmer. Cover with hot water to a depth of one inch above the jars, which should not touch each other. Process 10 minutes (this means bring water to a boil, reduce to a bubbling simmer, cover and sterilize for the time required).

Remove the jars with tongs to a tray covered with folded tea towels. Do not disturb until jars have cooled to room temperature—this takes many hours, so put the trays out of the way in some non-drafty place. When cool, test rings to see that they are firmly screwed down. However, the vacuum seal is already formed by the heating and cooling process. Label and date your product and store it in a dark, reasonably cool place. This chutney keeps well, properly stored, but once opened must be refrigerated.

Keep the cartons your canning jars came in, and as the jars are used up, wash them and replace them for use next year. Canning jars used to cost just pennies, but unfortunately even this humble item is no longer cheap enough to throw away. Once your canning equipment is on hand, it's a simple matter to put up a few jars of seasonal fruits or vegetables. Most modern recipes are for small amounts—in jams and jellies they are often for four, five or six half-pints. This recipe is so large simply because I had so very many green tomatoes on hand, pears were wonderful and cheap, and I got carried away. But it's easy to halve the recipe.

Old-timers never processed their high-acid chutneys, chow-chows, piccalillis, etc., at all. They simply boiled the jars and lids and filled them while very hot with the boiling product. Still, I think the hot-water bath is good insurance against spoilage, even though our ancestors would have thought it excessively cautious.

With the weekly market-basket price for feeding a family of four leaping above $100, it may be time for canning to make a comeback.

PEACH CHUTNEY

Peaches in all their blowsy voluptuousness display their charms along the roadside stands in late summer. I cannot resist their blandishments. So home I go with a bushel of local peaches knowing full well that there's just so much peach cobbler or shortcake that one can eat in a week or so.

As I thumbed through one of my favorite cookbooks, "Modern Cookery for Private Families," by Eliza Acton (1845), I came across this redoubtable lady's way to solve the mango shortage in England. There were no mangoes at all of course. Though I have adopted Miss Acton's use of peaches to replace mangoes, these are not first pickled. The chutney is a modern version of the chutneys brought home by retired Indian Service officers who, of course, anglicized them. My effort is to turn them home toward India. This is a highly spiced chutney.

Makes 6 pints

6 lbs. firm-ripe peaches
  (see Note)
2 tsp. pickling salt*
2 apples, peeled & chopped
rinds of 3 oranges, shredded
2 lemons, juice & shredded rinds
1½ cups seedless sultanas
1 cup dried currants, washed
2 lbs. yellow onion, chopped
  finely
4 or 5 fresh hot chilies, minced

6 large cloves garlic, minced
6 ozs. green ginger root,
  peeled & minced
1 orange, thinly sliced, seeded
  and cut in triangles
3 cups brown cider vinegar
2 lbs. white sugar
1 jar (12 fl. ozs.) molasses
2 tsp. cayenne (or to taste)
2 tsp. arrowroot mixed with
  ½ cup cool water

Note: Peaches are always picked hard; otherwise it would be impossible to transport them to even the next county. Buy them at least three days in advance, lay them out in a single layer in a dim, well-ventilated place that stays around 70°F.

* Pickling salt is simply plain salt with no additives of any kind. If you can't find it, use kosher salt and add a teaspoon.

Skin the peaches by dropping them, about four at a time, into boiling water for 20 to 30 seconds. Remove them to a basin of cold water. As you skin each batch, stone them and turn the halves in a little water that has been acidulated either with lemon juice, white vinegar or "Fruit Fresh."

Slice the peaches not too thinly and combine them with all the remaining ingredients except the cayenne and arrowroot. Use a heavy wide pan so that the mixture reduces without burning. Stir often with a wooden spoon and cook over medium low heat for about an hour. You must stir the chutney often or risk scorching this rather expensive mixture. Although few people go to all this trouble merely to save money on what must be considered a luxury food anyway, home-made chutney *is* immensely cheaper. You can change the ingredients around to suit your own preferences. But I would suggest trying the recipe as given before making alterations; the balance of sweet, hot, and sour is quite superior.

Finish the chutney by stirring in cayenne to taste and thickening the mixture slightly with the arrowroot—to be found in any supermarket spice rack. It leaves anything that needs to be thickened the most transparent. Cornstarch gives a similar, but more opaque result. Prepare Mason jars and follow the procedure as in the recipe for Spicy Tomato & Pear Chutney.

The Last Corn

William Cobbett, the eighteenth-century English radical writer, wrote after a stay in our country: "Roasted ears are certainly the greatest delicacy that ever came in contact with the palate of man . . . I defy all the arts of French cookery, upon which so many volumes have been written, to produce anything so delightful."

There is still corn, but autumn presses on all too quickly and there are only a few days left to enjoy "roasting ears" until next summer's crop. I suppose there must be people who can bid the corn season farewell without regret, but I'm not one of them.

To squeeze the last ounce of use from the end-of-season corn, here are a few suggestions. Procrastination has its virtues . . . corn that's preserved in September for winter use will taste fresher than if it had been put in the freezer in July. I really never thought there was much hope for frozen corn, but a farmer's wife assured me that the following method produces delicious corn of unimpaired texture and flavor.

FREEZING CORN

Shuck the corn and remove the silk with a soft brush under cold running water. Have ready a large stockpot of boiling water. Blanch the corn for one minute. Throw the ears into a sinkful of ice-cold water. Remove and slice the kernels from the cobs with a short, very sharp knife. Try not to cut too deeply—although the kernels won't separate readily if there is some of the cob holding them together at their base. (There is a corn cutter on the market, but it doesn't seem to fit over any but the manufacturer's dream of an ear of corn.)

Put the corn in zip-lock plastic bags and freeze.

To cook, sauté briefly in butter.

FANCY CORN BREAD

It is my policy never to recommend commercial products because, having done so once or twice, the thing has instantly seemed to deteriorate. However, I have recently discovered a cornbread mix I admire because it isn't cursed with the Great American Addiction: sugar. (I have never understood why manufacturers put sugar into bread and bottled salad dressings, to say nothing of corn muffin mix!) Aunt Jemima Corn Meal Mix is self-rising, made of white cornmeal and contains no sugar. It produces a very authentic Southern cornbread or fritter . . . or hush puppy.

Serves 8.

3 or 4 ears of corn
2 scallions, finely sliced
¼ cup parsley, minced
½ teaspoon red pepper flakes
Pinch of salt
2 eggs, beaten

1 cup milk
2 tablespoons bacon fat
1½ cups Aunt Jemima Corn
  Meal Mix
Butter

Preheat over to 400° F.
Shuck the corn and cut off the kernels. Mix together all remaining ingredients, in the order given, except for the butter. Use that to grease an 8-inch cast-iron skillet. Pour in the cornbread batter and bake about 20 minutes in the center of the oven. Serve hot, with lots of sweet (unsalted) butter.

Note: This Aunt Jemima stuff isn't essential; it just saves a little time by eliminating some measuring and sifting. Any good (unsweetened) cornbread recipe can be adapted to this skillet bread.

CORN PUDDING

Amazing, but you really can find something interesting to read in a doctor's waiting room—if you wait long enough. I copied out this traditional New England pudding, into which I have introduced some quite untraditional elements, from a 1976 edition of *Vermont Life,* found among the tatters of old copies of *U.S. News & World Report* and other such entertainments. (That region tends to find anything beyond salt and pepper an exotic frill, and the true Downeasterner is proud of it.)

Serves 6.

6 strips bacon, cut ⅛ inch
    thick
2 medium onions, finely chopped
2 mildly hot chili peppers, or
    2 small hot ones or 1 plain
    bell pepper, if preferred
¼ pound baked ham, diced
    (optional)
1 cup milk
1 cup light cream

2 tablespoons butter
3 eggs
2 cups fresh corn kernels
¼ cup flour
1 teaspoon salt
2 tablespoons parsley, minced
½ teaspoon dried thyme or
    marjoram leaves
Butter

Preheat oven to 325° F.

Cut bacon into small pieces and try out. Drain. Pour off all but three tablespoons fat. Fry onion in this until transparent. Seed and mince chilies and add to onions; sauté lightly. Add ham, if used. Warm milk and cream, add butter to melt. Beat eggs well, mix with corn, flour, salt and herbs. Combine the onions, chilies, milk and cream with the egg mixture. Crumble the bacon into the batter.

Butter a 1½-quart soufflé dish or something similar and pour the batter into it. Set this into a *bain-marie* (a pan half-filled with hot water) and bake the pudding on the middle shelf of the oven for about 40 minutes, or until a table knife comes out clean. Don't overbake—it's better to have the center a bit soft than to risk a dried-out pudding.

KATHERINE ANNE PORTER'S CORN PONE

Willie Morris, formerly the laureate of Bridgehampton, L.I. has returned to his Yazoo, Miss., roots. He sent me a charming cookbook compiled by William Faulkner's niece, Dean Wells. *The Great American Writers' Cookbook,* Yoknapatawpha Press, (Oxford, Miss.) has a lot of fine and/or arresting recipes by some serious writers along with some facetious balderdash by some (mercifully few) "macho" types. Miss Katherine Anne died in 1980 at the age of ninety, leaving behind a collection of recipes she was planning to publish eventually (if she hadn't passed away so untimely). She was an accomplished cook and her recipes are among the best ones in the book.

"CORN PONE, OLD STYLE

"2 cups white corn meal   ¼ teaspoon salt
2 tablespoons bacon fat

"Preheat oven at 450. Have baking tin ready, greased. Sift meal into bowl with salt. Add bacon fat. Scald with two cups boiling water, stirring with large spoon and pouring water slowly to avoid lumps. If necessary add a little more water to make a very heavy batter, not quite dough. Let stand to expand and soften until cool enough to handle.

"Form into small (two ounce) egg shaped pones. Press two fingertips into each one to make two dents (this is standard procedure, or custom, or tradition, what you like, I don't know why but I wouldn't think of not doing it). Place on baking sheet and put in the oven. Turn heat down to 350 at once, leave to bake until a bright smooth brown, about forty minutes. But look at them now and then to make sure.

"They should be served hot with butter. Very crusty outside, tender and melting inside. Ideal with cold buttermilk or sweet milk, with thick soups (split pea, black bean, black-eyed pea, potato) and meant to go with all sorts of good country messes, such as turnip greens, beet tops, boiled bacon with stewed fresh tomatoes."

Note: I realize that this recipe contains no fresh corn, but I found it irresistible, and after all, with winter coming on, you might need to know about corn pones from an unimpeachable authority such as Miss Katherine Anne. (—M. U.)

Scalloping Begins

On clear, calm days the immature individuals of this species
may often be seen in shallow water disporting themselves most
gaily, skipping about and snapping their valves in great glee.
—Augusta Foote Arnold, as quoted in
North Atlantic Seafood by Alan Davidson

These high-spirited bivalves had better have a care—the baymen are out in force chasing the prized blue-eyed scallops. And they fetch a charming price. This is one reason bay scallops are so seldom served "*nu et cru*" the way nature intended them: i.e., raw and unadorned. (When the price drops later in the season, try them raw with just a touch of lemon and salt.)

Scallops make a smashing seviche if you're feeling rich enough, or go scalloping yourself. I usually stretch out the scallops with a few fillets of the white side of the flounder. At any rate, there's a dazzling panoply of North Atlantic fish in early fall to combine with scallops in several ways: as a garnish, as a sauce, or as part of a fish chowder. While some fish dealers and restaurants go right on dealing flounder at you, the more enterprising could offer porgies, striped bass, bluefish, blackfish, fluke, tilefish, swordfish, mako and blue marlin, plus squid, mussels, clams and blue crabs. Generally speaking, the best fish is the one caught closest by. Any *really fresh* smallish white fish will do for the following recipes.

SEVICHE

Cebich and *ceviche* are some other spellings of this Mexican appetizer, which is traditionally made with mackerel. I prefer it made with flounder and, for *luxe,* with a combination of tiny bay scallops and flounder fillets. Weakfish could be used, but must be sliced no more than a quarter of an inch thick—skinned and boned, of course. This dish is normally served as a starter, but could serve as a light luncheon.

Serves 2–4.

½ pound bay scallops
½ pound flounder fillets (white sides)
½ cup fresh lime juice
⅓ cup scallions or red onions, minced
1 large, ripe tomato, peeled, seeded and chopped
1 to 2 tablespoons fresh hot chili peppers, seeded and minced or 1 or 2 canned jalapeño chilies, seeded and minced

2 tablespoons red sweet bell pepper, seeded, deveined and minced or same amount canned red pimento
2 tablespoons olive oil
Salt and white pepper to taste
Fresh coriander and/or parsley, minced (to taste)
Slices of ripe avocado, rolled in lime juice

Rinse the scallops and fish fillets briefly under cold water (do not wash away all their flavor). Cut the fish into thin flat squares of about one inch. Combine them with the scallops and the lime juice in a plastic bag. Tie it securely, put it in a deep bowl and refrigerate, turning the package from time to time, for about five hours. The texture will be firm and the fish will turn an opaque white.

Drain the fish, reserving the lime juice. Combine everything but the ripe avocado. Taste and add some of the reserved lime juice if needed. Garnish each serving with a few thin slices of avocado (rolling them in lime juice prevents the gold-green fruit from turning black when exposed to air).

This recipe can be prepared ahead up to combining the fish and scallops with the other ingredients, which should also be chilled, except for the oil, which must not be allowed to congeal.

SCALLOP AND FISH CHOWDER

Blackfish, sometimes called rockfish, turn up at this time of year, but there never seem to be any dependable quantities at any time of year. Its proper (common) name is the *tautog*, a type of wrasse that feeds on mollusks. There's a type of sea bass also called blackfish, but it is not so good for chowder. In winter, this stew is very good made with fresh cod.

Makes about 3 quarts.

1 tautog (blackfish), about 4 or
5 pounds
2 quarts fish fumet: 1 rib
celery, 1 sliced carrot, 1 sliced
onion, 1 bay leaf, 1 pint
dry white wine, 1½ quarts
water, salt to taste
¼ pound butter (1 stick)
1 large onion, chopped medium
fine
3 cloves garlic, peeled and
minced

3 medium size all-purpose
potatoes, peeled and diced
1 pound bay scallops
2 cups light cream
(half-and-half)
3 egg yolks, beaten
½ cup fresh parsley and chives,
minced together
Salt and white pepper to taste

Have the blackfish cleaned, gills removed and fins cut off. Have the head severed but keep it for the *fumet.* Have the fish cut into two or three pieces across the body.

Make the fish *fumet* by combining all the *fumet* ingredients listed, plus the head of the fish. Simmer for 30 minutes. Strain and discard all solids. As this chowder contains wine, egg yolks and cream, it should be made in a non-aluminum pot; an aluminum one could give the chowder a grayish cast.

Put the chunks of blackfish into the strained fish *fumet,* bring it to a slow simmer and cook, just under the boil, covered, for about 20 minutes, until barely firm and opaque. Strain, reserving the fish broth. Remove all trace of skin and bones from the fish and break it (or cut it) into bite-sized chunks.

In a heavy chowder pot (an enameled iron pot such as that made by Le Creuset is good, as is flame-proof earthenware glazed on the inside only), melt the butter and slowly simmer the onions and garlic, covered, until transparent. They should take on no color. Add the potatoes and strained fish *fumet.* Simmer about half an hour or until the potatoes are very soft.

Put the fish and raw scallops into the stew and bring to a simmer. At once add the cream, which you have beaten with the egg yolks, to the chowder, stirring constantly so it will not curdle. For extra insurance, do this off heat. Stir the mixture gently over a low fire until it thickens a little. This is a delicate, rather thin chowder and if you would like it thicker, cook 2 tablespoons of flour in the onion, butter and garlic mixture before adding the fish *fumet* and potatoes.

Serve in heated bowls sprinkled with a little of the mixed herbs. Hot corn muffins and a salad of mixed greens would complete a pleasant fall supper and still leave room for a substantial fruit pie made with seasonal plums, peaches, apples or pears.

Scallops, the True and the False

Behold congenial Autumn comes,
The sabbath of the year!
—John Logan, "Ode on a Visit to the Country"

Even so, I cling to summer. Each autumn tests my unshakeable faith in the "Indian summer" I believe to be lurking just ahead. No matter that more realistic folk have, by late September, closed their swimming pools and aired out their woollies, and that even my cat Rufus has sense enough to come in at sundown, I'm always sure that summer is not finally, irrevocably, over.

The tomatoes don't believe it; the eggplants go serenely on about their purple ways, and the impatiens proliferates idiotically. And I court disaster leaving houseplants outside that are probably pining for the warmth of indoors. Once you're too old to get outfitted for back-to-school, the autumn becomes a somewhat melancholy time. But even if my Indian summer never materializes, I'm always cheered by the simultaneous opening of two of my favorite seasons: scalloping and football.

No matter how many restaurants list them, no matter what fishmongers may advise you, there are no fresh, genuine, blue-eyed bay scallops to be had except from September through March. There is, however, an impostor: the calico (sea) scallops from Southern waters that masquerade—in appearance if not in flavor, they are similar—as Long Island bay scallops. The real article, the nonpareil bay scallop, has a creamy color with a very faint pink cast and, at this early season, is about the size of a quarter. Calicos are stark white (the calico refers to their shells, not their flesh) and very small, about the size of the end of your thumb. Bay scallops have a rich, sweet flavor, and for this reason I decided recently that I have made my last *Coquilles St. Jacques*. This classic dish is just too much embellishment for the delicate bay scallop. Here is a much simpler dish with, I think, a superior, more cleanly defined, taste.

BAY SCALLOPS IN BUTTER SAUCE

The sauce, a famous French one called Beurre Blanc, is made from a reduction of the poaching liquids and good fresh sweet butter. For all its apparent simplicity, it takes a fine judgment to get it just right. French legend has it that the classic Beurre Blanc is a "woman's sauce" because the great women cooks of France, Mère Clemence and others, made it their specialty. Ths rich first course looks lovely in shallow but heavy earthenware bowls or in large scallop shells that are sold in cookware stores (local scallop shells never get that big).

Serves 4.

Buy 1¼ pounds of bay scallops to serve four as a first course. The recipe is in three parts: preparing the court-bouillon, cooking the scallops, making the sauce.

COURT-BOUILLON

This makes a little over a quart of poaching liquid, just enough to cover the scallops. Save the leftover broth and freeze it for future soups or sauces. Court-bouillon is enhanced by having several fish poached in its lovely vapors.

1 carrot, peeled and thinly sliced
1 stalk celery, peeled and thinly sliced
1 medium onion, thinly sliced
2 cloves garlic, cut in half
1 sprig fresh thyme (or big pinch of dried)

1 sprig fresh tarragon (or big pinch of dried)
4 white peppercorns, cracked
1 teaspoon coarse salt
1 cup dry white wine
1 quart water

Combine all ingredients and simmer together, covered, for 30 minutes. Strain.

COOKING THE SCALLOPS

Rinse them very lightly in cold water, or you can just pick them over for bits of shell that sometimes cling. Put the scallops in a deep saucepan, cover them with the strained court-bouillon, bring it to the simmer. Turn off the heat, and let the scallops stand, covered, for 5 minutes. Pour off the liquid, cover and set the scallops aside in a warm place. Heat the dishes or shells for the scallops and quickly make the sauce.

BEURRE BLANC
(Creamy Butter Sauce)

The trick here is in incorporating the butter to a creamy emulsion without letting it melt. If that happens, you are stuck with a lot of melted butter, which you had probably better turn into a hollandaise by whisking it into three egg yolks (or use a blender). I don't know of anyway to reverse a collapsed (melted) Beurre Blanc, so be on your toes and don't let it melt.

Makes about 2 cups.

¼ cup court-bouillon
1 tablespoon shallots, minced to
  a pulp
1 tablespoon white wine vinegar

¾ pound (3 sticks) sweet
  butter
Salt and white pepper to taste

If you have a heavy, small copper saucepan you've never seen a use for, this is the ideal time to bring it out. Otherwise use Calphalon or enamel-lined cast iron—the weight is important, but it must be small so that you can lift it hastily from the fire from time to time.

Reduce the bouillon, shallots and vinegar until the liquid has almost evaporated. Cool the saucepan until you can comfortably cradle it in your hand. Cut each stick of cold butter into four pieces and begin whisking them in, one at a time, over a very low flame. Lift the pot from time to time and work as quickly as you can. When all the butter is incorporated, season with salt and pepper. Divide the warm scallops on the plates and instantly blanket them with the sauce. Your guests should have their forks at the ready and their Muscadet (the ideal wine with this dish) already poured.

Fall Vegetables

If condos and cluster housing grow where once the stately rows of cauliflower,
cabbages and little trees of Brussels sprouts held ground, we may indeed see the
day when all fresh vegetables are luxuries. At the moment we have plenty of crisp
fall vegetables to compensate for the loss of summer's lush produce. (I can face the
end of the zucchini season with the same calm as the death of the last gypsy moth.)

Unlike artichokes and avocados, Brussels sprouts have never had much glamour.
But a few years ago, some smart East End farmers figured out that they looked
quite exotic left on their central growing stalk—like tiny Christmas trees in fact.
City folks marveled at them and took them home to tempt little Alison into trying
a mouthful of this weird "new" veg. Frozen vegetables are so pervasive in America's
eating habits that relatively few people even know what a live vegetable looks like
in its native state.

The following recipes accord our fresh local vegetables the respect they deserve,
and several can even serve as the centerpiece of a meal rather than as a casual
adjunct.

SAUTÉED BRUSSELS SPROUTS AND POTATOES

The sort of little brown potatoes usually left in the fields for the gleaners are
wonderful for this dish. But first-quality "boiling" potatoes, or russets, peeled and
cut into chunks, will do as well. In this dish, the vegetables are partially cooked
separately, then sautéed together, with bacon and a bit of onion, until all the elements
are crisp and lightly browned.

Serves 4.

1 quart basket small Brussels sprouts	*2 shallots or 1 medium white onion, minced*
1½ pounds small brown potatoes (or equivalent)	*Salt and freshly ground pepper to taste*
3 to 4 slices thick-cut bacon, cut into small squares	

Wash and trim the sprouts. Cook them in an open pot of salted boiling water until barely tender at the root end. Run cold water into the pot to stop the cooking, which will take barely 5 minutes. Drain them in a colander and spread them out on paper towels to dry.

Wash and scrub the potatoes (or pare and cut large potatoes into chunks). Either steam them over a little boiling water or cook them in a small amount of boiling salted water until barely tender. Do not overcook, or they will fall apart during the subsequent sautéing.

Put the bacon into a cold iron skillet large enough to hold all rest of the ingredients (a deep-sided French *sauteuse* is ideal). Try out the bacon slowly until almost crisp and until some fat is rendered.

Stir the shallots or onion into the bacon. Add the sprouts, and roll them around in the pan to coat them with bacon fat. Raise heat and sauté, moving the pan frequently for about 3 minutes. Add the well-dried potatoes and continue sautéing for several minutes more. You must stand over this operation attentively, moving the pan every few seconds and not allowing anything to burn. The sprouts improve in flavor when they take on a rather dark-brown crispiness, but the potatoes should be just a golden color. Season to taste with coarse salt and plenty of freshly milled black pepper. This is a wonderful country supper in autumn and is so satisfying that a small lamb or pork chop is all that is needed to round out a meal nicely. Vegetarians could easily adopt it for a one-dish meal with a salad added. An especially lovely addition to this vegetable combination would be a weisswurst, a delicate white veal sausage, originally German. These can be bought at food specialty stores and at German butcher shops. In New York they are made by Karl Ehmer and Schaller & Weber.

PURPLE CAULIFLOWER SALAD

Purple "cauli" is the result of some horticultural hijinks over the past several years, and it can now be found on most farm stands. (Royal Burgundy string beans are another of these hybrids that start out dark purple and turn a delicate green when cooked.) The purple cauliflower has a mild broccoli flavor and meltingly tender texture. Great care must be taken not to overcook it.

Serves 4 to 6.

2 small heads purple cauliflower
4 tablespoons walnut oil or
   3 tablespoons olive oil mixed
   with 2 teaspoons brown
   sesame oil

1 tablespoon fresh lemon juice
Salt and pepper to taste
4 scallions, minced

Wash the heads and trim them down to small flowerets (you can use the stems to make soup). Bring a large pot of salted water to a boil and drop in the vegetable. Boil gently, uncovered, about 2 to 3 minutes, until barely tender. Drain and refresh in a basin of ice water. Drain again and arrange on paper towels to absorb any excess moisture.

Mix together whichever oil you have chosen with the lemon juice, and add salt and pepper to taste. Season it rather highly, as it is difficult to add to the dressing once it is on this tender vegetable, which breaks easily.

Put the cauliflower in a bowl and pour on the dressing evenly. Mix it *very* gently with your hands. Sprinkle on the minced scallions and serve at room temperature.

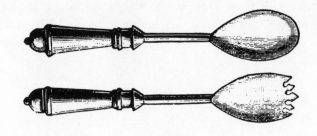

CAULIFLOWER SOUP WITH CROUTONS

How something can be at once elegant and rustic I can't quite explain, but this soup is exactly that. It is thickened with potatoes, not flour, and is hearty enough to serve as a luncheon main course.

Serves 4–6.

*1 large head white cauliflower
  with leaves
2 "boiling" potatoes (about
  1 pound)
Handful of fresh celery leaves
1 small onion, minced
2 cups chicken broth*

*2 cups cauliflower water
Salt and white pepper to taste
1 cup heavy cream
2 tablespoons fresh parsley,
  minced
Croutons*

Wash and trim the cauliflower, retaining the pale-green inner leaves that cling to the head. Separate the head into flowerets and cook it in a large pot of lightly salted boiling water for about 3 minutes. Drain it, reserving 2 cups of the cooking water.

Wash, pare and dice the potatoes. Put these and the minced onion and celery leaves into a pot. Add the chicken broth and cauliflower water, bring to a simmer and season to taste with salt and white pepper. Cook on slow heat until potatoes are tender, then add reserved cauliflower and simmer until cauliflower is very tender. Purée the soup, then return it to a clean saucepan and heat thoroughly. Stir in the heavy cream, heat a bit more, then divide among hot soup plates, sprinkle with parsley and fresh croutons and serve.

HOMEMADE CROUTONS

I have tried innumerable brands of packaged croutons because I'm very fond of them in soups and salads. Unfortunately, I've had to throw them all out after one tasting. I can't imagine why they're so awful . . . unless it's the preservatives added to give them the shelf-life of an Egyptian mummy. Homemade ones aren't much trouble, and they add a wonderful crunchiness to counterpoint the smooth, creamy soup.

4 thick slices "home-style"   *½ stick butter*
  white bread   *2 tablespoons plain salad oil*

Trim the crusts from the bread and cut the slices into ½-inch cubes. Let them dry out for an hour. Heat the butter and oil together in a large sauté pan or black iron skillet. Toss in the bread cubes and fry until crisp, moving them around constantly. Drain on paper towels and use at once. If you prefer a lower-calorie crouton, simply cube the bread and spread it out on a cookie sheet or jelly-roll pan and bake in a 400° F. oven, stirring occasionally, until very lightly browned and dry. These can be kept in an airtight canister for several days.

Some Useful Sauces

While French and Italian cookery could scarcely exist without sauces, Americans have rather stoutly resisted coming to grips with even the simplest of them. This severely restricts one's culinary range and condemns one to eating the same vegetables with as much variety as, in S. J. Perelman's words, "tracer bullets."

BÉCHAMEL SAUCE (MEDIUM)

Anyone unable to make this sauce really cannot cook at all, as it is *the basic sauce*, not terribly exciting in itself, but essentially to a number of derivative sauces and a variety of dishes from soufflés to croquettes. Béchamel and velouté sauces are used to enhance and/or transform eggs, fish, poultry, veal and vegetables in every course from hors d'oeuvre to savory.

If this sauce is made with chicken, veal or fish broth, it is called a velouté (which may or may not be enriched with cream or eggs); if with milk or light cream, it starts out as a béchamel. Besides dressing vegetables or fish and shellfish, it is useful for combining leftovers and can be varied with herbs, spices and cheeses. If a thin sauce is needed, use one tablespoon less flour; if a very thick sauce is wanted, use one tablespoon more flour and ½ tablespoon more butter than the basic recipe calls for.

Makes 2 cups.

2 tablespoons butter
3 tablespoons flour
2 cups milk simmered with
   1 small onion, quartered, and
   1 sprig parsley

Salt and white pepper to taste
1 teaspoon lemon juice

OPTIONAL ENRICHMENT
*1 to 2 tablespoons softened
butter whisked in just before
serving*

Melt the butter in a small, heavy-bottomed saucepan (avoid iron or unalloyed aluminum, which could discolor the sauce). Stir in the flour with a wooden spoon and cook, stirring, over very low heat about 2 minutes to eradicate the raw flour taste. The roux (that's what you have now) should not color at all—if it scorches, start over. The hot milk, which should be gently simmered 30 minutes with the quartered onion and parsley sprig, should be strained into the roux, whisking vigorously. Season to taste with salt and pepper (if no white pepper is available, use cayenne so that there will be no visible specks in the finished sauce). Add the lemon juice a few drops at a time until you get the desired effect. A béchamel should not actually taste of lemon; it is only there to subtly point up the sauce. For use with vegetables, in particular spinach, grate in a tiny bit of nutmeg.

Unless the sauce is to be combined with something else and cooked further, you must simmer it carefully over an asbestos pad on low heat for at least another 15 minutes, stirring often. This sauce used to be cooked for hours and hours, but as the flour is first cooked in the butter and the milk is also simmered in this technique, the need for long simmering is obviated.

You may keep this basic sauce warm for hours in an improvised *bain-marie*—a pan of hot water with the saucepan set into it. If you choose to enrich your béchamel or velouté to a French lushness with egg yolks and cream and more butter, wait until serving time before doing so, as the butter tends to break down and separate if the sauce is kept hot too long. The extreme direct heat of a broiler has the same effect, so a sauce to be used in a *gratin* dish should not be enriched with more butter, although it is perfectly all right to add egg yolk and cream.

For an herb sauce, just before serving beat in three or four tablespoons of finely minced parsley, chives, tarragon or chervil, or a mixture of these herbs, depending on what food the sauce is to be served with. If you must use dried herbs (though there can never be any excuse for dried parsley), they must be infused in the hot milk for at least 15 minutes to reconstitute their flavor. Unfortunately, dried herbs are not a fresh green color, and my recommendation is to omit them from any white sauce and use fresh parsley and the tops of scallions if nothing else is available.

THICK CREAM SAUCE

Make a thick béchamel using 3 tablespoons butter and 4 tablespoons flour. In addition to the milk, finish the sauce by stirring in heavy whipping cream by the spoonful until you have the consistency you want. The cream is to make the texture silky, not to thicken it, so do not cook it to a paste.

SAUCE MORNAY

Restaurants invariably serve this cheese sauce with cauliflower and it can be very good—if the cheese was any good to begin with. Sometimes the "sauce" seems to consist of nothing but melted Velveeta, a noisome orange dairy product that bears little resemblance to actual cheese. This cooked "processed cheese" molded into waxy loaves is to be avoided at all costs. I can't imagine why it was ever invented except for its almost limitless shelf-life. (This gives the dairy farmer something to do with his surplus milk, which is bought and stored forever by the government.) Use any natural cheddars, Swiss (Emmenthaler) or the Norwegian Jarlsberg cheese for a good Mornay. If Gruyère from France or the Swiss side of the Jura is available to you, that should be the first choice.

Makes 2½ cups.

*2 cups basic béchamel or
velouté sauce
1 cup grated natural hard cheese
(as above)*

*Pinch of nutmeg (freshly
grated)
2 tablespoons grated Parmesan
(optional)*

Bring the basic sauce to a careful low simmer, stirring constantly. Remove it from the fire and beat in the grated hard cheese, then put it back over low flame and continue stirring until the sauce is perfectly smooth. Grate in a little nutmeg but do not get carried away; this strongly flavored nut from Jamaica can overpower other flavors all too easily. Always check the balance of salt and pepper in any sauce at the end of the cooking.

HOLLANDAISE

Some truly weird concoctions have come my way under the guise of hollandaise . . . and they keep getting weirder. As the brunch date proliferates, thus condemning hundreds of thousands of eggs to go forth every Sunday dressed as "Eggs Benedict," some company had to come up with an "instant" hollandaise. Except for its somewhat lurid hue, the powdered mix looks exactly like the genuine article, but the taste is rather like artificial lemon pudding. Very few sauces are simpler or quicker to make; it consists of egg yolks, butter, hot water, salt, cayenne or Tabasco and a few drops of lemon juice. It is not meant to be sour; in fact, one should not really be aware of the lemon juice, although most contemporary American versions taste of little else. (My war with lemon-juice-on-everything is very likely as hopeless as my husband's battle with the misuse of the word "hopefully"—lost.)

3 egg yolks (U.S. Grade A
"large")
Pinch of salt
6 ounces (1½ sticks) unsalted
butter

Few drops of lemon juice
Few drops of Tabasco or a bit
of white pepper

There are many ways to get the yolks and butter amalgamated; this is the one I prefer. Select a heavy china bowl, a good bit narrower at the base than at the top, and set it over a steady deep saucepan of *almost* simmering water. Put the egg yolks and 1 tablespoon of hot water into the bowl and whisk vigorously a few seconds.

Cut half a stick of the butter into six slices. Melt the other stick and let it cool somewhat.

Add the salt and slowly trickle in the melted butter, whisking constantly. If the sauce seems to be getting too thick or the bowl too hot, remove it from the saucepan, set it on a folded towel and whisk in some cold butter, one piece at a time. Return the bowl to its place over the hot water and continue beating in the remaining melted butter alternately with the cold butter. Season with lemon juice and Tabasco and more salt if needed. This sauce can never be more than lukewarm or it will curdle—if you see this developing, beat in a few drops of cold water to smooth out the sauce. The whole process takes about 5 minutes.

BLENDER HOLLANDAISE

The only thing that has ever gone awry using this technique is when I have rushed the butter into the yolks, without cooling it sufficiently, causing the sauce not to thicken correctly. As it can be made at least an hour ahead of time and the whole blender jar set into a saucepan of warm water to hold, there's no point in a last-minute rush to make this sauce.

3 egg yolks (U.S. grade A "large")
½ teaspoon salt
Dash Tabasco or sprinkle white pepper

1 tablespoon lemon juice (or less, to taste)
6 ounces (1½ sticks) sweet butter

Put the eggs, salt, Tabasco and lemon juice in the blender jar. Melt the butter over low heat, skim off the foam, and cool slightly. Blend the egg yolks at high speed for three or four seconds. Remove the center from the blender top and, with the blender at high speed, slowly trickle in the melted butter. If the machine begins to clog, pour the butter a bit faster; if it still clogs, add a teaspoon of very hot water to get it going.

When the butter is in and the sauce thick (it should plop, not run weakly), taste for seasoning and add more salt, Tabasco or lemon juice—but do not obliterate the delicate flavor of the fresh egg yolks and butter.

Serve the sauce in a slightly warmed sauceboat. This recipe may be doubled easily, but as hollandaise is such a rich sauce most people will not care to eat it in great quantities. There are exceptions of course; even in my own family there are members who would confiscate the entire sauceboat for themselves alone. Besides cauliflower and broccoli, this luscious sauce is wonderful with hot artichokes and broiled fish.

If there is any leftover sauce, store it in a tightly covered jar in the refrigerator. Allow it to return to room temperature before stirring and do not try to reheat it. The heat of the food it is served on should be adequate to do that.

MAYONNAISE AND DERIVATIVE SAUCES

A twelve-year-old friend dropped in on me one afternoon when I was making some mayonnaise. He couldn't have been more astounded had he discovered me grinding my own wheat. Yet commercially bottled mayonnaise was uncommon in this country until the thirties and is still an expensive rarity in European stores (Hellmann's can be found in their *recherché* food sections). But at last American cooks are getting back to basics, and reintroducing the voluptuous fresh flavor of homemade mayonnaise. Perhaps the myth that mayonnaise is a terribly tricky thing to make has disappeared with the coming of the food processor.

Since there are so many possible formulas for this delicious sauce, it can be either more, or less, expensive than the commercial product. But aside from possible economy, the chief thing about homemade mayonnaise is that its texture, flavor and density, not to mention its pureness, can be controlled by the maker. And the basic sauce can be varied in so many interesting ways.

Commercial mayonnaise is not made with olive oil; more likely, cottonseed or cheap soya oil is used. If you are going to bother with making your own mayonnaise, it should be at *least* half olive oil for general purposes and 100 percent olive oil for such specialties as *aïoli* and the fancier sauces. A decent grade of oil from the Italian province of Lucca is good for general use, but of course your mayonnaise will assume greater finesse if you are able to invest occasionally in the fine cold-pressed virgin olive oils of France and Italy.

Just as you may elect to use various types of oil in differing proportions, you may alter the number of egg yolks. It is safest to allow one egg yolk per ½ cup of oil. It is possible to incorporate 8 ounces of oil into a single yolk, but the risk of curdling rises tremendously, and I see no point in courting disaster when eggs are cheap and oil is not. An exception to this is blender mayonnaise, in which a whole egg must be employed in order to keep the machine from clogging.

It is possible to make mayonnaise in a mortar with a pestle; in a bowl with a wooden spoon or wire whisk; or in a soup plate with a table fork; in an electric mixer; with a hand-held electric beater; or in a food processor as well as in the aforementioned plain old blender. Blender mayonnaise is less rich and golden than those made with only yolks, but there are occasions when a lighter sauce is preferred. Additionally, it is the only kind of mayonnaise which, in my experience, absolutely *never* "breaks down." This problem, idiosyncratically, can happen even when apparently you have done everything exactly right. Fortunately this is rare and it can be cured.

Whichever method you choose, the ingredients should all be at room temperature; the oil emulsifies quicker if it is tepid.

Processor Mayonnaise

The very best result with the least effort is obtained via the food processor method. It produces a rich, stiff yellow sauce undetectable from a mayonnaise laboriously whisked together by hand. (However, watching the mayonnaise slowly develop is enjoyable, and many people really prefer the hand method.)

Makes about 1¾ cups.

3 egg yolks (U.S. grade A "large")
1 teaspoon Dijon-style mustard or ¼ teaspoon dry mustard
½ teaspoon salt (optional)
1½ cups light olive oil or ¾ cup olive and ¾ cup salad oil

2 teaspoons lemon juice*
White pepper or cayenne to taste
1 to 2 tablespoons boiling water (if needed)

If the eggs are directly from the refrigerator, drop the separated yolks directly into a small bowl which has been heated with boiling water and dried. Warm the oil by placing it, in its container, in a pan of warm water until it is tepid.

Fit the food processor with the metal blade. Put the egg yolks, the mustard, salt and 1 tablespoon of the oil into the bowl of the processor. Cover it and turn it on. Dribble the remaining oil through the top opening until the sauce begins to thicken. At this point you may pour it in a thin, fine stream, and when the mayonnaise becomes really thick, run the oil in faster and add the lemon juice. If it is too thick, thin it with a tablespoon of boiling water, then another, if needed. Some say this stabilizes the mayonnaise and it seems to keep longer in the refrigerator. However the hot water also turns the mayonnaise from glossy and translucent to a paler, opaque color, which is preferable when the sauce is to be used in combination with other foods, as in chicken salad, for instance.

Store in a tightly covered jar in the refrigerator with as little air as possible between sauce and lid. It will keep quite well for a week, but not if you allow it to stand out in a warm room too often.

* White wine vinegar is more commonly used, but I prefer fresh lemon juice.

Handmade Mayonnaise

Ingredients are the same as for Processor Mayonnaise (preceding recipe). The main problem with this method is that you really need three hands. However, people have been making mayonnaise this way since 1756, when, legend has it, the cook of the French commander beseiging the English at Port Mahon in Minorca invented it. Ah, those French! Even under battle conditions, a sauce emerges that will live forever.

The English know a thing or too about mayonnaise also: they invented a heavy china bowl with one flattened side at the base, so that it will stand tilted and steady while one pours oil with the one hand and beats with the other. It is called T. G. Green's "gripstand" bowl and can be found at fine kitchenware shops. An ordinary heavy bowl of about 3-quart capacity can be used if it is propped up on one side with a heavy wet cloth. The bowl must not slip.

Beat the yolks, freed of any white specks, with the mustard and salt until thick and sticky. Whisking constantly, dribble in the oil, drop by drop, from a spouted pitcher. When it stiffens—you do not have to beat madly, just steadily—after about 5 minutes, you may pour the oil in a thin, thread-like stream. Add drops of lemon juice or vinegar from time to time to thin the sauce. When it is finished, season to taste with pepper. If the mayonnaise is to be used immediately, the boiling water isn't necessary and you may thin, if you choose, with tap water.

Electric Mixer Mayonnaise

Use the same ingredients in the order given for Processor Mayonnaise. Set the beater on medium speed and again, very slowly, dribble in the oil. With this method you only need *one* hand.

Blender Mayonnaise

This is the easiest and quickest of all the methods. It is also lighter and less caloric—it is also a little less divine.

Makes about 1 cup.

1 whole egg (U.S. grade A "large")
¼ teaspoon dry mustard
¼ teaspoon salt
½ cup olive oil plus *½ cup salad oil* or *1 cup olive oil, at room temperature*

1 teaspoon lemon juice or white wine vinegar
Cayenne or white pepper to taste

Put the whole egg in the blender jar with the dry mustard and salt. Whirl at highest speed a few seconds, then remove center of top and through the opening pour the oil in a very fine, thin stream directly into the vortex of the eggs. If machine starts to clog, increase rate of oil. Add lemon juice and pepper. If the machine clogs before all the oil is incorporated, thin the sauce with a little warm water (or boiling water dribbled from a spoon).

RECONSTITUTING A "BROKEN" MAYONNAISE. If the mayonnaise breaks down, that is, separates into a helpless ugly bowl of oil and curds, it is because the oil has been added too rapidly. The egg yolk is a capricious thing and must be fed the oil drop by drop (like an orphaned squirrel) until it emulsifies well. Otherwise the yolk simply collapses and releases whatever oil you've managed to beat into it.

Fortunately there is a great Humpty Dumpty act that always works. Pour your curdled mayonnaise into a pitcher. Wash out the bowl you made it in and rinse with hot water. Dry well. Put another room-temperature egg yolk into the bowl, whisk until dark and sticky, then, beating all the time, whisk in the turned mayonnaise, tablespoon by tablespoon, until you have incorporated about half the sauce into this new egg yolk. You may then continue with the whisk or transfer the mixture to a processor or mixer and add the remaining curdled sauce in a very thin stream. The reason for not starting over in the machines is that a single egg yolk does not provide enough mass for these rather large containers to work successfully.

AÏOLI

Until about ten years ago this most famous of Provençal sauces, a heavily garlicked dense mayonnaise, was unfamiliar to most Americans. Now there are addicts in every part of the country. *Aïoli* (pronounced eye-o-lee; *ail* is French for garlic) is the most important part of an *Aïoli Garni,* boiled fish and fresh vegetables, which was the standard Friday dinner in Provence. It also adorns the classic *bourride,* a white fish stew more highly regarded by many Frenchmen than the now touristy *bouillabaisse.* It is wonderful on baked potatoes instead of butter and I long ago made it the dipping sauce for my cocktail parties' *crudités. Aïoli* is powerful stuff, and people who have eaten it together probably should stay together until the fumes die down.

Makes about 1½ cups.

1 *slice day-old white bread,* *crustless*	*Pinch of salt*
3 *tablespoons wine vinegar*	1 *cup tepid olive oil*
6 *cloves garlic (or 4 large ones)*	2 *tablespoons lemon juice* *(approximately)*
1 *egg yolk*	3 *tablespoons boiling water*

Just as in French grammar, we immediately have an exception to the egg yolk–oil ratio. It is the bread in *Aïoli* that holds the oil together in this sauce.

Soak the bread in the vinegar about 5 minutes. Remove and squeeze nearly dry. Put the garlic and bread into a mortar and pound it to a smooth paste. Pound in the egg yolk and salt. When it is thick and very sticky, add the oil by droplets and after about ⅓ is incorporated, you may pour a little faster and use a wire whisk to complete the beating. The whole process can be done with a mortar and pestle (traditionally it *was*) but I find the sauce works up faster and with less exertion using the whisk.

To keep the mortar from bouncing around, either wedge it into a pot lined with damp dish towels, or hold it clenched between your knees—again the old three-hand problem. Add some lemon juice when the sauce becomes very heavy. Thin with the boiling water, using only as much as necessary. *Aïoli* should be a very stiff paste that holds its shape.

You can make this sauce with minimum exertion in a food processor. Add an extra yolk and ½ cup oil to the basic recipe (the bowl is rather large and the steel blade must have a little more volume to work with), adding the ingredients in the order given.

MAYONNAISE VERTE

Make a mayonnaise by any method you choose and add to it:

2 *tablespoons parsley, minced*	1 *tablespoon chives, minced*
2 *tablespoons tarragon, minced*	
2 *tablespoons watercress leaves,* *minced*	

Blanch all the herbs in boiling water for twenty seconds, drain, refresh, drain and pat very dry. Stir into the mayonnaise or put the herbs in during the final beating of the sauce. If you want a pale-green sauce with few flecks in it, add the herbs at the beginning of the mayonnaise making. Good on fish, shellfish, chicken, hard-boiled eggs and raw vegetables as well as hot boiled potatoes and cold cooked broccoli or asparagus.

SAUCE GRIBICHE

This sauce, pronounces Escoffier, "is usually served as an accompaniment to cold fish." I wish someone would tell America's restaurants about that: how much nicer a shrimp cocktail would be with a Sauce Gribiche instead of that obliterating catsup and horseradish usually served.

Makes 1½ cups.

1 raw egg yolk (U.S. grade A "large")
2 hard-boiled egg yolks
1½ cups olive oil
½ teaspoon dry mustard

Juice of ½ lemon (or equivalent in vinegar)
Salt and cayenne to taste
1 tablespoon boiling water

Make the basic mayonnaise, using the above ingredients, by any of the preceding methods. This sauce should be a little thinner than a regular mayonnaise, so you may have to thin it further with another spoonful of hot water. When the mayonnaise is finished, stir in the following:

Whites of 2 hard-boiled eggs, julienned
2 small kosher dill gherkins, finely chopped
2 tablespoons scallions (or chives), minced

2 tablespoons small capers
¼ cup parsley, minced
1 tablespoon fresh tarragon leaves, minced
1 teaspoon prepared Dijon-style mustard

SAUCE RÉMOULADE

This sauce has, in addition to the above additions to a basic mayonnaise, a bit of anchovy paste and minced chervil.

Autumn's Silver Lining

It was a struggle not to accept second or even third helpings of
soup and so risk having no appetite left for the dishes to follow.
This is one of the dangers of a good soup.
—Elizabeth David, *French Provincial Cooking*

Turning this "danger of a good soup" to advantage, this is the most felicitous time
of year to enfold all the last flavors of summer in the famous *Soupe au Pistou* of
Provence. The Niçois, whose cuisine shares many characteristics with that of northern Italy, have simply appropriated "minestrone," given it their own interpretation
and added the Gallic version of pesto sauce to flavor the soup at table. (Just when you
thought you'd seen the last pesto ride into the sunset!)

Even though I heartily endorse a moratorium on most things *al pesto*, this stu-
pendous peasant soup is such a soul-warming comfort on crisp fall evenings, it would
be a shame not to try it while all the makings are in such good supply. Actually a
winter version is entirely possible if you have managed to salvage some basil in preserved form . . . more on that later.

Richard Olney writes in his fine book, *Simple French Food,* of *pistou:* "The thing,
in itself, is like some unleashed earth force, sowing exhilaration in its wake—but, in
that wake, nothing else may be savored, for it has a distinctly paralyzing effect on
the palate; one may as well make it in quantity and plan to make a meal of it . . .
And it is a sure wine-killer, so one may as well settle for a well-chilled, lightbodied,
dry rosé."

Good country bread of any ethnic persuasion and some fine fresh butter are the
only other requisites to round out this meal. It should be served in large, heavy soup
plates (well heated), so there is plenty of room for stirring in the *pistou* and mopping
the plate with bread. This is not a genteel soup, but a meal to engulf the senses. For
a *pistou* dinner party one might want to serve a simple fruit dessert such as pears
simmered in spiced red wine or a warm apple crisp with cream.

There's no way of making this dish in small quantities, but even if you have not
invited guests to share it, *Soupe au Pistou* remains in delicious condition, refrigerated,
for four or five days. I suppose you could freeze it, but the texture of the various vegetables would certainly be altered. But being able to enjoy *pistou* on a cold December
day might be worth the sacrifice of a little texture.

SOUPE AU PISTOU

Makes about 6 quarts.

½ pound dried white beans
 (Great Northerns)
¼ pound lean slab bacon, cut
 in julienne strips
1 tablespoon olive oil
3 medium onions, chopped
2 leeks, finely sliced
3 long carrots, peeled and sliced
 (2 cups)
2 large baking potatoes, peeled
 and diced
3 large celery stalks, peeled and
 diced fine

½ small head of green cabbage,
 shredded
1 quart light chicken stock
1 quart water
2 cups fresh green beans, cut in
 2-inch lengths
2 small zucchini, cut in short
 sticks
Salt and freshly milled pepper
 to taste

SAUCE PISTOU

4 cloves garlic, peeled and
 chopped
2 cups basil leaves, lightly
 packed
½ cup parsley, leaves only
1 teaspoon salt

Freshly milled pepper
1 cup grated Parmesan cheese
1 cup olive oil
1 ripe tomato, peeled, seeded
 and chopped

Never use freshly picked basil leaves (they should be a day old, refrigerated) for this sauce, warns Mireille Johnston, author of *The Cuisine of the Sun,* a book about Provençal food. Since she was born in Nice and I wasn't, I do what she says . . . but not altogether. Her *pistou* uses five whole cups of shredded basil leaves, but the palates around my table basil-out on that much of this rambunctious herb.

I might add that there are many ways to make an "authentic" *Soupe au Pistou,* just as there are for making a champion vegetable soup. The bacon in my version is unorthodox. And this is considered an early summer soup in France . . . but our seasonal vegetables don't gibe with theirs. Finally, nearly all versions of this sturdy soup include some kind of macaroni, but I feel that a soup carrying both potatoes and white beans has quite enough body without throwing in pasta. In any event, the pasta gets somewhat waterlogged if all the soup isn't eaten at the first sitting.

Wash and pick over the dried beans the night before you plan to make the soup. Cover them with cold water and soak overnight. Next day, cover with fresh cold water (no salt) and boil them slowly, covered, until firm-tender—about one and a half hours.

In a large, heavy casserole, sauté the bacon in the olive oil. When the bacon is almost crisp, add the onions and cook over very low heat. Wash the leeks well,* trim off the roots and most of the green (the upper leaves are extremely tough and inedible). Slice finely crosswise and add to the soup pot. Add carrots, potatoes, celery, cabbage, chicken stock and water. Add the pre-cooked white beans, drained of their liquid. Cover the pot and boil the vegetables slowly about 30 to 40 minutes (this depends on the age and conditions of your vegetables). Add green beans and cook 5 minutes if the beans are young and tender, longer if not. Add the zucchini sticks last, as they require about 5 minutes cooking. Add salt and pepper to taste.

If the soup is not to be served at once, remove the cover and take the pot from the stove. Cool it in a cold pantry so that the vegetables don't continue to cook. Do not leave it on the back of a warm stove, as the soup could sour. A cool porch or garage is a good place to store it until you reheat it later. In any case, do not worry about the vegetables being crisp. This is an old-fashioned French country soup, and the French were as guilty as any of us of overcooking veggies before the *nouvelle cuisine* burst on the scene. And indeed the vegetables are supposed to meld flavors and textures in this sort of dish.

While the soup is cooking, make the *pistou*. Traditionally this is pounded to a paste in a large marble mortar. I have done it this way many times, and cannot see that it is in any way superior to a *pistou* made in a food processor. Put the garlic in the processor bowl and mince it as finely as you can. Add the basil, parsley and salt to the container and mince, but do not purée it. Grind in some pepper, half of the cheese and pour in half of the olive oil. Blend. Add tomato, remaining olive oil and cheese and turn the motor off and on several times until all is well blended, but by no means a smooth purée. The *pistou* should have some texture, and it will have to be re-stirred by each person before he or she adds it to the soup. Because the Parmesan is salty, I have indicated very little additional salt. You may like more. I always like more fresh pepper than other people do, so taste and season as you blend the sauce.

Put the *pistou* into a heavy mortar or stoneware bowl along with a small ladle.

---

* Slit the leek from the top to within an inch of the base of the vegetable, slit it again similarly so that the leek is almost in fourths, and, spreading the leaves, wash it under cold running water to rid it of sand.

After the soup is served, each diner should add the heady sauce to his personal taste. If all the sauce is not used, run a thin film of olive oil over it, cover and refrigerate. It keeps well up to two weeks. A little *pistou,* with its obvious relationship to pesto, is excellent with egg pastas.

Note: To keep basil for several months, pick it in dry weather, lay it in salted layers in a plastic box and cover it completely with olive oil. Cover air-tight.

Oysters

I need no oyster
　　to be in love with you.
Nor, when I roister,
　　raw roots to chew; . . .
　　　—A. P. Herbert, "Love Song"

Oysters have been thought to be an aphrodisiac since man first had the wit to investigate those craggy, recalcitrant shells. They are also reputed to be "brain food." So it is small wonder that Roman consuls, European princes and American railroad barons have gorged on them. They are, it's true, very high in phosphorus, which may or may not turn up the lights in some dim bulbs. But I need no excuses to down a couple of dozen freshly opened plump and creamy Northwest Bay oysters.

M. F. K. Fisher wrote an essay years ago called "Consider the Oyster," in which she did just that. In it there are reminiscences, meditations, dogma, myths and recipes from everybody and every place. Mrs. Fisher's own oyster expertise ranges from the tiny Olympias of the Pacific Northwest to the famous Whitstables of England and the many varieties of France (the French cultivate more oysters than any other nation), then back to our own Atlantic coast varieties. Although every oyster fancier makes bellicose claims for the creatures of his native region, I offer this testimony from the supremely unbiased, superbly sensitive M. F. K. Fisher (a native of Whittier, California).

"In America, I think I like best the oysters from Long Island Sound, although I have eaten Chincoteagues and some others from the Delaware Bay that were very good. Farther south, in spite of my innate enthusiasm, I have had to admit that the oysters grow less interesting served in the shell, and almost cry out for such delicious decadences as horseradish or even cooking, which would be sacrilege in Boston or Bordeaux."

Which brings up a matter about which I am passionate: sauces on raw oysters in the shell. If these prized mollusks be fresh, from clean cold waters, and just opened, they need no adornment save perhaps a grind or two of fresh pepper. After the first dozen have been downed in this pristine state, it just might be allowable to add one drop of lemon juice to the body of each oyster right before drinking them off their shells. But that dense, obliterating, red catsup-and-horseradish sauce—never, no, never. It is a barbarous sauce, created for people with stone palates or those who eat in fast-food chains and neither know nor care what they are feeding on.

OYSTER STEW

My father used to rise from his reading chair about 10:30 of an evening and announce, "I think I'll just slip downtown for a bowl of oyster stew." He never invited anyone else along and I think really regarded this dish with such reverence that it had to be eaten in solitary with no distractions. To be a little more sociable, this recipe is designed for two.

12 large "stewing" oysters (with
their liquor)
3 tablespoons butter
1 tablespoon flour
1 tablespoon scallions, with some
green tops, minced

1 cup milk
1 cup half-and-half or light
cream
1 tablespoon minced parsley
Salt and pepper to taste
Oyster crackers

Cut the oysters in half and put them in a small saucepan with their liquor. Melt the butter in another saucepan and stir in the flour, then the scallions. Cook over low heat, stirring constantly, for a few minutes. Beat in the milk with a wire whisk; when it comes to a simmer, beat in the half-and-half and let stand over very low heat. Poach the oysters in their juices until the edges *just* ruffle, then add them to the milk-and-cream base. Heat this to just under the simmer, then stir in the parsley and season to taste with salt and pepper (or cayenne). Pour into two heated bowls and serve the oyster crackers on the side. Some people like to crumble them into the stew, but I prefer the crisp texture to nibble on between bites of the steamy, succulent stew.

GRILLED OYSTERS ON THE HALF-SHELL

Oysters cook, in fact overcook, in a matter of minutes, so this is a rather tricky preparation and should be attempted only for a few close friends who are willing to stand in the kitchen with you while you tend to the broiling very, very carefully.

Serves 4.

2 *dozen fresh oysters in their*
  shells
4 *tablespoons butter*
4 *to 6 large mushrooms, minced*
4 *shallots* or *mild onion, minced*

24 *squares of bacon, half cooked*
1 *lemon, quartered*
Rock *salt* or *a roll of*
  aluminum foil

If you cannot open oysters yourself, have the fish dealer do it for you, leaving the oyster on its deep shell, loosened. Ask him to save all the juice and give it to you in a container. Rush the oysters home and start cooking. (Actually, if you get them home a few hours in advance, they are perfectly wholesome—it's just that shellfish opened far in advance (as in some restaurants) lose their plumpness and fresh briny flavor.)

Melt the butter and sauté the mushrooms over medium heat for a couple of minutes. Add the shallots or onion and continue sautéing until they are translucent, stirring constantly.

Preheat the broiler for about 10 minutes. Use two jelly-roll pans or shallow roasting pans, and either fill them with an inch of rock salt on which to steady the shells, or crumple up a fairly large quantity of foil and place it in the bottom of the pans to serve the same purpose. Push the rough side of the shells down into the salt or foil so that they do not move. Divide the sautéed mushrooms and shallots among the shells and top each with an oyster and a bit of the liquor. Top each oyster with a bacon square.

Carefully slide the two pans under the broiler about 4 inches from the flame. (I have a huge, restaurant-style broiler—this may have to be done in two batches in a normal-sized broiler.) Watch the oysters constantly; when their edges begin to curl, snatch the pans from the heat and place them on trivets in the middle of the dining table. Give each diner a plate, a fork and a lemon quarter to use at his own discretion.

Country Pâté

Spring forward,
Fall back
—Anon.

It is now officially fall. I often wonder in what mythical part of the world the seasons occur as advertised. On eastern Long Island they are usually half over by the date they arrive. After an exceptionally long and gaudy autumn, for which I'm always grateful, there's a chill in the air and more briskness in the kitchen.

I begin to think of firing up the oven for some serious cooking—earthy pâtés and stews, cabbage soups and bean pots. Pâté and soup make a soul-satisfying autumn meal for families (or loners), and besides that are ideal for country parties in winter.

I've hesitated to present a pâté recipe principally because most people are under the impression that they are too difficult (or impossible) to make. Pâtés do take time to explain, but require no more skill than it takes to make a good meat loaf—at least the simple *pâté de campagne* (country "block," according to one French dictionary) that follows here doesn't. And, too, the ingredients, cheap though they are, have not been that easy to find except in large cities. These are cheap stewing veal or patties, pork shoulder and hard pork fat in sheets. But I've been able to find all these things with little or no trouble as sophistication creeps toward Montauk. Leaf lard and caul fat (the lacy veil of fat surrounding the pig's stomach used to enclose homemade sausages or pâtés to be baked in a crust) still have to be special-ordered from the butchers, but they freeze well and are nice to have on hand in case a fit of pâté-making overwhelms one on a winter afternoon. Any shop with a real butcher in it should be able to provide the sheets of fresh, unsalted pork fat needed to line the pâté tins.

Do not make the mistake of using "better" or leaner or more expensive cuts of pork, because the fat content of shoulder is just right—even at that, extra pork fat is added. The commonest and absolutely fatal mistake made by Americans is cutting down on the rather alarming proportion of fat in French pâté recipes. It is essential to the correct texture and flavor and cannot be compromised on. It is better to just forget the whole matter than to attempt to make a "diet" pâté. Because of its unctuousness, pâté is always served chilled, in thin slices accompanied by pungent pickles and plain good bread.

PÂTÉ DE CAMPAGNE
(Country Pâté)

If you have never attempted a pâté before, it would be wise to observe the recipe rather strictly. However, after even one successful trial run, you should be confident enough to make a few conservative alterations. These could be some strips of raw breast of chicken or duck, or pieces of boneless rabbit marinated in wine or cognac, a very few chopped, peeled pistachios, perhaps tiny cubes of ham or tongue. This pâté can be made a week or two in advance quite safely, as it is sealed in its own fat. It should be made at least three days in advance for the flavors to blend and mellow.

French pâté pans are not wide like our bread pans that double as meat-loaf pans. They are longer, deeper and narrower as a rule, thus requiring a shorter cooking time. This recipe will fill a 1½-quart rectangular pâté tin or any terrine of that capacity (an oval terrine is a bit more tedious to line than the straightforward loaf shape). Cooking times vary with the depth of the pâté, and the surest way of determining doneness is with an instant-read cooking thermometer small and finely tuned enough to take a chop's temperature. Although split seconds aren't involved, don't imagine that a pâté cannot be overcooked. Too lengthy a time in the oven releases too much fat and juice from the meats, and you wind up with a dry, rather shriveled little loaf floating in a sea of very tasty fat and natural gelatin. An hour and a half is usually sufficient for this amount of meat.

Makes 1 terrine.

1 pound ground veal (or
    1½ pounds veal stew meat)
1 pound fresh pork shoulder
    (boneless)
½ pound fresh hard pork fat
    (trimmed from a loin of pork)
1 tablespoon salt
¼ cup cognac
¼ cup dry white wine
½ pound barding pork fat
    (sheets ⅛th inch thick)
⅔ cup fresh white breadcrumbs
3 eggs (grade A "large")

¼ cup parsley leaves, minced
1 tablespoon juniper berries
2 cloves garlic
1 medium onion
1 teaspoon dried thyme
1 teaspoon freshly ground
    allspice
2 teaspoons freshly milled coarse
    pepper
2 small or 1 large truffle
    (optional)
3 bay leaves

Mix the veal with the pork shoulder, which should be ground together with the pork fat. If you are using stewing veal, remove any membrane or fat before grinding it. A food processor is even better, as it doesn't squeeze out the juices of meat and is an invaluable tool in making pâtés. Process the meat to medium coarse and do not pulverize it. Mix in the salt, cognac and wine, cover and set aside in a cool place for an hour or so, or refrigerate overnight.

Line a 1½-quart loaf pan with the thin sheets of pork, leaving enough overhang to bring up over the top of the pâté, completely enclosing it.

Make the breadcrumbs in a processor or blender and add them to the meats. Beat the eggs and add them along with the minced parsley (or process the parsley and add eggs to clean processor before adding to meats).

Put the juniper berries and the garlic into the processor with a few grains of salt. When this is almost a paste, add the peeled onions and chop finely. Add this to the meat mixture, then add thyme, allspice and pepper. Mix all together lightly but thoroughly with your hands and avoid squeezing the mixture. At this point, test-fry a quarter-sized patty to taste for seasoning, which should be rather high. Otherwise the pâté will taste quite flat after chilling.

Pack half the pâté into the fat-lined tin. If using truffles, chop them into about ⅛-inch dice, arrange the pieces down the center of the forcemeat and pour on some of their juice.

Pack the remainder of the forcemeat into the pâté tin then fold over the pork strips to enclose it completely. Align the three bay leaves down the center. Cover with a double thickness of foil and secure it tightly under the rim of the pan. Set the pâté tin in an underpan and pour boiling water around it to a depth of 2 inches. Put the whole contraption into the center of an oven that has been preheated to 375° F. After 30 minutes, reduce the heat to 350° and continue baking for another 45 minutes. Remove the foil and bake, uncovered, an additional 15 minutes or until the fat runs clear, the pâté begins to float and/or the instant-read thermometer indicates the interior is 170° F. (Don't use those huge meat thermometers inserted at the beginning of the cooking—they are inaccurate and leave a big gaping hole for the juices to rush out of.)

Let the pâté rest for about 15 minutes, then lift it from the underpan. Pour out the hot water and replace it with cold. Pour all the fats and juices into a fat separator or a wide bowl that will enable you to skim off all the fat. When the fat and juices are separated, pour the juices back over the pâté (reserve the fat), cover it with a double layer of foil and a weight it with a board with evenly distributed canned goods on top weighing about two pounds. Heavier weights are added if there are large chunks or fillets of meat in the pâté, but it is not recommended for this rather soft mixture. If you haven't a board of the right size (or anyone to tailor one to your pans) use two 1 lb.-packages of spaghetti piled on top of each other.

When the pâté is cold, remove the weights, re-liquefy the reserved fat and pour it evenly over the pâté to seal it.

Note: This separating of the fats and juices while the pâté is being pressed is my own technique to ensure that the pâté will be well sealed. If it will be eaten within a few days, this is not necessary. The jelly in the bottom of the pâté is delicious and a little should be served with each slice of pâté.

To serve, run a table knife dipped in hot water around the inner rim of the pâté. Dip the bottom of the pan in hot water briefly (15 seconds) and invert the pâté on a long platter. Try not to melt the jelly on the bottom. Usually a couple of good, sharp downward jerks will make the pâté fall out into the platter.

This is a simple pâté that could be splendidly embellished with the addition of some fillet of venison, wild hare, pheasant, duck or turkey laid upon half the force-meat, then covered with the remainder.

Cordially Yours

Take the juice of a quart of gin . . .
—Eddie Condon, *We Called It Jazz*

Making cordials for the holidays was a ritual for both city and country wives in colonial America and continues to be so for farm wives in many European countries. They make wonderful, thoughtful Christmas presents without too much expense or work on the part of the giver. However, now is the time to get the fruit and alcohol together, so that they will have several weeks to embrace in the dark.

Early November isn't too late to start bottling a few of these lovely concoctions for your own or your friends' after-dinner tipples. Incidentally, it is quite legal to make wine, beer or spirits for your own consumption or as gifts—*selling* it is a no-no with the Feds.

Vodka is an especially congenial medium for making fruit-flavored liqueurs. These most closely resemble the now astronomically priced *Eaux de Vie* of France and Germany such as *Poire, Framboise* (raspberries—which I should have started in July), *Kirschwasser* and my favorite, *Mirabelle,* which is made of little yellow plums that grow in Alsace, and now costs about a dollar a drop. But any kind of plum makes a very engaging drink. *Eaux de Vie* are, of course, distillations of the fruits or berries—it requires 60 pounds of raspberries to make one liter of *Framboise.* So their priciness is understandable, though that doesn't make them any closer to affordable.

The homemade *Eaux de Vie* ("water of life") that I propose in the following directions won't require your setting up a still or doing anything very strenuous at all. Nice cheap American vodka—such as Gordon's or Georgi—is just ideal for these delicious spirits. August would have been a better time to start all this, but I wrote my notes on this subject and forgot all about it until I discovered a bottle of *Poire* I'd made and put away about a year ago. It is simply smashing. But it really isn't necessary to put by your homemade cordials and liqueurs for so many months. Fruits and berries seem to release their essences very quickly into the vodka or brandy. Six weeks' aging is adequate, though I suppose three months would really intensify the fruit flavors to an ideal degree. One of the really convenient things about some of these concoctions is that after some of it is poured, the bottle may be topped up with additional spirits to extend its life. Of course, too many raids too frequently will diminish the flavor rather seriously. Some of these cordials are strained and clarified and naturally they cannot be "topped up."

I talked with Joseph Luppi, a friend of mine who is a bartender, ball-player, cook and connoisseur, about base spirits that would give pleasing results for these home-made drinks. Christian Brothers makes a good, clean-tasting American brandy suitable for combination with apples and peaches. Smirnoff (of Hartford, not Moscow) might be used for some other fruit cordials. But it is not recommended to grow too fanciful when doctoring up expensive imported vodkas such as Absolut (Swedish), Finlandia (like it sounds), Stolichnaya (Russian), or Wyborowa (Polish). However, Mr. Luppi enjoys a thin strip of lemon zest curling inside a bottle of Finlandia, and I like a long thin strip of orange peel floating in a bottle of Absolut. These should be kept in the freezer and served in tiny cold schnapps glasses. Some people advocate the addition of pepper, but I've never tried it.

The first thing you need to know in preparing these drinks is how to make a simple syrup to sweeten them a little. Of course, you do not have to sweeten them at all, but a little sugar smooths out the flavor of the fruit or berries.

SIMPLE SYRUP

Makes 1 quart.

2 cups water   *4 cups sugar*

Stir the two together in a heavy-bottomed saucepan, set over low heat and stir until sugar is dissolved and syrup is clear. Cool very thoroughly (overnight is best) before using.

PEAR "WATER OF LIFE"

Buy 3 or 4 good firm pears and let them ripen until just pressable at the stem and blossom end. Wash carefully, and slice them in vertical quarters. Put them in a 2-quart jar and cover them with one cup of the simple syrup. Fill up the jar with vodka, seal it closely, then gently upend it several times to distribute and mix all the ingredients. Put it on a dark cool shelf (cool is very important), and remember to invert it once a week from now until about the middle of December, when it will be ready for broaching. Or giving.

This does not make a sweet cordial. It tastes light and rather dry, with just a faint sweetness. For a heavier drink, use more simple syrup. Also I strain out the pears, as they become quite dark. If you want to keep them in the jar and have them retain an appetizing color, roll them about in a solution of Fruit Fresh, which is mainly ascorbic acid without the sourness.

KIRSCHWASSER

2 cups fresh cherries　　　　　　　　*1 quart vodka*
1 cup Simple Syrup

Wash and bruise the cherries—do not pit them. Put them in a jar large enough to hold all the ingredients. Mix with the simple syrup and vodka. Close up tightly and store as in the preceding recipe. When ready to broach, strain out the cherries. If you have a Melitta coffee funnel, put a filter in it and drip the *Kirschwasser* through it. This should clarify it adequately. If you wish the brew to be even clearer, repeat the process. Pour your completed product into an attractive bottle and stopper it up. Dividing it into two pint bottles would be a practical idea. Some of the French olive oil bottles with corks make especially pretty containers. But you must remember to scour both well and soak the cork so that it will expand. The bottle should be filled to the brim so that the cork remains moist. This type of spirit evaporates once it is opened and air gets in the bottle.

APPLEJACK

Get three or four Cortland, MacIntosh or Greening apples, wash and cut them in quarters. Put them in a tall, narrow jar and pour about 1½ cups simple syrup over them. Add 1 quart of brandy, and store in a cool, dark place as advised in the foregoing recipes—or formulas as the case may be. After six weeks, this should be strained and rebottled in an attractive decanter. It need not be clarified.

PEACH RATAFIA

Ratafias were ladies' drinks in the nineteenth century, possibly in the century before as well. They appear in many old Southern cookbooks, and if the following recipe from *The Carolina Housewife* is any indication, it must have permitted many a gentlewoman to get quietly smashed in a dignified way.

"Steep for several months in a gallon of brandy twelve hundred peach-kernels (blanched). When the flavor is extracted from the kernels, pour off the brandy, and add to it one quart of Frontignac wine, one quart of strong hyson tea, one pint of orange-flower water, and three pounds of white sugar; stir all well together, and bottle it. Aso soon as it becomes clear it may be used, but improves with age."

MODERN PEACH RATAFIA

This is a much simplified adaptation—I don't know what hyson tea is, but I know I wouldn't want it in my drink.

4 large ripe, blemishless peaches	*1½ quarts brandy*
2 cups simple syrup	*Handful of blanched almonds*

Skin the peaches and cut them in quarters. Crack the stones lightly and put them in a jar with the peaches, simple syrup, brandy and almonds. Seal it up and leave six weeks, turning from time to time. I think this looks best in a large canning jar, because it's nice to eat a nibble of the fruit with the ratafia.

Late Vegetable Trio

As I write there's still no November frost on the punkin' and we've plenty of those, as well as snowy cauliflowers and trees of Brussels sprouts almost too pretty to eat. Well, not *that* pretty.

Butternut squash seems to be increasingly in evidence on the East End. It is a type of pumpkin, and can be crossed with, say, an acorn squash. Any two or more varieties of the same species will cross if you want to save some seeds (stored in a cool, dry place), plant them together and see what odd result comes up next autumn.

The ornamental gourds, the exotic result of many accidental crossbreedings, used to comprise a considerable amount of the household equipment in earlier days. They were made into dippers, bottles, spoons, bowls, even musical instruments and pipes. This might be an interesting project for schoolchildren. But to return to my own turf: some recipes for the splendid produce in the fields right now.

CAULIFLOWER/BRUSSELS SPROUTS CROWN

If you want to think ahead to Thanksgiving, this is quite spectacular for holiday tables—beats the old creamed peas and onions hands down.

Serves 10–12.

*1 large spotless white head
  cauliflower
1 quart (approximately) fresh
  Brussels sprouts*

*¼ pound sweet butter
Salt and freshly milled pepper*

Although the vegetables may be trimmed and refrigerated early in the day, this dish cannot really be cooked until every other part of the dinner is ready to go on the table. There are few things worse than either cauliflower or Brussels sprouts that have been "kept warm." Better to let them get cold entirely and reheat them in butter. The white head of cauliflower ringed with bright green sprouts should be served in a shallow bowl, pre-heated of course.

Trim the cauliflower but leave a few of its more delicate leaves on. Remove the center core. Wash the head in cold running water. Trim the Brussels sprouts, removing any scraggly leaves. Wash them in cold running water.

Put two pots of water on to boil, each holding about 4 quarts, and add 1 tablespoon of salt to each. Put the butter in a small heavy pot to melt slowly over very low heat.

Cook the cauliflower in one pot until it is barely fork-tender at the base (about 10 minutes, a bit more if very large). Do not cover. Meanwhile, drop the sprouts into the other pot of boiling water and cook, uncovered, for 8 to 10 minutes—again, until just tender at the stem end. Drain well, refresh in ice water and turn out onto a towel.

Pour half the butter into an iron skillet and when it foams, add the sprouts. Sauté them over fairly high heat, shaking the pan often, until they begin to brown a bit. Grind on fresh pepper and add more salt if needed.

Arrange the drained whole head of cauliflower in the center of a very hot bowl. Spoon the sprouts around the perimeter. Pour the remaining melted butter over the cauliflower and serve. If you want to make this a truly royal dish, nap the cauliflower head with hollandaise sauce instead of butter.

BUTTERNUT SQUASH PURÉE

A creamy-tan, gourdlike squash with brilliant orange flesh, the butternut and many similar squashes were cultivated by the Indians and probably served at that fabled first Thanksgiving. It is a particularly complementary dish to serve with roast duck, capon, turkey or pork.

Serves 4.

1 butternut squash (about
  2 pounds)
2 to 3 tablespoons butter
¼ teaspoon salt
1 tablespoon soft light-brown
  sugar

Dash of ground allspice
Tiny grating of nutmeg
Peeled green ginger root, grated
  (optional)

Stand the squash up and peel it from neck to base with a swivel-blade vegetable peeler. Split it lengthwise and cut off a slice from both ends. Scoop out the seeds and pith with a sharp spoon and discard. Cut the squash into large chunks. (You can, if you like, just serve the vegetable in chunks with butter, salt and pepper.) Put the chunks into a steamer basket and set over boiling water. Cover and steam about 10 minutes, or until fork-tender but not mushy. Purée the squash in a food mill (I did not use a food processor because that machine turns mashed potatoes into a ghastly sticky mass, but it may be all right for squash). Beat in all remaining ingredients with a wooden spoon. For a fluffier concoction, beat the purée with an electric mixer.

Although it is the same color, this dish is not to be confused with that time-honored oddity made of sweet potatoes and marshmallows (nominated at my daughter's school as the positively worst dish ever created). The puréed squash is definitely a vegetable, not meant to be sweet, just to have a tantalizing, elusive flavor that marries well with pork and poultry. For a little added zing, grate in a small piece of peeled green ginger root.*

* Powdered ginger is not the same thing at all and cannot be used as a substitute in any recipe where green ginger root is called for.

A Quiet Country Thanksgiving

All happy families resemble one another, but each unhappy family
is unhappy in its own way.

—Leo Tolstoy, *Anna Karenina*

If there's one day on which all American families try to resemble one another, it's Thanksgiving Day. Generally I think most of us succeed in making this a fine family get-together, and ours is usually enhanced by extending the family as far as the leaves in the table permit. However, there *is* the shrinking family syndrome, as members fan out into impossibly distant geographic locations, and Great Big Bird is no longer feasible.

Fresh breast of leviathan turkeys weighing about 4½ pounds are a wonderful substitute for the whole bird, and a lot easier to carve. (If there are dark-meat lovers in your group, buy a big leg, also sold separately nowadays, and roast it along with the breast.) I recently roasted one on a covered charcoal grill using the indirect method. A handful of soaked hickory chips thrown on the coals at the beginning of the cooking gives the meat an elegant smoky flavor. Chilled and sliced thinly, smoked grilled turkey breasts are convenient and filling for holiday parties coming up. The following recipe, however, is for a steadfastly traditional Thanksgiving meal for about six people.

TURKEY BREAST WITH GOLDEN EGGS

1 large fresh turkey breast
(about 4½ pounds)

BRINE
3 quarts cold water
2 tablespoons mixed pickling
  spices
4 tablespoons coarse salt
½ cup dark-brown sugar (not
  packed)

1 recipe cornbread stuffing or
  use your favorite stuffing
  recipe

¼ pound sweet butter, softened

1 cup onions, chopped
2 cloves garlic, minced
1 to 2 cups chicken broth
1 cup wine plus 1 cup water
1 tablespoon cornstarch
Salt and pepper to taste
1 cup sliced mushrooms
  (optional)
6 hard-boiled eggs
2 teaspoons turmeric
2 bunches watercress

Mix the brine ingredients together and pour them over the turkey breast, which you have placed in a deep, non-metallic container. Leave it for about twenty-four hours, turning it as often as you think of it, which you will every time the refrigerator door is opened.

Make the cornbread stuffing, or whatever kind you prefer. Rinse the turkey breast briefly in cold water, then dry it well. Using your fingers, gently lift the skin up away from the flesh and fill this space about a ½-inch thick with stuffing. If the skin has loosened up too much, skewer it down with little metal turkey pins so that the stuffing does not escape. This is both an attractive and practical way to keep the breast meat—usually inclined to be a bit dry—moist. Rub the breast skin with some of the softened butter. Melt the remainder and sauté the chopped onion and garlic in it. Place these in a roasting pan and arrange the turkey breast on top of it. Cover the breast with a loose tent of foil. Put the remaining turkey stuffing in a casserole and ladle a few cups of chicken broth over it.

Preheat the oven to 350° F. Put the turkey breast in the center of the oven and roast it for one hour, then baste it with more melted butter and put the casserole of stuffing into the oven along with the turkey, which should now have the foil cover removed so that the skin will brown nicely. Baste with butter every 15 minutes until it registers 165° on a meat thermometer and is tender when pierced, probably another 45 minutes. These large turkey breasts have such dense meat that they take rather a long time to cook.

Remove the turkey to a platter and let it rest at least 30 minutes (an hour won't hurt) in a warm place. Turn off the oven and leave the casserole of stuffing in it, covered with a loose piece of foil so that it doesn't dry out.

Deglaze the roasting pan with a cup of wine and a cup of water (I use red wine) and pour this into a small saucepan. Simmer and season to taste with salt and pepper. Thicken it with a tablespoon of cornstarch mixed to a thin paste with cold water. If you like, simmer a cupful of sliced mushrooms in the turkey sauce.

Drop the shelled hard-boiled eggs into the turmeric mixed with boiling water and leave them for about ten minutes, agitating them often so that they color evenly to a deep gold. Drain the eggs on a rack; when dry arrange them around the turkey breast and decorate the platter with a wreath of watercress.

Unexpected Treasures, New Old Friends

St. Matthew inveighed against putting new wine into old bottles, but I think he would approve of putting some old favorites into new guises. Except for the noble turkey, the single most traditional (some may call it unavoidable) dish at the Thanksgiving feast is pumpkin pie. And with the jack-o'-lantern season gone, this handsome gourd lapses into another year of neglect.

Cranberries, too, seem to come in just three forms: canned, jellied and whole fresh berry sauce. At least, that was the case until a few years ago, when some genius stuck with a bog full of unsold cranberries figured out cranberry juice cocktail, cranapple and on and on. (And it's not bad stuff, shaken with vodka and ice.)

So with the prospect of two holidays with the same traditional foods closely following each other, I thought you might like a couple of changes to ring on the old standbys. Either of these desserts can be made a day or two in advance of Big Bird Day, and will be the better for it.

PUMPKIN MOUSSE

Choose a fairly fancy mold of about 2-quart capacity for this (or a bundt cake pan will do). Oil it and chill it before you start. The mousse *should* be made a day or two in advance to develop firmness and flavor. Unmold it, then replace it in the refrigerator before you sit down to dinner.

Serves 12.

1 tablespoon plus 1 teaspoon
   plain unflavored gelatin
¼ cup cold water
4 eggs, separated
½ cup heavy cream
½ cup milk
1 pound puréed cooked
   pumpkin (canned or fresh)
1 cup brown sugar, not packed

¼ teaspoon each: cinnamon,
   nutmeg, ground ginger
Pinch of ground cloves
¼ cup white sugar
1 tablespoon bourbon or cognac
½ cup black walnuts, chopped
   (for garnish)
1 cup heavy cream, whipped
   (for garnish)

Sprinkle the gelatin over the cold water to soften. In the top of a double boiler or a very heavy non-aluminum saucepan, beat the egg yolks until light, then beat in the cream, milk and half of the pumpkin purée.

Beat in the brown sugar and spices, then cook, stirring constantly, over low heat or in the top of a double boiler until mixture becomes a thick custard. Remove from heat and stir in gelatin and remaining pumpkin, making certain it is smoothly incorporated.

Cool to tepid—otherwise the hot custard will collapse the egg whites to be added. To speed this, you can set the custard pan into a pan half-filled with ice and water and stir the custard until it is cool (about 5 minutes).

Beat the egg whites to a fairly stiff meringue, adding the white sugar last. Add bourbon or cognac, then fold the meringue into the custard with a rubber spatula, using an up-and-over motion to avoid breaking down the air bubbles. Scrape the mousse into your chilled, oiled mold, cover it tightly with plastic wrap and refrigerate it for a day or two.

Unmold it at least half an hour before you wish to serve it so that it has time to "set up" in the icebox again.

Lightly oil the plate you want to serve the mousse on (so you can move it if your unmolding technique is somewhat less than terrific). Lower the mold into very warm water (the mold should not be filled higher than ¼ of an inch from the top) for a few seconds and invert it onto the serving plate. Holding the plate and mold together, give the whole thing a sharp jerk and the mousse should drop out. If not, place towels wrung out in very hot water on the botton of the mold—this usually does the trick.

Sprinkle the mousse with walnuts (the native black walnut has a unique flavor, quite distinctive from the bland English walnut) and put it back in the icebox. Just before serving, garnish it with whipped cream, or pass the bowl of cream separately after presenting the mousse to be admired. If you have a pastry bag, pipe rosettes of whipped cream around the base of the mousse.

CRANBERRY SHERBET

Since the revelation of all the iniquitous doings by commercial manufacturers, home-made ice creams and sherbets haven't had a bigger vogue since T. Jefferson brought his recipe back to Monticello from France. Good, efficient electric ice-cream freezers are available at reasonable cost—I strongly recommend the inexpensive Waring, which uses ordinary table salt and plain ice cubes. However, if you don't feel like investing in this equipment, this sherbet can also be made in a bowl placed in the freezer section of your refrigerator. However, the texture will not be as fine as sherbets made in an electric (or hand-turned) ice-cream freezer.

Makes about 1 quart.

2 cups raw cranberries
½ cup superfine white sugar
⅔ cup sweetened condensed
   milk

1 tablespoon lime juice
2 "jumbo" egg whites

Wash the berries and put them into a large shallow saucepan. Add the sugar and heat slowly until berries burst. Cook, stirring, for about 5 minutes, then grind coarsely in a food processor or a manual food mill.

Stir in condensed milk and lime juice and cool the mixture. Beat the egg whites stiff and fold into the cranberry mix. Turn this into a fairly shallow metal bowl or ice trays. When it has frozen solid about 1 inch around the edges, turn it out into a chilled bowl and beat it with a hand or electric beater. Turn it back into a chilled container just large enough to hold the sherbet, cover it tightly and return it to the freezer of your refrigerator until firm.

If you have an ice-cream maker, follow the manufacturer's directions for freezing, then pack the sherbet into containers and keep it in your freezer until half an hour before serving. The sherbet will be too rock-hard if not allowed to "temper" in the refrigerator. This sherbet looks especially Christmassy if served in wineglasses or coupes with a sprig of holly on top. And it makes a nice alternative for guests who may not be able to handle a heavy dessert after our traditional paralyzing holiday meals.

MINCEMEAT AND PEAR CREPES

Crepes are among the easiest of desserts to make. But there are so many processor, blender and mixer recipes, and so many types of crepe pan, I'll just say make your own favorite crepes according to your own system.

Serves 12.

3 fairly ripe pears
Juice of half a lemon
½ cup sugar
1 jar (28 ounces) mincemeat
(Nonesuch)

3 ounces black walnut meats,
coarsely chopped
½ cup brandy or cognac
Whipped cream or crème fraîche

Make 24 crepes in advance, wrap them in foil and refrigerate for up to three days. Return to room temperature before using.

Peel, core and slice the pears, dropping them into the lemon juice as you go. Put them in a small, heavy saucepan with the sugar and slowly bring to the simmer. Stir often and cook until just tender. Combine with the mincemeat and walnuts, heat the mixture and set aside. Unless you want to flame the crepes at the table, add the brandy now to the mincemeat.

When you are ready to serve, whip the cream and sweeten it very slightly if at all. Heat some dessert plates (or a large platter), heat the mincemeat and heat the crepes in a low oven. Working quickly, put about 1 heaping tablespoon of mincemeat into each crepe and roll up. Arrange two crepes on each plate and put them on a cookie sheet. Put the cookie sheet in a very slow oven to keep the crepes warm while you finish the others.

If you feel up to a production number, put all the crepes on a warm platter and carry it into the dining room. With lights dimmed, heat a ladle of brandy over a candle until it catches fire, then pour this over the crepes and you have mincemeat crepes flambées. Otherwise you can just put the brandy into the mincemeat in the first place. But I must say, flaming desserts impress the socks off most people and nothing could be easier to do. That's why all those headwaiters collect a huge tip for learning to strike a match.

W·I·N·T·E·R

A Couple of Quick Meals

Hardly have the plastic Pilgrims and papier-mâché turkeys hit the road before we're awash in Christmas wreathes and twinkling Santas. But this was not always the case. Originally, Thanksgiving was celebrated in October, at the true end of harvest time. And as any farmer on the East End can tell you, harvest time ends quite a spell before the third Thursday in November. (F.D.R. fixed that day as Permanent Thanksgiving after some centuries of shilly-shallying between Thursdays.)

One Thanksgiving morning my favorite radio sage told a rattling good yarn about how two mosquitoes were responsible for a plague (typhoid probably) that downed some early Pilgrims and put off the celebration until the weather turned safely chilly. So *that* is why—to go on with this shaggy mosquito story—we have two major holidays crashing headlong into each other.

Christmas shopping moves into high gear with all kinds of sales and blandishments on the very Friday after our day of national thanks. It is to the tired, the hungry, the impoverished shopper that this is dedicated.

SPAGHETTINI "CASINO" WITH CLAMS AND BACON

Clams "Casino" have always been one of my favorite things, so I thought, why not Spaghettini "Casino"? There are unfortunate parts of the world where canned clams would be permissible in this recipe—but not here. You can use any kind of hard-shell clams, but big cherrystones are my preference. Quahogs are all right, but it takes an expert to pry open those giants. (Almost any fishmonger will shuck clams for you if you call in advance.)

This sauce can be made in the time it takes the pasta to cook, so have heated bowls in readiness and hungry people ready to carry them in to table. A quickly made simple green salad adds a refreshing note to the meal.

Serves 2.

2 to 4 slices bacon	*Red pepper flakes*
½ pint shucked cherrystone	*½ pound #9 spaghettini*
clams (about 1 dozen)	*2 large pats butter*
2 tablespoons olive oil	*2 tablespoons parsley, minced*
1 large clove garlic, minced	

Put about 4 quarts of salted water on to boil. Cut the bacon in half (I use rather thickly cut slab bacon—you will need 4 slices of the wispy kind) and fry it very slowly until just crisp; drain on paper towels and reserve.

Chop the clams coarsely with a sharp knife, reserving the juices. You can do this in a food processor if you're quite careful not to turn the clams to mush.

Heat the olive oil in a small heavy skillet and sauté the garlic a few minutes on low heat. Add pepper flakes and turn off heat.

Cook the spaghettini *al dente,* drain it, add butter and place it in hot bowls. Keep warm in a low oven. Turn the heat back on under the skillet and toss in the clams, their juices and the parsley. Stir around until clams are just heated through and barely cooked, about one minute. Divide this between the waiting bowls of pasta and crumble the reserved bacon over the top of each serving.

CHICKEN LIVERS AND MUSHROOMS BORDELAISE

Rice takes approximately 20 minutes to cook, and is the best underpinning for this speedy concoction. Minute rice is awful and takes about 14 minutes. Broad egg noodles can be substituted if you're too rushed or hungry to wait for the rice to cook.

Bordelaise indicates a dish that has been cooked in red wine. It certainly need not be a Bordeaux. Any decent dry, full-bodied red from California—for instance a Zinfandel or a Cabernet Sauvignon—will do. And you can drink the rest of the bottle with dinner.

Serves 2.

1 pound fresh chicken livers
Flour
3 tablespoons butter
1 medium onion, chopped fine
10 medium-sized fresh
  mushrooms

¼ teaspoon dried thyme
1 cup dry red wine
Salt and freshly milled black
  pepper
Rice or buttered noodles
Minced parsley for garnish

Rinse the chicken livers in cold water, dry them and cut each whole liver into 4 pieces. Remove any bits of fat or stringy tissue. Put them into a plastic bag with a little flour—just enough to coat them lightly. Then turn them into a colander to shake off excess flour.

Melt the butter in a heavy skillet and sauté the livers about 4 minutes, browning them on all sides. They should remain pink inside. Remove them with a slotted spoon and keep warm. In the same pan, sauté the onion until transparent.

Rinse, dry and slice or quarter the mushrooms and add them to the onions. Sauté, stirring constantly, about 2 minutes. Add the thyme and red wine and cook down rapidly a couple of minutes. Return the chicken livers to the skillet with the other ingredients, heat well (but do not cook further) and add salt and pepper to taste. Serve Chicken Livers Bordelaise over hot steamed rice or buttered noodles and sprinkle it lavishly with fresh parsley or some minced scallions.

Fresh ingredients, briefly cooked with a little care and imagination, take less time, to prepare than a great many frozen dinners. But I'll have to admit that there is nothing quicker than the Toucan School of Cookery: take a can of Cream of Something soup and add it to a can of Something Else and there you are—eating miserably.

Dr. Edouard de Pomiane, a professor at the Institut Pasteur in Paris, wrote a little cookbook in 1930, now translated into English, titled *French Cooking in Ten Minutes or Adapting to the Rhythm of Modern Life*. Frozen foods were then unknown and even commercially canned vegetables a bit of a novelty, so most of the dishes in this charming little book are freshly made from raw ingredients. Not all of them come in under the 10-minute wire, but it's a delightful book and here is one of his recipes.

"OYSTERS AND SAUSAGES

"No one, except maybe your doctor, would tell you that you shouldn't start your lunch with half a dozen fresh oysters, opened for you by the man who sells them.

"You can make a whole lunch of oysters if you eat them the way they do in Bordeaux. Buy a dozen oysters. [Have them opened—M.U.] Fry some link sausages. Take a bite of burning hot sausage, then soothe your mouth with a cool oyster. Twelve times . . ." Dr. de Pomiane also prescribes a glass of cold, crisp white wine. The recipe serves one happy person.

Happy Christmas shopping.

Thoughts on Kitchen Gifts

There's some what will and some what won't,
There's some what do and some what don't . . .
—Anon. *Early blues*

Cook, that is. But the non-cooks are just as passionate about eating as the stove-bound. Gifts of food, homemade or not, are particularly apt for the non-cook. And rare or expensive ingredients or unusual kitchen tools make especially pleasing presents for the accomplished *cuisinier*. My own personal Christmas list is divided not by sexes or ages but by "Cooks" and "Non-Cooks," and so these suggestions will be, too.

FOR COOKS

Really dedicated cooks would rather be in their kitchens than out trying on fur coats—behavior that seems demented to most of the world, but there it is. Since a lot of them spend hours slouching along the aisles of fancy cookware shops you might think this type "has everything." This, of course, is never true. Just as no woman can be "too rich or too thin," no cooking fanatic can have too many gadgets, terrines, turk's-head molds, *soufflé* dishes, pans for babas, or baskets for *coeur à la crème*. For instance, I bought myself an advance Christmas present just the other day—something I really needed: a terra-cotta pig terrine for pâtés (at Dean & DeLuca*). After all, as I explained the whole shameful business to myself, "these things cost a fortune in France, this one's American-made, cheap and so well done, etc., etc." There's also a duck and a rooster I may go back for some day. Dean & DeLuca, the mecca for kitchen as well as food gifts in both East Hampton and New York City's SoHo, will fill written requests, though they do not have a formal mail-order business. They always stock a rather hard-to-find instant-read thermometer made by Taylor that no serious (or even foolish) cook should be without.

My local hardware store, The Emporium, whose manager would rather eat cedar

* Newtown Lane, East Hampton, N.Y. and 121 Prince St., NYC.

shingles than sell cutesy kitchenware, also carries this professional chef's thermometer. When I first moved to Sag Harbor over a decade ago, this store carried graniteware and cast-iron cooking ware and nothing else much flossier than paint, rope and nails-by-the-pound. Now they even sell the Atlas pasta machine. The range and sophistication of kitchen things in even small-town stores across America is truly amazing nowadays.

It's an intelligent approach, when selecting a kitchen gift, to pander to special interests: ice-cream and sorbet making, barbeque or smoke cooking, fancy baking or candy making, are particular interests for some cooks. (I think all the fondue sets that need ever be given, have been—also crock pots and electric woks.)

Henckel or Sabatier knives, sturdy and thick grooved carving boards, large serving platters, efficient food warmers, professional pastry bags and baking tins are some non-special things any good cook would be pleased to get. And no one could ever be surfeited with oven-to-table baking dishes—either earthenware or the magnificent French high-fired porcelain. Bennington Potters in Vermont makes fired ceramic ware that are practical works of art.

For people with limited space, peripatetic lives or who simply hate electric kitchen machines, make a collection of little gadgets such as the Mouli line of cheese graters, parsley grinders, the food mill with different plates. These things will perform, by hand, most of the functions of a food processor. For lovers of the esoteric there are lemon zesters, melon-ball cutters, citrus knives, ravioli cutters. For campus cooking: a wok, a good Chinese cleaver, four large, inexpensive wineglasses and maybe a set of measuring cups and spoons, which beginners never seem to think they need. I've given this grouping to several of our offspring—many students like to cook their own food to avoid the expense and tedium of college dining rooms.

When choosing gifts for good cooks, select kitchen things that are sturdy, cleanly designed, unornamented and of manifestly professional intention.

Besides equipment, there are plenty of food gifts for cooks that are always eagerly received—but these are usually ingredients, not finished products. Cooks moon around displays of expensive walnut, hazelnut and *très vierge* olive oils, liters of fine aged wine vinegars, tins of truffles and saffron. A bottle of "extra" cold-pressed olive oil is far more appreciated than yet another bottle of wine. Some other good choices are imported wild dried mushrooms or herbs, good fresh spices, green or red peppercorns —none of which should be bought in very large quantities because they deteriorate if not used fairly quickly. Premium quality dried fruits and nuts bring joy to the cook who knows how to use them well.

But then, there's a welter of great things to buy for cooks, who, God bless 'em, are easy-to-please, even-tempered, kind, gracious and grateful for an addition to their kitchens. Just ask any good cook.

NON-COOKS

The hardened, unregenerate non-cooks, despite their often keen appreciation of the culinary arts, really want effortless food that needs almost no transformation of any kind. Open and eat (or drink)—that sort of thing. One of the nicest gifts for this type is a selection of imported cheese. The staff at many fine food stores will help you to make up variety baskets or they will do the selecting for you at a predetermined price. Honey fanciers would be delighted with a little collection of honeys from Tasmanian and other far-flung bees. Or one might make a collection of several kinds of coffee beans, a small electric coffee grinder and a Melitta for an (either-sex) bachelor-type present. A selection of teas and a lovely teapot (the glass pot from the Museum of Modern Art permanent design collection is available at specialty kitchen stores and the fine brown English teapot can be found in most good hardware stores) accompanied by a Chinese bamboo tea strainer is another thoughtful gift suitable for those who only boil water.

Homemade gifts of food are undoubtedly the most loved by those who don't know how to cook. Jams and preserves are among the easiest things to make. Of course, there's little point in making up a batch of something that Smucker's gnomes do just as well. Pick out unusual fruits and spruce them up with a bit of rum or Grand Marnier. Greengage preserves are easy to make and almost impossible to find commercially. Clementines (thought to be descendants of wild Algerian oranges) make wonderful marmalade spiked with dark rum. Remember to gather beach plums next September—a true delicacy in jelly.

The Ball Blue Book of Canning and Preserving, available at any country hardware store, will instruct you in all this and gives concise, simple, small-quantity recipes. Marmalades, jams and preserves are among the easiest and most beautiful food gifts one can make. The French and Italian glass canning jars, though less well sealed than ours, make lovely presentation jars and are not expensive.

Tea breads—pumpkin, cranberry, lemon or banana—are good "keepers" and make nice homey presents that are quick to make. Pâtés baked in small foil pans (see *Pâté de Campagne* recipe, page 167) are welcome gifts to party givers. People who live alone might like to get your own special soups or stews frozen in small foil loaf pans. And only you can make special things for special people with special problems—say, salt-free sausages or sugar-free preserves. Here's an annual gift I make for one of my daughters who is convinced that white sugar is deadlier than heroin.

PEAR RAISINÉ

This is a resurrected centuries-old recipe from Burgundy that uses grape juice instead of sugar, which they did not have. The reduced grape juice sweetens the fruit and colors it a lush reddish amethyst.

Makes 2 jars.

3 pounds "firm-ripe" pears
1 quart pure, unsweetened red
   grape juice

3 cloves
1 cup Catawba grape wine
1 tablespoon cognac

Buy good, firm, blemishless pears and let them ripen a couple of days at room temperature (not in the sun). They should be fragrant and give slightly when pressed at the blossom end.

Simmer the grape juice and cloves until the liquid is reduced by half. Remove cloves. Stir in Catawba wine.

Wash, peel, core and slice the pears. Cook them in the grape juice and wine in a heavy saucepan until thick and jammy. Use low heat and stir often to avoid scorching. Divide between two glass or stoneware containers (I like to use old stoneware mustard pots) that have been sterilized. Pour some of the cognac on the surface of the *Raisiné*. This gives added flavor and retards spoilage. Still, this should be refrigerated unless it is sealed with paraffin. Paraffin is sold in blocks at hardware stores. Melt a little over low heat (it is quite flammable) in a small heavy pan. Pour a layer about 1/8-inch thick over the surface of the preserves and tilt it very slightly to seal it. Cool the preserves. Cut circles of white parchment paper about 2 inches larger than the diameter of the jar top and fit one over each top. Crease the paper down over the neck of the crock and tie it in place with string or yarn.

Focaccia, a Genoese Pizza

The great thing about baking with yeast is the difficulty of failure.
—George and Cecilia Scurfield, *Home Baked* (1956)

And who has time for failures with all the holiday hustle and hassle coming up? I've only recently come upon a really interesting party or snack food that is the soul of simplicity: *focaccia,* a yeast-risen flat bread similar to pizza. Genoese bakers have been turning it out for centuries to test the heat of their morning bread ovens. *Focaccia* is unembellished with tomato paste, garlic or oregano (three items whose dreary repetitions in Italo-American cookery have made it pall on me).

My belated discovery of *focaccia* (which would probably seem inane to Italians, but I excuse myself for this ignorance because I've never seen it in New York), came about through Francesco de Rogati, an Italian journalist. He was waxing lyrical about the food of his native region, Liguria, and bemoaning the mystifying lack of *focaccia* in a city (New York) so filled with Italians. He had to resort to making his own with dough cajoled out of a neighborhood Italian baker.

Focaccia is the favorite snack of Genoa, eaten for breakfast (a "string" bought from a baker), between meals, on the street and in cafés—Ligurians pull open the hot bread and fill it with prosciutto and other nice things. For this reason I thought it a good thing to be able to put together quickly during the busy holiday season.

The basic *focaccia* is but a sheet of yeast-leavened dough, usually pulled out to a thin rectangle before being fitted into an oiled and salted pan. Then it is dented all over with two fingertips to make little wells to collect the olive oil that is dribbled over it. Finally it is sprinkled with coarse salt before being baked on the floor of a very hot oven. A pizza stone is nice to have for this, but you can get the same effect by laying enough quarry tiles to nearly cover the lowest rack of your oven and pre-heating it for about 30 minutes.

If you use the stone or tiles, you do not, of course, need a pan. But you do need a "peel," a thin flat paddle from which the dough is slid onto the hot stone or tiles. However, a simple jelly-roll pan is all you really need to try out the following *focaccia* recipe. Should you get interested in pizza or *focaccia*-making on any scale, cookwares stores sell the stone and bread peels, and quarry tiles are easy to come by in flooring stores. Get nine unglazed tiles 6" x 6" square, and for little cost you can have a real baker's oven that is quick to assemble and dismantle. Once you see how extremely simple it is to make pizza and *focaccia* and how much superior and cheaper the home-made article is, you may never buy another one at the pizza parlor.

Focaccia al Formaggio is made much the same as described above except that a layer of coarsely shredded Fontina is put over the bottom crust, then covered with another sheet of dough, then oiled, salted and baked. It is best hot, but it's not bad just warm. Once you have the basic dough on hand, either in the refrigerator or the freezer, it's quicker to make your own pie than to go sloshing out into the cold to the nearest pizzeria. If even processor dough-making is beyond you (and I don't believe this is possible for anyone), you may find the frozen dough in some supermarket deli departments. But really, it is incredibly simple to make at home. And it is indestructible, as are nearly all yeast breads. If they collapse, you just knead them and the ever-living yeast mold will make them rise again.

FOCACCIA AL MIRIAMO

Naturally, the dough can be made by hand, but the kneading takes about 10 to 15 minutes. A food processor zips through the job in about 2 minutes. Amounts of flour to be incorporated in any yeast-leavened bread dough are always variable, because flour itself is.

Makes 2 12-inch pies or
1 large 9- x 12-inch oblong.

BASIC YEAST DOUGH

2 packages active dry yeast (check date on package before using)
1 cup warm water (110° F.)

3½ cups unbleached white flour (approximately)
2 teaspoons salt
¼ cup olive oil

Proof the yeast in about half a cup of the water—it should bubble a bit after about 10 minutes. Then put the yeast, remaining half cup of water, flour, salt and the oil into the work bowl of a food processor. Turn it on and off several times. Then let it run until the dough cleans the bowl and begins to ride the blades. If the dough is too sticky, add more flour; too dry, add a bit of water. Remove and knead by hand on a floured board for about a minute. When it is smooth and elastic, put it into a floured bowl, cover with a damp tea towel (wet it and wring it nearly dry) and put the dough in a warmish, draught-free place to rise for about an hour. The unlit oven of a gas stove with the heat of a pilot light is ideal.

Punch the dough down and divide it in two. If you only want to use half the dough, put the remainder in a plastic bag, twist it closed and freeze it for another day. Or it may be kept refrigerated for two or three days.

Heat the oven to 425° F. for about 30 minutes. If using the quarry tile or pizza stone they must be put into the *cold* oven, on its floor or a very low rack, otherwise they will crack.

Roll out the dough on a floured board as far as you can. Then pick it up and with your fists doubled up, pull the dough out, moving it around so that it is evenly thin. This is not at all like short pastry. It can take any amount of abuse, and if it starts to tear, just ball it up and start over. This kind of dough should not be terribly thin anyway, about ¼-inch thick.

Oil your jelly-roll pan liberally with good olive oil (if baking directly on stone omit this step) and put your oblong or circle of dough on it. Poke it all over with two fingers. Make the topping:

THE TOPPING

3 tablespoons fine olive oil
Half a medium red Italian
  onion, thinly sliced
4 or 5 large fresh mushrooms,
  sliced
6 to 8 large black Greek olives,
  pitted

6 ounces Fontina cheese, coarsely
  shredded
4 to 6 flat anchovy fillets,
  cut in pieces
Coarse salt

Heat the oil in a skillet and sauté the onions until limp. Spread them over the surface of the *focaccia*. Toss the mushroom slices in a little more oil and lay them on top of the onions, pressing them into the dough. Cut the pitted olives into quarters (those water-packed black California olives won't do—they have no taste whatsoever) and press them into the dough. Add the cheese and poke the anchovy pieces into it. Sprinkle with a little coarse salt.

Slide the jelly-roll pan directly onto the floor of your preheated oven and bake the *focaccia* for about 10 to 15 minutes. Its edges should be just golden and the cheese bubbly. Remove, cool a few minutes and cut into wedges or squares. Squares are easier to handle as party food. To avoid ruining my pans or bread peel, I cut the *focaccia* with a long-bladed scissors.

This bread has a crisp freshness totally unlike the often sodden crusts of commercial pizzas. And you can bake one up to order in just a few minutes, varying the ingredients as you like. Purists use only salt or Fontina, but that's a little strict. However, please, please, do not smear this lovely crust with tomatoes. The plain version is nice with a bit of chopped fresh marjoram or sage leaves.

Ever-ready Holiday Hors d'Oeuvre

So little done, so much to do.
—Last words of Cecil J. Rhodes

I'm delighted to live in an area where the shops close firmly and early on Christmas Eve. This takes matters out of my hands and I am free to collapse into the Christmas spirit. 'Tis the season to be jolly whether you like it or not. And to be hospitable at the drop of an earmuff: cold weather makes people crave both food and companionship.

The British, surprised by the cold in those wonderful old houses with no central heating, crowd in the pubs and celebrate a month-long Christmas season. Winters were even colder in mid- to late nineteenth-century England, and then as now, innkeepers had to be able to serve food and drink to frozen patrons at any hour of the day or night. One of the most famous tavern owners and cooks of the period was John Farley, famous for his "Cold Table." He left a cookbook giving some of his best dishes, and they are wonderfully suitable for modern cocktail parties or just the odd drop-in guests. I've up-dated some of the receipts for the Brits' beloved potted meats and fish. These foods keep well over a period of a week or ten days and this also makes them attractive for working hosts who must cook well in advance.

POTTED SPICED TONGUE

With the advent of the food processor, all kinds of potted food can be pounded senseless in a trice, where before it was necessary to labor with a mortar and pestle. A whole smoked beef tongue, which you must cook to begin with, makes a passel of potted meat, so you may wish to have your butcher slice the choicest part (after you cook it) and use the rest for this recipe.

Poached Beef Tongue

1 whole smoked beef tongue
2 tablespoons mixed pickling spices (ready-mixed)

4 cloves garlic

Rinse the tongue in cold water. Put it in a fairly deep pot and add the spices and garlic, which should be lightly mashed. Cover with fresh cold water to a depth of 3 inches and bring to a simmer. Poach, at a very low heat, with a lid slightly askew, for about three hours. The tongue should be very tender when pierced. When it cools to tepid, peel off the skin and discard. Remove and discard the small bones in the root end. Select the plump middle of the tongue for slicing unless you are preparing for a large party. Turn it on its side, cover with foil and weight it overnight to obtain the thinnest possible slices. (If the entire tongue is to be potted, the weighing is, of course, unnecessary.)

Potted Tongue

Weigh the amount of tongue you wish to pot and cut it into 1-inch chunks. Add ⅓rd of its weight in unsalted butter and cream the two ingredients together in a food processor. Add pepper to taste. Pack into a terrine and seal with a thin film of melted butter and doubled foil. Serve cool (larder temperature) but not icebox cold.

Potted Shrimp or Finnan Haddie

Buy small fresh shrimp (about 28 count to the pound) and rinse them lightly. Bring a large pot of water to the boil, throw in 2 tablespoons or so of Old Bay Shrimp Boil (fish stores usually sell this mixture in tins) and simmer 10 minutes. Add the shrimp, cover, turn off the heat, and let sit for 10 minutes. Drain, peel, de-vein and chop roughly. Proportions remain the same no matter how much you are making: For 1 pound of shrimp (before shelling), add 3 ounces sweet (unsalted) butter, a pinch of grated nutmeg, a pinch of white pepper and ¼ teaspoon lemon juice. Pulverize everything in a food processor and pack it into a crock. Cover tightly, refrigerate for at least twenty-four hours to develop flavor. Serve at room temperature with thin, fresh, trimmed toast triangles.

This "receipt" and the one that follows are ideas I got from Eliza Acton's wonderful *Modern Cookery for Private Families* first published in London in 1845. She used the shrimp to point up the flavor of the lobster she was potting, and you may do the same if you can afford it.

FINNAN HADDIE PÂTÉ

This is Scottish smoked haddock, which may be bought, often frozen, in good fish markets. Buy it filleted and defrost if necessary.

1 pound finnan haddie, filleted
½ pound (2 sticks) unsalted
  butter

Cayenne pepper and a few
  drops of lemon juice
Salt if necessary

This form of haddock is "hot-smoked," therefore already cooked, but quite dry. Poach it, covered, in a mixture of half water, half milk for 10 minutes but do not let the liquid boil. Remove and discard any skin or small bones that may lurk in the flesh. Cut it into chunks. Gently melt, *do not boil,* the butter. Put the fish and butter into the food processor and whirl to a smooth mass. Season to taste with cayenne, lemon juice and salt if the haddock wasn't already salted enough. Pack into a couple of small crocks and seal with foil and a rubber band for long keeping in the fridge. This is rather like something the English love called "bloater paste." It can also be made with kippers, skinned and filleted. And you could use smoked bluefish instead of finnan haddie in the above recipe and it would be equally delicious.

Pease for Luck

You cannot fight against the future. Time is on our side.
—William Gladstone, 1866

Maybe you can wring a little cheer from the old British prime minister's words. On New Year's Day, it's time to relax and enjoy before we have to gear up for whatever beastliness may be lying in wait for the coming year.

Around our house, football obtains from noon to midnight—Bowl follows Bowl: Rose, Orange, Cotton, Sugar—I think there's even something called the Bluebonnet Bowl that comes on at midnight! I like to watch with as much fanaticism as anyone, and I try to get the day's nourishment together in advance so I won't be stamping around the kitchen in a pet because I'm missing plays.

Good luck food for the first day of January in Charleston where I grew up was always ham and Hoppin' John, a mixture of black-eyed peas and rice cooked with a ham hock. This is wonderful food, easy to make ahead and serve at half-time.

Ham can be many things, some of them simply awful. Canned hams top the list of dreadfuls, then down on through the pre-cooked, water-injected messes that are touted as "ready-to-eat." I can't imagine by whom. I have found one brand that, with a bit of doctoring, tastes very ham-like indeed. This is the bone-in Boar's Head pre-cooked ham, but even *it* is not "ready-to-eat," no matter what the label says. There are ways to improve this type of ham, but if possible I always try to get my hands on a real country ham—such as a Smithfield—about a week in advance. These are aged, raw hams and must be soaked in several changes of water before they are simmered to tenderness. Although they are often referred to on menus as "Baked Virginia Ham," all hams must be simmered before they are finished in the oven with a glaze or nailed down with cloves (which is pretty, but ruins the ham).

I think a fine country ham plainly simmered in good pure water, then skinned, cooled and sliced paper thin, is the ultimate ham. Hot baking-powder biscuits and butter or those big stone-ground wheat crackers and green peppercorn mustard are the best accompaniments for a buffet.

Slicing a firm-fleshed country ham is a chore, and one you should never permit your guests to attempt unless you are absolutely certain they know what they're doing. Badly carved ham is tough and inedible as well as being a visual disaster.

HAM MADEIRA

Buy a whole or half good quality pre-cooked ham—indeed, it is becoming increasingly difficult to find one that has *not* been pre-cooked. These are nearly always injected with water to increase their weight, a practice that is legal for some odd reason. This is what creates the wet, cottony texture that meat-packers apparently strive for.

Remove the ham from its wrappings, string or whatever it comes in. Rinse it well with cold water. Dry it very thoroughly with paper towels. If you have a bulb injector, fill it with Madeira (there are some fairly decent cheap brands one can cook with) and inject the ham near the bone and in 8 or 10 places in the flesh, as deeply as you can. If you haven't this device, just baste the ham in Madeira every 15 minutes. Put the ham in a shallow pan just large enough to hold it. Bake it in a pre-heated 350° F. oven for about an hour, basting often. If the Madeira and juice start to dry and burn in the pan, add some hot water.

Cool the ham at least an hour—two is better—before attempting to slice it as thinly as possible across the grain. Arrange the slices in a neatly overlapping pattern, saving the most attractive slices for the top. For grandeur, set the uncarved portion of the ham in the center of the platter. Take it back to the kitchen for carving when you see that more slices are needed. Otherwise, some well-meaning friend will butcher it.

COUNTRY HAMS

A good ham that has been cured, smoked and aged is a considerable piece of work and is, accordingly, expensive. But the deep red, salty meat is so rich and delicious that a little goes a very long way. You must take it home with you about three days before you want to serve it.

If any directions come with the ham, pay attention to them, but many have very skimpy instructions or none at all. So . . . remove it from its wrappings and put it to soak in a large container of cool water. Very old hams need to be scrubbed with a stiff brush and hot water before being put to soak—don't let bits of green mold distress you; they will scrub off and are harmless. Change the water twice a day for two days.

On the third day, put the ham in a large vessel of cold water (wash boilers were used for this in the old days and I think you might substitute a very large granite-ware turkey roaster or canner—but be sure to measure your ham before you buy or borrow a ham pot). The ham should be completely immersed and brought very slowly to the simmer. Skim, if necessary.

Cook the ham very slowly with the water just at the tremble for 18 to 20 minutes to the pound. Many wrappers instruct the cook to allow 30 minutes to the pound, but this overcooks the ham and makes it stringy. Pierce it with a skewer or trussing needle to see if it is tender. The ilial bone near the shank should be easy to remove.

Turn off the heat and let the ham cool in its water about two hours. Then remove it, still warm, and take off the rind. Pare the fat to a smooth ½-inch thickness and let the ham get completely cold. Don't refrigerate unless you must—just put it in a cold room, covered loosely. Carve exceedingly thin, in long diagonal slices, starting at the shank end. If you've ever watched an Italian butcher carve a prosciutto ham with the bone in, this is the same method. The carving system illustrated in most American cookbooks seems to assume that huge, thick slabs of ham are the ideal. Get a book on carving and practice, practice, practice. This is the essential skill for elegant and economical meat cookery.

HOPPIN' JOHN

The peas for this dish come both frozen and dried at this time of year. The frozen ones are fresh, slightly greenish beans with a black "eye" in the center. Dried ones are tan with a black "eye" in the center. These beans are always called "peas," whether cow peas or black-eye peas. The dried ones are very easy to find in most grocery stores. The quantities given are rather large because people are expected to eat a lot of Hoppin' John for luck and a few thin slivers of ham for contrast. A green salad is almost a must with this rather starchy, but utterly delicious, New Year's Day tradition.

Serves 8 to 10.

1 pound dried black-eye peas
¼ pound smoked slab bacon
   or 1 ham hock
1 onion stuck with 2 cloves
1 bay leaf
Salt and freshly milled pepper

5 cups cooked white rice, very
   dry and firm-grained
Chopped parsley
Hot-pepper pickles or relish
   (optional)

Wash and pick over the peas. Put them in a deep pot with cold water to cover by a depth of about 4 inches. Bring to the simmer, skim if necessary, and add the bacon or ham hock and the onion and bay leaf. Do not add salt yet. Simmer very gently with a lid slightly askew for about half an hour. Add salt to taste. Continue cooking the peas until tender but not mushy, and add pepper. Drain them, reserving the "pot liquor," and mix the peas with the rice, using two forks to avoid mashing things up. Pour over a few ladles of pot liquor to moisten well. Serve in a shallow hot dish sprinkled with lots of fresh parsley and minced hot-pepper pickles.

Southerners tend to drink iced tea with this dish, but then they tend to drink iced tea with almost everything. It's a taste I've grown away from, however, and I think either good beer or a chilled rosé or white wine would be the best choice. This is a fattening but comforting meal—and who knows what the New Year will bring besides higher prices.

Good Intentions, Slimming Thoughts and Japanese Food

I don't think anyone really makes resolutions on New Year's Eve. No, that's no time to study the glumness of our moral and physical decay. The hour of grim decision is the first Monday after the New Year of *any* year. And this day should have a name: All Fat Souls Day, maybe.

Forced to meditate on an array of jeans in three or four sizes—all mine—has caused me to reconsider Michel Guérard's *cuisine minceur*. But not for long. When a diet entrée for two servings demands seventeen ingredients (among them *fromage blanc, crème fraîche* and truffle sauce) tediously amalgamated, I know I couldn't possibly stand in the kitchen that long without having a little snack.

I have to admit that even the mindless compliance of the Scarsdale Diet has at least *that*—no decision-making—to commend it. Upon close examination of almost any "new, never-be-hungry, eat-all-you-want" diet, it turns out to be a low-fat, low-carb, daily food allowance of less than 800 calories. And for some odd reason all dieticians assume that fat people are crazy about grapefruit and bales of raw greens without any salad dressing. These same skinny sadists also assume that a sweet tooth —easily assuaged by half a cup of diet raspberry jello—is probably responsible for the whole problem in the first place. The diet-makers never consider the people like me, whose sweet tooth died in adolescence and who ingest a pound of sugar every other year. For dieters like me, a no-cal wine or hollandaise would be the answer to eternal slimness. A de-calorizing powder to sprinkle on everything that's fattening is another of my hopes for the future.

But until then, I have found a way. The paths of righteousness have been shown me by my daughter, Dominique, who stays thin by eating a lot of her meals in Japanese restaurants. Obviously, that poses a problem on the East End of Long Island. But Japanese cookbooks are available and most of the ingredients can be found in local grocery stores. I see bean curd and bean sprouts, bamboo shoots, rice wine and various soy sauces in Bridgehampton and Southhampton food shops. And green ginger root is no stranger in these parts. We have terrific fish, poultry, pork and beef, and if the fresh produce is not to be compared with our fabulous summer farm vege-tables, we have plenty of mushrooms and scallions and food supplies that are im-mensely more sophisticated than they were ten years ago.

205

Small amounts of carefully prepared, artfully arranged food served on appropriate plates is the fundamental idea of Japanese cuisine (from which the *nouvelle cuisine* chefs have helped themselves quite liberally). There are few rich sauces, and cream, butter and cheese are virtually unknown. The Japanese do eat a lot of noodles—but usually floating in a plain thin broth rather than accompanied by a glob of rich, calorie-laden meat sauce. Rice fills you up and it is always served quite plain as a background to other tastes. The average Oriental rice bowl holds about half a cup of cooked rice—or 90 calories worth. Eating with chopsticks is a good way to slow your eating RPMs. (Too keep track of calories, buy a reliable guide to basic foods so that you can easily figure out totals of home-cooked dishes. Avoid all books with references to brand names or canned or processed foods. Who cares how many calories there are in a Hershey bar? You *know* you're not supposed to have one.)

Until recently, when the West introduced the Japanese to refined sugar, potatoes, beer and Scotch whiskey, which they have embraced with brio, there were almost no obese Japanese. (The sumo wrestlers deliberately fatten themselves to grotesque size for their "art.") *Aisukurimu*—ice cream—is a big hit in Japan, as are most American sweets, and the indefatigable "Kentucky Fried Chicken" man has crossed the wide Pacific.

Conversely, the popularity of Japanese cuisine has grown so rapidly in New York that there are now hundreds of *sashimi* and *sushi* parlors, formal restaurants and even "take-out" shops. We accept raw oysters, clams and scallops, so why not raw fish? Especially in an area where good, really fresh fish is abundant. I am such a *sushi* and *sashimi* freak that I sit at the counter of New York's Hatsuhana restaurant so that I can point wordlessly to all the marvelous *sushi* ingredients the chef makes up one at a time to lay on the shining clean eucalyptus leaf befere me.

Chinese food is another of my great passions, but most of it is far from slimming and best avoided until enough poundage is shed to go on an occasional spree. Even if you have never eaten Japanese food in your life, the principles are there to be adapted to American ingredients. If for a month you skip alcoholic drinks and desserts (Japanese sweets are horrid), cook Japanese and walk briskly away from the table, it will be the most enjoyable diet you're ever likely to find.

Some books to help you on this project are *Home-Style Japanese Cooking in Pictures* by Sadako Kohno (Japanese Publications) and *At Home with Japanese Cooking* by Elizabeth Andoh (Knopf, New York). When you really want to get into it, the most complete work is a gorgeous book called *Japanese Cooking: A Simple Art* by Japan's master chef, Shizuo Tsuji (Kodansha). My favorite beginner's book, which I got in 1973, is a cheap paperback called *Japanese Home Cooking,* written and illustrated by Barbara Farr, published by a little house called Potpourri Press in Greensboro, N.C. It's out of print but copies turn up in secondhand shops. This book has one grave, but easily corrected, fault. Omit the vast amounts of sugar which the author seems to find necessary in everything from clam soup to salmon salad. Here is a simple and delicious dish that illustrates how easily one can make Japanese dishes with American ingredients. It is adapted from Barbara Farr's book, which is really only a primer. Should you be drawn to this delicate and interesting cuisine, Shizuo Tsuji's book is the unparalleled guide and teacher.

YAKITORI

Small bamboo skewers soaked an hour in cold water are normally used for this. They are cheap, disposable and available at any good cookware shop.

Serves 4.

*1 whole chicken breast, skinned
  and boned
8 chicken livers, washed and
  trimmed*

*½ pound fresh mushrooms
4 large scallions*

SAUCE

*½ cup soy sauce (Japanese
  brand: Kikkoman)
2 tablespoons light brown sugar
  (I omit this)*

*2 tablespoons dry sherry
1 tablespoon toasted sesame
  seeds (my addition)
Plain oil*

Cut chicken breast into 1-inch cubes. Halve chicken livers. Dry both meats well. Cut mushrooms into pieces same size as chicken. Cut scallions into 1-inch lengths. Mix the sauce in a long shallow dish.

    Alternate chicken breast and mushrooms on four bamboo skewers. Alternate livers and scallions on remaining four skeweres. Place the skewers in the bowl of sauce and marinate while the broiler or hibachi (a small hibachi can be used in the fireplace in winter) is heating. Broil chicken and livers until just done, brushing often with the sauce and a little oil. The livers should be slightly pink inside and the chicken is done when it springs back to the touch—about 5 minutes total cooking. The skewers should be watched constantly and turned several times.

Serve two yakitori skewers across a small bowl of rice to each person. With this you can serve the traditional Japanese salad, *Cucumber Sunomono:* Peel one large cucumber leaving thin stripes of green down the sides. Slice it thinly and salt lightly. Marinate it in a dressing made of: 3 tablespoons cider vinegar (rice wine vinegar is better) and a few drops of soy sauce. I have omitted Miss Farr's addition of 3 tablespoons of sugar, and I would add fresh black pepper, although it is not at all the Japanese thing to do. Alter the dressing as you like. Chef Tsuji says "as long as you know the rules, and know what authentic Japanese food is, there is almost no limit to the variations you can make with local ingredients."

There are a few items you might get from any of the numerous Japanese food stores* in New York: *wasabi,* a fiery green horseradish powder which is mixed to a paste with water, then stirred into soy sauce to make a smashing *sashimi* sauce. *Kombu,* an edible seaweed to make the basic Japanese cooking broth, *dashi. Miso,* a fermented soy-bean paste widely used in this cookery. Rice wine vinegar and bonito flakes are other common ingredients and all keep well for months, unrefrigerated.

Although we westerners usually think of tempura, the deep-fried shrimp and vegetable combination, as typical Japanese food, actually most of it is broiled or steamed, making it splendid food for fatties, as well as being utterly delicious for everyone.

* These include Katagiri Company, 224 East 50th Street, New York, New York 10022, and Tanaka and Company, 326 Amsterdam Avenue, New York, New York 10023. The major supplier of Oriental foodstuffs in the continental United States, The Japan Food Corporation, 445 Kauffman Court, South San Francisco, California 94080, will gladly supply enquirers with the names of stores in other areas that handle mail orders.

The Duck Debate

Wanna' buy a duck?
    —Joe Penner, vaudevillian

Penner was an early baggy-pants comic and one of those who helped mightily in killing vaudeville with that famous unfuny routine of his. A lot of restaurants are doing about as much for the famous Long Island duckling—a lovely creature when properly cooked, which it seldom is. The "menu-ese" entices us with "moist, succulent flesh, crackling skin," etc., etc. Unless the place offers almost nothing but duck dishes, or you have ordered a day in advance, this is highly unlikely. A domestic duck requires upwards of two hours roasting and a great deal of careful prepping for the oven beforehand. (Wild ducks play by altogether different rules, and are not being discussed here.)

Most restaurant ducks are, perforce, precooked—unless you are in a *nouvelle cuisine* joint, where it is served half raw. What usually arrives is a reheated, dry, stringy bird with a soggy skin cowering under a cloying blanket of fruit sauce. I admit to a personal prejudice against any sweet sauce on any meats of any kind, but I realize that other people do enjoy them—there are plenty of recipes for these sauces in English and German cookbooks.

The French passion for rare, bloody duck simply dumbfounds me, but I *have* had some faintly pink duck breast I enjoyed. The legs of a rare duck are inedible and should be reserved to put into a cassoulet or some such dish. I don't think French ducks—usually citizens of Rouen or Nantes—can have much in common with the descendants of the nine Peking ducks that rounded the Horn in a Sag Harbor whaler in 1873. Their average market weight is about 4½ pounds, and about half of that is fat. (It does seem that, with modern genetic engineering, farmers ought to be able to breed out some of that excessive fattiness.)

The Chinese—who, after all should know how to cook a Peking duck—go to great lengths to extract this fat and still achieve a crisp duckling with moist flesh. Over the years I've read hundreds of duck recipes and tried many of them. Of them all, I think the easiest way to cook a perfect duck is by spit-roasting. A lot of electric ovens are equipped with rotisseries (which most people never use), and this method produces the most succulent roasts and birds of all without requiring much attention from the cook. There also seems to be a good deal less shrinkage in spit-roasted meats, and sauce-makings are improved because the drippings fall into a pan removed from the heat source and therefore do not burn.

I am impressed by the performance of my electric countertop rotisserie, which operates smokelessly in the kitchen air and produces truly roasted and not baked meat or poultry. An alternative to the rotisserie is to roast the duck upright in the Chinese fashion. There are metal frames on the market that hold poultry in position as long as there is sufficient oven height. Unfortunately there seldom is because manufacturers of home ovens seem to be cutting them smaller and smaller. And outdoor barbeque grills grow ever more gigantic, even though the entire American population is not, as yet, residing in California.

SPIT-ROASTED DUCKLING

Even though the duck farms are fast disappearing on Long Island, it is still relatively easy to find a fresh bird if you shop around a bit. A 4½- to 5-pound raw duck looks hefty enough to serve a family of four. It doesn't. The average domestic duckling will satisfy only two or at most three appetites. The rendered fat, however, can be salvaged and used for general frying and the carcass may be converted into a good soup after discarding the stuffing, which is not edible.

1 fresh L. I. duckling, about
    4½ pounds
2 medium onions, thinly sliced
1 thin-skinned orange, unpeeled,
    thinly sliced

Salt and pepper
Softened butter
1 bunch watercress

You will need a length of soft white string to truss up the duck and a very large sharp needle both to sew it closed and to prick the skin. The skin and only the skin is pricked to release the fat underneath—the meat must remain unpunctured so that the juices do not run out. To do this, after the duck is stuffed and fully prepared for cooking, take long, shallow, running stitches through the surface of the duck skin as though you were basting up a hem. This extremely effective technique occurred to me as I was working with great care to preserve the integrity of an expensive Christmas goose, which has a lot of the same anatomical problems as the duck.

Remove the neck and giblets from the duck and rinse them. One duck liver doesn't do much for anybody, so my cats usually get it. If you want a sauce, put the neck and other innards into a pot with an onion stuck with two cloves, a piece of carrot and some marjoram, bay leaf and thyme. You can save this broth for a soup if you prefer your duck unembellished, as I do. (I can see no point in going to all the bother of obtaining a perfect, crisp skin and then pouring something wet on it.)

Rinse the duck, dry it well and pull out all the solid white fat you find in the vent and crop. Discard it. Gently lift the duck skin away from the breast with your fingers. Try to get your hands completely under the skin, so that you can stretch it away from the body and thus break up the fatty tissue. (The Chinese do this by blowing up the skin with a bicycle pump.)

Place a few onion and orange slices between the duck breast and the skin. Salt and pepper the cavity, and put the remaining onion and orange slices into it. Sew the neck skin to the back. Snap the wings into place behind the duck's back. Push the legs close to the body and tie them together, then run the string around under the tail and up along the sides of the breast, across the back and down along the other side of the breast and tie the string to the original knot at the legs. Make shallow running stitches all over the duck's skin, piercing the skin well, but *not* the flesh of the duck.

Center and balance the duck on the spit so that it will turn evenly and not flop and cook unevenly. Adjust and tighten the prongs that secure the bird to the skewer. Rub the duck's breast and legs with softened butter and salt and pepper it.

Preheat the rotisserie, then put the skewered duck in place as close as possible to the heat source in the open table model unit (or follow directions for your own oven rotisserie). Turn on the motor and check to see that the duck is revolving slowly and evenly with no slipping or flopping over. If it does this, you have not balanced the duck correctly and must take it off the spit and re-balance it; this it not normally necessary. As the duck roasts, continue to make a few new needle holes as described in the foregoing instructions—if you work fast it can be managed without turning off the rotisserie. The fat will fall into the drip pan underneath and it should be removed from time to time with a bulb baster so that it won't overflow.

Roast the duck for two hours, then turn off the heat but not the rotisserie motor. Allow it to turn about 15 minutes longer for the juices to settle and facilitate carving.

Remove the duck from the skewer and cut away the strings. Cut off both wings, then both legs and thighs, which should remain in one piece. With the knife slicing along the keel bone, cut away each half of the breast in one piece. Then slice each half into three or four diagonal slices. Arrange on a heated platter and encircle with fresh watercress sprigs.

Apple slices sautéed in butter are nice with the duck, as well as a dollop of spicy Indian chutney. Scalloped potatoes or lentils braised in broth are pleasant, juicy accompaniments to the crisp, unsauced roast duck. A Zinfandel or Cabernet Sauvignon from California are good to drink with duck.

Frozen Improvisations

Oh! the weather outside is frightful,
But the fire is so delightful . . .
—Sammy Cahn and Jule Styne,
"Let It Snow! Let It Snow! Let It Snow!" (1945)

And, the song continues, "since we've no place to go . . ." the road being kneedeep in snow, a fortuitous time to inventory the refrigerator presents itself. (We would all probably buy and waste less food if we had to cook by our wits two days a week.) My freezer elicits glad cries from almost no one because it's full of frozen stock, bags of beef and chicken scraps for making said stock, herbs, hot peppers, odd ingredients that are not easily available, puff paste, pizza dough. My only frozen vegetables are spinach and artichoke hearts and the occasional box of lima beans (my husband's favorite fruit). But except for a few soups and stews, there's little that can simply be thawed out and eaten without further ado. My family tends to groan and say, "Why can't you ever have anything to *eat* in here?"

They are utterly justified. And my refrigerator is scarcely any better, because although it's jammed to the gunwales, all the food is what the Chinese cooks call "food materials." This means that they must be transformed into an edible dish by some form of preparation and/or cooking. That was my challenge for a snowed-in weekend: to see how many good things I could make out of my "food materials."

When my children return on visits they immediately swing open the refrigerator door, expecting it to look like an Amana showroom: those plastic turkeys, hams, pâtés and salamis arranged artfuly to exhibit plenitude and spaciousness. The reality of the typical American fridge is a jumble of plastic boxes, jars and bags of half-used foods and accursed leftovers. But as I cook with the object of a restaurant—exact portions—I seldom have even leftovers except at holiday time. But, it turns out, I do have a lot on hand for fresh beginnings. The fridge/freezer/store cupboard yielded up this lovely meal for us.

Snowed-In Saturday Luncheon
Dry Sherry
Braised Sauerkraut & Weisswurst
Steamed Parsley Potatoes
Pinot Grigio   Camembert & Rolls

212

SAUERKRAUT AND WEISSWURST

Kraut keeps indefinitely if refrigerated in sealed plastic bags; canned kraut is not worth the space it sits on. Weisswurst are pale veal sausages with a touch of nutmeg. These and Italian sausages freeze well, thaw quickly, and are prudent to keep for emergencies.

Serves 2.

1 pound fresh sauerkraut	*1 medium onion*
1 cup chicken broth and	*1 bay leaf*
drippings or *butter*	*½ cup dry white wine*
1 clove garlic	*Freshly milled black pepper*
6 to 8 juniper berries	

Drain the sauerkraut in a strainer and rinse it briefly with cold water. Let it drain. (I had the broth and pan drippings from the previous day's roast chicken, and these infused the sauerkraut deliciously.) In place of that one can use butter to sauté the garlic and onion, which should be minced in the food processor with the juniper berries (or crushed in a mortar, the vegetables chopped fine with a knife). When they are just transparent, add the sauerkraut, bay leaf, broth, wine and enough water to cover the kraut. Stir in some pepper, cover and braise over low heat for an hour.

Peel two fairly large potatoes, cut them in quarters and arrange them in a steamer basket. Sprinkle with a bit of salt and steam about 15 to 20 minutes. Chop some parsley and have the butter nearby.

Melt 1 tablespoon butter in a small heavy skillet and add the sausages (one per person—they are large) after pricking them with a needle. These veal sausages are quite fragile and burst easily, so should be cooked over a fairly low flame. Mince a small onion finely and scatter it over the sausages. Turn them around occasionally; they will be done and nicely browned in about 10 minutes—at the same moment as the steamed potatoes, which should be timed to finish with the sauerkraut.

Lift the steamer basket out of the pot, throw out the water and put a little butter into the empty pot. Add the potatoes and roll them in melted butter. Sprinkle with chopped parsley—quite a lot of it.

With a slotted spoon, arrange a big mound of sauerkraut on each heated plate.

Flank it with a sausage and some parsleyed potatoes (the parsley is not a frippery, but essential to the goodness of a simple boiled or steamed potato). Enjoy it while it's smoking hot, with glasses of crisp, cold white wine. We lunched in the greenhouse, warmed by our Victorian wood stove, and watched the snow fall and fall and fall.

Midwinter Fantasies and Fish

Last season's fruit is eaten
And the fullfed beast shall kick the empty pail.
—T. S. Eliot, "Little Gidding," from *Four Quartets*

And we shall shuffle through the pages of the newly arrived seed catalogues. The Burpee people feature a salacious cover of bursting-ripe, indecently red tomatoes. Upsetting, when you realize how far away the reality of all those stunning seed-packet pictures still is.

Gazing out over the ice-choked harbor and the bays it seems impossible that our fishermen can haul anything from that frozen, forbidding seascape. But somehow they do. I thought the scallops had closed their blue eyes in horror until warmer times, but some have been gathered. And there are mussels, and both hard and soft clams. And there is cod, a fine, firm, winter fish that makes the best of all possible chowder (and is exotic fried in tempura batter).

So there's always *something* in the old Long Island larder without resorting to frozen fish sticks and dreaded parsnips. (Remember that expression "fine words butter no parsnips"? Who'd want to!) However, I do esteem those big ugly yellow turnips that seem to last until Palm Sunday. But I have been singularly unsuccessful in convincing others of their worth. Just try adding a few pieces cut in small dice to discover what richness and flavor the unlovely rutabaga can add to a beef stew or a thick vegetable soup.

Something I've never had to persuade *anyone* to eat is my winter fish chowder, which is varied according to what's available (except for the cod, which is essential). Sometimes you will find monkfish (a.k.a. anglerfish) or pollack at this time of year; halibut also makes a fine chowder, but rarely can be found in the non-frozen state. Flounder and weakfish are too fragile and tend to disintegrate in a chowder.

EAST END WINTER CHOWDER

As will be obvious from the ingredients, this is a substantial main-dish chowder. A salad and some hot biscuits or cornbread would complete a warming meal for a blustery night. Avocados and oranges are cheap and plentiful now and add a tropical touch to these frigid times.

Serves 6–8.

3 pounds fillet of cod

FISH FUMET
Head and skeleton of the cod
1 quart cold water
1 tablespoon coarse salt
Several grindings fresh white peppercorns
2 cups dry white wine
1 bay leaf
1 teaspoon dried tarragon (in summer use fresh tarragon)

6 slices thick slab bacon
1 tablespoon butter
2 or 3 cloves garlic, minced

2 large onions, chopped (about 2 cups)
2 tablespoons flour
3 baking potatoes, peeled and diced
½ pint bay scallops
½ pint shucked oysters (cut in half if large)
1 pint half-and-half (or milk for a thinner stew)
3 tablespoons fresh parsley, minced

Remove the skin, if any, from the cod, and cut it into 1-inch chunks; return it to the icebox. Be sure the gills are removed from the head of the fish or they will impart a bitter taste and also discolor your chowder. Put the head and the fish bones, chopped in several places, into a large pot with the water, salt, pepper, wine, bay leaf and tarragon—this will make your foundation broth, or *fumet*. Simmer all this together for about 30 minutes, uncovered, then strain it before adding it to the chowder pot.

Note: Long boiling makes fish broths taste rancid and they don't keep well, even when frozen. Since a fish *fumet* is so quick and simple to make, there's no point in cluttering the freezer space with it anyway. Fresh clam juice is another matter—I always save mine and freeze it when opening clams; it is extremely useful to add to poaching broth and other fish preparations.

Cut the bacon into sticks and slowly fry it in the butter until crisp but not hard. Drain and reserve it to garnish the chowder. In the bacon fat remaining in the pan, sauté the garlic and onions until soft and transparent, but do not let them take color. Sprinkle with the flour and stir it into the onions well. Cook, stirring, a couple of minutes over very low heat. Pour the fish *fumet* over these ingredients, stirring constantly. Add the potatoes and simmer about half an hour. Add the cod and simmer for about 5 minutes or until opaque. Add the scallops and oysters and half-and-half or milk. Bring to the simmer, then turn off the heat and cover for 5 minutes.

Dish up the chowder in heavy heated bowls and garnish with crumbled bacon and a dusting of minced parsley.

Another Note: Despite all the anti-flour propaganda expounded, it is necessary in this chowder to bind the fish *fumet* with the cream, which would otherwise be curdled by the addition of the shellfish. In fact, sauces thickened with *crème fraîche* reductions, while delicious, are infinitely higher in calories and fats than the much-maligned flour-thickened sauces. The chief thing to keep in mind about flour is that it must be cooked long enough to eradicate the raw flavor. And it must be used in extreme moderation to avoid that thick, pale, pasty "gravy" so beloved by school and hospital cafeterias.

ORANGE AND AVOCADO SALAD

This combination may seem a little eccentric, but if you consider the classic Brazilian accompaniment to their national dish, *feijoada*—oranges and onion slices—it will seem less odd. California avocados, the little wrinkled ones, have a dense, creamy flesh, much superior to the big pale-green Florida variety. The Florida avocados are often quite watery and tasteless.

Serves 6.

½ *lemon*
3 *California avocados*
4 *large oranges, (temple or navel)*

1 *tablespoon red wine vinegar*
1 *teaspoon salt*
2 *tablespoons olive oil*

Squeeze the half lemon and put the juice into a bowl large enough to hold the avocados. The citric acid is necessary to prevent the avocados from blackening, which happens almost instantly without this precaution. (This is what accounts for gray guacamole.)

Peel, stone and slice the avocados in crescents and turn them in the lemon juice to coat them completely. Peel the oranges, removing both skin and pith at once. Slice into ¼-inch circles and arrange them on a platter in an overlapping pattern. Mix the vinegar, salt and olive oil and pour it over the avocado slices. Arrange them on top of the orange slices and serve. The salad is quite an attractive buffet dish and the chowder is certainly a handy one when there are too many guests for a seated dinner. For a simple family dinner, the expensive oysters and scallops could be omitted and a few minced fresh clams substituted.

A Lincoln Day Dinner

When Abraham Lincoln came into this world in 1809 in the Kentucky backwoods, his mother, Nancy Hanks, probably had about twenty dollars a year in "discretionary income." That is, of course, any money you have left to throw around after paying for the necessities. Money was tight, and while Lincoln was studying law in Illinois he was also a postmaster-storekeeper. Of all the changes since then—moon shots and motor cars, jet planes and foreign wars—none could have astonished the former storekeep more than the current price of groceries.

Here's a simple and direct menu to commemorate the Great Emancipator's birthday or anybody else's that happens to fall this month. It's traditional American food treated with some modern methods to lighten the meal. Salt fish, beans and lamb, cornbread and cabbage are some of the everyday foods made special. Authenticity probably cries out for fried bear paws and burnt hoecakes and a lot of other early American stuff that no one would eat now. But it's important to maintain the spirit of the old dishes. This menu is for eight people.

Menu
Maatjes Herring with Dill
Backwoods Cassoulet
Cornbread with Bacon Bits
Shredded Cabbage and Beet Salad
Apples, Pears and Walnuts

MAATJES HERRING WITH DILL

Salt fish was a mainstay in the diet of frontier Americans, though I doubt they had anything so refined as Maatjes herring, a dusky-rose, sweet-sour Scandinavian herring. The fillets are quite large and half of one is enough for each person. Arrange each half on a small plate with a sprig of fresh dill and some sour cream mixed with chopped dill. Garnish the plates with a few thin cucumber slices. Serve black bread and sweet butter with this course.

BACKWOODS CASSOULET

Cassoulet is of course, one of the most famous provincial dishes of France. Much of the gastronomic writing on the subject makes the construction of the dish seem only slightly less forbidding than the raising of the cathedral at Reims. It is in reality just a farmwife's winter dish of dried beans and savory meats gently baked in an earthenware casserole. Preserved goose is supposed to be among the meats in an authentic version, but few people can find that (and it's frightfully expensive), so I often substitute a half-roasted duck to finish cooking on top of the beans. Or try this native approach to cassoulet that uses only ingredients available nearly everywhere. We have a lot of Polish farmers who supply us with kielbasa, but there are very good brands sold nationally, Boar's Head for one.

2 cups dried Great Northern white beans
2 cups dried pink (California) beans—not kidney beans
1 quart strong chicken broth, homemade if possible
2 tablespoons salad oil
1½ pounds meaty lamb neck or shoulder
1½ pounds center cut slice fresh ham (pork leg)
Flour, salt and pepper
3 fat cloves garlic, minced

2 large onions, chopped medium fine
2 cups good broth (veal, beef or turkey)
2 cups canned tomatoes including juices
2 small bay leaves
2 teaspoons dried thyme leaves
1 teaspoon dried marjoram (optional)
1 whole kielbasa sausage (about 1½ pounds)

Wash the beans in cold water and pick them over for any that are discolored or badly shriveled. Cover with cold water to a depth of about 3 inches above the beans. Bring to a boil, simmer 2 minutes, turn off heat and let soak for an hour.

Meanwhile, brown the lamb and pork, which should be cut into roughly 1-inch cubes, in the oil heated in a deep heavy skillet. Sprinkle the meats with about 1 tablespoon of flour, which will help the browning, and a little salt and pepper, stirring often with a wooden spoon to brown all sides. Add the garlic and onions and cook over low heat until these ingredients are soft but not brown. Add the 2 cups of meat or turkey broth, the tomatoes, bay leaf and thyme to the meats, and the marjoram, if used. Marjoram has a rather pronounced flavor that I like very much in small quantities. Some people don't care for it at all, so it's best to proceed with caution in using this herb.

Stir up the ingredients in the skillet, cover it and simmer over low heat for about an hour.

Drain the beans, put them in a pot with the cold chicken broth, adding cold water if necessary to cover them by an inch. If you cook them in a fairly deep pot, this should not be necessary. Cover the beans and bring to the simmer. Cook them for an hour, checking occasionally to see that the broth has not evaporated. This will not happen if you maintain a low, even heat under the pot.

Pre-heat the oven to 325° F. In an earthenware casserole about 3 inches deep, combine the beans, their liquid and the meat mixture. Mix it gently to avoid mashing the beans, which will in any event still be quite firm as they should be only half done. Taste for salt and pepper and add more as needed. Cover the casserole with a double thickness of foil and its own lid if it has one. (Most earthenware casseroles lack lids, and the ones they occasionally have do not fit tightly.) Bake the cassoulet about an hour and a half or until beans and meats are tender and have absorbed most of the juices.

At this point you can set it aside, uncovered, in a cool place until an hour before serving time. At that point, broil the kielbasa under a low flame about 6 inches from the heat until its skin is browned and crisp—about 5 minutes on each side. Cut the sausage into 2-inch lengths and half imbed them over the surface of the cassoulet. Reheat in a preheated 325° F. oven until all is very, very hot throughout. The only tricky part of a cassoulet is in getting the beans to absorb nearly—but not all—the liquids while cooking to a meltingly tender, but not mushy, state.

This dish may be made a day ahead, except for broiling the kielbasa, which would become sodden, but it must be returned to room temperature before the cassoulet's final heating.

CORNBREAD WITH BACON

English visitors to America in the first half of the nineteenth century—Frances Trollope, Harriet Martineau, and the great Charles Dickens among others—almost routinely returned home to write scathing reports of American food. They were particularly revolted by the excessive amounts of corn and salt meat eaten here. But as Henry Adams explained: "The rich alone could afford fresh meat . . . except for poultry and game." The ordinary rural American was brought up on salt pork and Indian corn, or rye. We have stubbornly persisted in our love of corn and salt meats such as ham and bacon. This recipe combines several of our native lapses of taste.

4 to 5 slices thick bacon
2 cups yellow cornmeal
2 teaspoons baking powder
½ teaspoon salt

1 cup buttermilk
2 eggs
2 tablespoons melted butter

Preheat oven to 400° F.

Butter an 8- x 8-inch baking tin or an 8-inch black iron skillet.

Slowly fry the bacon until crisp, but take care not to let it blacken or the fat burn. Drain it and reserve the fat.

Sift the dry ingredients together. Beat together the buttermilk and eggs. Stir them into the dry ingredients along with the reserved bacon fat and melted butter. Blend, but do not beat, the batter. Pour it into the buttered pan or skillet. Crumble the reserve bacon and sprinkle it over the top of the batter. Oil your knuckles well and press the bacon bits lightly into the batter. Bake on the middle rack of the oven for 30 minutes or until lightly browned and a skewer comes out clean.

SHREDDED CABBAGE AND BEET SALAD

Of course it's possible to get salad greens at any season these days, but a century and more ago, the cook had to stick with the winter vegetables. This is a rather attractive change from the usual mixed green salad.

1 small head dark green cabbage
4 tablespoons olive oil
1 teaspoon salt
1 teaspoon freshly milled pepper
½ teaspoon prepared mustard

1 tablespoon cider vinegar
1 8-ounce jar pickled julienne beets
½ cup red Italian onion, minced

Wash and core the cabbage and cut it in half. Shred it finely, by using a manual slicer or food processor with the slicing attachment. The cabbage should be in long thin shreds, not chopped.

Mix the oil, salt, pepper, mustard and vinegar together with a whisk and pour it over the cabbage. Use your hands to mix the cabbage well with the dressing, then put it in a shallow glass bowl. Drain the beets and pile them in a mound in the center of the cabbage. Scatter the minced onion over the surface of the salad.

Staying Alive

A little of what you fancy does you good . . .
—Fred W. Leigh and George Arthurs, old music-hall song

Unfortunately, almost nothing I fancy is reported to do anyone any good these days. Just ten minutes with *Jane Brody's Nutrition Book* spins me into almost irreversible depression. All should be fatless, careless, sugarless and, in fine, weightless, if one is to be a healthy, nicotine-free, teetotaling, running, hopping, skipping, with-it Modern Person.

People should look nice. People should also be happy and feel satisfied once in a while, and with guilt-free conscience enjoy some anachronistic unchic food of the kind that made winters bearable. What, I asked myself one February day, could fortify body and soul in this endless slough of icy days? So I turned to my old, pre-"Me Generation" cookbooks to hunt for something rich, filling, suffused in every mouthful with sheer pleasure in taste, texture and aroma. And I made this gloriously fattening ragout of adamantly unfashionable oxtails. I don't know if it's good for you, but it's both cheap and delicious—a meal to which you can beckon your friends and relations.

OXTAILS RAGOUT

While oxtails are seldom displayed in supermarket meatcases, if you ask your butcher, he can order them. They will probably be frozen, because they are so perishable, but this seems to do them no harm. The tails should be cut in 2-inch lengths and the terminal 3 or 4 inches discarded, as it is meatless. I have adapted this recipe to modern taste to the extent of eliminating the excessive greasiness characteristic of earlier recipes. This improves the texture tremendously, as well as rendering it fairly harmless in the cholesterol department.

Serves 6.

6 pounds oxtails, jointed	Salt and pepper
¼ cup brandy	12 to 14 small imported black
3 medium onions, finely chopped	olives, pitted and rinsed with
2 large cloves garlic, minced	boiling water
1 cup dry red wine	3 to 4 tablespoons flour
8-ounce can tomatoes	Lots of minced parsley
Pinch dried thyme	Cooked rice or boiled or
Thin paring of orange rind	mashed potatoes
2 inches long	

Skimming the fat from an oxtail stew can be a tiresome piece of repetition, so here is a way to get rid of most of it in the begining and also to brown the meat effortlessly. Simply dry the pieces of oxtail, spread them out in one layer in a large, lightly oiled roasting pan, sprinkle with salt and pepper and put them in a hot oven (approximately 425° F.) for half an hour, stirring them up and over after 15 minutes. Pour off all the accumulated fat into a clean jar and save it to use for frying —it makes delicious fried potatoes. Reduce oven temperature to 325° F. Reserve about ¼ cup of the rendered fat to sauté the onions and garlic; you will need some more at the end of the recipe to make a roux for thickening the stew.

Heat the brandy over direct flame in a large ladle. When it flames up, pour it swiftly over all the oxtails. This strengthens the flavor immensely and burns off more fat. Remove the oxtails to a large oven-to-table casserole. Deglaze the roasting pan with hot water, scraping up all the browned bits, and pour this over the oxtails.

Heat a few spoonfuls of the rendered fat in a large skillet and sauté the onions and garlic gently until transparent. Add these to the oxtails along with the wine. Purée the can of tomatoes in a blender (do not use canned tomato purée—it is too sweet and thick); add them, along with a large pinch of dried thyme. Add enough hot water to barely cover the oxtails and stir the ingredients well, adding the orange rind last. Taste for salt and pepper, remembering that the ragout will reduce considerably. Cover tightly and braise in the center of the oven for about two hours. Add the pitted and rinsed olives to the ragout, and cook for another half hour. The meat should be almost, but not quite, falling from the bones.

Melt some of the reserved beef fat (2 or 3 tablespoons) in a small, heavy saucepan and stir in the flour. Cook this roux, stirring over low heat, about 5 minutes. Skim the ragout well, removing as much fat as possible. Take about a pint of the sauce from the casserole and stir it into the roux. Whisk thoroughly and stir over low heat about 5 minutes. Return this to the oxtails and mix well. Sprinkle the finished ragout with parsley, and serve on very hot plates with plenty of fluffy hot mashed potatoes, plain boiled potatoes, or my favorite: firm, dry white rice. I tried this ragout once with noodles, but the combined textures were too similar. Braised carrots are good with this, and, winter yielding so little in the way of crisp fresh vegetables, serve a big green simple salad or a bowl of shredded green cabbage dressed with a plain oil and vinegar vinaigrette—no creamy dressing with such a rich stew.

Just to be sure that everyone will stay immobilized in front of the fire, an apple brown betty with a light trickle of cream may be served for dessert. But if you want to be righteous, simply serve a bowl of apples.

Long Island Passion Fruit—Potatoes

Then a sentimental passion of a vegetable fashion
must excite your languid spleen,
An attachment à la Plato for a bashful young potato,
or a not too French French bean!
—W. S. Gilbert, *Patience*

How *can* I have gone on with this hymn to Long Island produce for such a time without discussing the passion fruit of the South Fork? The potato—not as flashy as a kiwi, but demure, nutritious and filling.

The potato, which is a South American immigrant, had a tough time gaining acceptance, both here and in Europe. It was taken to France as early as 1540, but grown only as an ornamental plant. The French considered potatoes unfit for human consumption and just possibly the cause of leprosy. Parmentier defended the tuber in a thesis written in 1771, and by clever subterfuge finally got the French people to realize what a delicious and valuable food they were passing up. He planted a plot of potatoes, set a heavy guard around it by day and removed it by night. Now there are more than a hundred potato recipes in *Larousse Gastronomique*.

"Weight for weight, potato contains two and a half times less carbohydrates than bread," according to the unimpeachable *Larousse*. It is also rich in potassium and highly digestible, particularly when it is baked or boiled in its jacket. I can make no such claims for the limp and greasy "French fries" that partner nearly every steak and hamburger served in America. To say nothing of the unspeakable "chips" that in England are the other half of "Fish and."

"Bangers and Mash" is another English specialty—awful in England because of their cereal-filled sausages, but a very good winter dish here when made with spicy pure pork link sausage laid across a mound of hot, fluffy mashed potatoes. The potato has a death-grip on the English cook's imagination and almost no meal is considered complete without potatoes in some form.

In Ireland, one is often served not one, but *two* kinds of potatoes on the same plate. Although potatoes were planted in Ireland in the late sixteenth century, they were regarded with suspicion for a couple of hundred years before becoming the mainstay of the Irish diet. (In the American South, all white potatoes are called "Irish" potatoes to differentiate them from sweet potatoes.) A commonly served supper—which is called "tea"—for the Irish workingman is a "fry." This consists of bacon—Irish bacon is lean and much more substantial than American bacon—eggs and potato cakes fried in the bacon fat. Maybe not a nutritional triumph, but a "fry" is delicious nonetheless.

COLCANNON

Irish cookery is not, as the Irish themselves say, very "sophistica-ated." For centuries, just getting enough to eat was such a struggle that even a plain dish like Colcannon was something of a little celebration. It is traditionally served on All Hallows Eve (the same as our Halloween) studded with various trinkets of forecast such as a thimble (spinster), a button (bachelor), a ring (a marriage proposal) and so forth. If you plan to do this authentically, it would be well to warn people before they dig into a sturdy mixture of mashed potatoes and cabbage. Originally, Colcannon was made with kale, but that leafy green vegetable isn't common any more, so cabbage or spinach is substituted. In Ireland this is the entire meal, but you might add a touch of luxury with a slice of ham, a sausage or even a couple of meatballs.

Serves 4.

3 pounds Russet or Green Mountain potatoes, peeled and quartered
Half a head of green cabbage
¼ pound (1 stick) butter, softened

1 cup hot milk (approximately)
½ cup minced scallions, both white and green parts
Salt and freshly milled pepper to taste
4 tablespoons melted butter

Boil the potatoes in just enough salted water to cover. They will be done in about 20 minutes. While they cook, shred the cabbage and steam it (on a rack) until barely tender. Set aside and keep warm until potatoes are mashed.

Drain the potatoes when done, put them back over the low fire with a folded tea towel on top to absorb excess water. Put them through a food mill or ricer, then beat in the ¼ pound of butter and enough of the hot milk to make creamy, but not too soupy, mashed potatoes. Beat in the scallions and salt and pepper to taste. Fold in the steamed, drained cabbage and divide the Colcannon in heaped-up mounds on four hot soup plates. Make a well in the top of each mound and pour one tablespoon of melted butter into each. You can also use chopped spinach, but it should be fresh and just barely cooked or there will not be enough textural contrast.

POTATO OMELET

The origin of this dish, which I like for a quick supper, is the German *Bauern-fruhstück*—meaning "farmer's breakfast." You can add a bit of ham, bacon or sausage, cooked and chopped, but the basic thing is potatoes.

Serves 1.

2 tablespoons butter
¾ cup potatoes, peeled and
   diced fine
½ cup onion, chopped
Salt and pepper

3 eggs
1 teaspoon milk
2 tablespoons fresh parsley,
   chopped

Melt the butter in a non-stick, 8-inch frying pan. Dry the potatoes, add them to the butter and cook, stirring often over low heat, until they are lightly browned and tender—about 10 minutes. Add the onion and salt and pepper lightly. Stir and cook gently about 5 minutes.

Heat a plate to receive your omelet. Beat the eggs with the milk and parsley, then pour it over the contents of the frying pan. Turn up the heat slightly and lift the edges of the omelet to let the uncooked egg run under the cooked portion. This takes about a minute. When the omelet is still somewhat runny on top, fold it in half and slide it out onto the waiting plate. (If you attempt to roll the omelet in three turns, as for a French omelet, it will break up, as it has too much filling in it.)

OSPREY NESTS

These aren't really as big as osprey nests but I named them this because they are shaped like an osprey's nest. If you have a food processor, these are simplicity itself but must be made quickly to prevent the potato discoloring.

Serves 1.

1 medium-small baking potato	*Salt*
Fresh peanut or corn oil	

Peel the potato and rinse it in cold water. Have ready a bowl of cold water. Use the shredding disc of the food processor or the very largest holes on a hand grater to shred the potato. Put the shreds instantly into cold water. Pour the oil to a depth of about a ½ inch into an 8-inch frying pan and heat to about 375° F. (as for French fries).

Drain the potato shreds and dry them well on paper towels. Loosen the shreds and drop them in an even layer into the hot oil. When they form a crisp cake, turn them over and cook on the other side a minute or so. Drain on paper towels, salt and serve.

Note: To make a number of these cakes, use two pans and keep the completed ones warm in a 300° F. oven. Lay them in a single layer on paper towels.

These make a delicious crisp nest under a hamburger or a small tender steak which must be cooked before starting the "osprey's nest." These are a scrumptious cooking project to do with children when making popcorn palls.

Meat-Loaf Season

Second marriages are a triumph of hope over experience.
—Samuel Johnson

March is much the same. As a month, it falls between the cracks, offering alternate despair of winter and hope of spring. It's the time when couples fall to quarreling about their taxes, who laid the last fire and whether there's really any point to taking a vacation this late in the year. Those of us who stick it out through the winter on islands have to come up with some fairly bizarre antidotes to the bleakness of this final awful month.

Journalist Shana Alexander, a neighbor who was hunkered down in Wainscott all winter, invited a bunch of us to her Great Hamptonian Meat-loaf Bake-off. An inspired idea! Nothing, but nothing else is in season right now, so why not The Meat-loaf Season for beastly early March? Why not an *annual* "Meat-loaf Week" nationwide: a contest, prizes, bathing beauties (OK, long-john beauties) displaying winners. In a couple of years, when meat disappears completely, we can have a Fake Meat-loaf Contest, with entries made *entirely* of Hamburger Helper. Oh, black thought!

Meat loaf and meat-loaves-I-have-known can sustain lengthy conversations among total strangers. There may be a few cranks who won't admit to an occasional longing for this humble dish, but they were probably raised in institutions. I put in some years in a convent boarding school and can understand this.

Although it groomed my fortitude, the convent did not, thank God and the BVM, form my culinary character. One does not even *see* a convent kitchen (and one has no desire to), much less learn to cook. So the first things I learned to make when I finally gained access to pots and pans were fudge, brownies, penuche and angel cake. But the first real entrée I ever learned to make was—you guessed it—meat loaf.

In those days it wasn't much of an investment for the family to let a young girl mess up a few pounds of ground meat. Relatively speaking, it still isn't, thus making meat loaf an excellent "Beginners' Dish." My first meat loaf was crafted from instructions in the 1947 edition of the *Good Housekeeping Cookbook*, which was apparently the only cookbook in our house. I still have it.

Because of the recent war shortages, cookbooks were obsessed then with saving and stretching things. There was, mercifully, no "hamburger helper" at the time but meat loaf, for instance, was "extended"—perfidious word!—with rolled oats. I knew instinctively not to put any rolled oats—whatever *they* were—into *my* meat loaf.

Since those first halting meat loaves, I've experimented with adding dozens of other ingredients, but always with the purpose of improving the texture and flavor (not "extending"), and I cannot resist this urge even now. I have never made exactly the same meat loaf twice, and most likely no one else has either.

WILD MUSHROOM MEAT LOAF

Dried black mushrooms from Japan and spicy, pungent French chanterelles make this a meat loaf for royalty. As well it might, since the imported dried mushrooms cost a king's ransom. One way to economize on this, if you wish to, is to use only half an ounce of the highly flavored chanterelles augmented by one cup of sautéed domestic mild mushrooms. (Never add uncooked vegetables to a meat loaf or pâté mixture as they will not amalgamate properly, thus causing the meat loaf to crumble.)

Serves 6.

1½ pounds lean ground beef
1 pound ground pork shoulder
(fatty)
1 pound lean ground veal
⅓ cup bourbon
2 teaspoons coarse black pepper
2 ounces dried black Japanese
mushrooms
1 ounce dried French
chanterelles
1 cup onions, minced

2 cloves garlic, minced
2 tablespoons butter
½ cup soft fresh white
breadcrumbs
1 large egg, beaten
¼ cup fresh parsley, minced
½ teaspoon dried thyme
3 teaspoons salt
4 to 5 thin strips Virginia bacon
(best quality, cut from slab)
Watercress

Mix together the beef, pork, veal, bourbon and black pepper, cover with plastic wrap and refrigerate ovenight . . . or several hours at least.

Wash the mushrooms well, as they are apt to be a bit sandy. Put them in a deep narrow bowl and pour boiling water over them. Let stand 20 minutes. Save the water to use in soup. Drain the mushrooms, dry them and cut out the hard centers of the Japanese type and just the very tips of the chanterelles. Chop these into about ¼-inch dice and add them to the meats.

Preheat oven to 350° F.

Sauté the onions and garlic in the butter until limp and add them to the meats along with all remaining ingredients except the bacon and watercress. Mix the meat loaf well, using your hands and a light, quick motion. Do not squeeze the meat as this will make the meat loaf tough, and do not use a dough hook, as this beats all life out of it. Shape the loaf into a long oval about 4 inches high. Put into a low-sided gratin dish and cover the meat loaf firmly with as many bacon strips as required. Place this in the center of the preheated oven and bake for one hour, or until an instant-read thermometer registers 170° F. Do not overbake, or all the flavor and juiciness will stay behind in the pan juices. Let the meat loaf rest at least half an hour before serving. It is fine served at room temperature, but this is not highly spiced enough to be served cold. Slice in ½-inch servings, put the loaf back together tightly and serve it on a platter surrounded by sprigs of watercress, lots of it.

On no account allow anyone to introduce catsup to this meat loaf (there has not ever been, nor will be, a bottle of this stuff in my house). Make a dill-mustard sauce for it with Dijon-style mustard thinned with heavy cream and laced with chopped fresh dill.

Lent and Eggs

Lent is a time for secret heroics. Lent is a time for our renewal in reality.

—Florence Berger, *Cooking for Christ*

As Mrs. Berger puts it in her "liturgical year in the kitchen," "the purple days of Lent are upon us." Rules governing what Catholics may eat during this doleful period of sacrifice have been eased considerably. In fact they're almost sybaritic compared with the diet of the early Christians, who took only one meal a day and abstained from meat for the entire six weeks before Easter. The fast became increasingly strict until on Good Friday only bread, salt and vegetables were eaten.

Fasting and abstinence are, of course, practiced in many religions. Moslems eat no pork, and on the Feast of Ramadan they don't eat anything at all. High-caste Hindus are vegetarians and so are most Buddhists. Orthodox Jews are forbidden pork and the laws of keeping a strict kosher kitchen are so complicated it's no wonder that few Jews even attempt it any more. Episcopalians as well as Catholics are required to abstain from meat on all the Fridays of Lent. But they can live it up on fish and eggs. The Greek Orthodox, still hewing to the rules of the primitive church, forbid even eggs—which is why Easter Sunday is such a festival of hard-boiled eggs.

Then there are The Vegetarians. This cult used to be made up primarily of flakes like Isadora Duncan's mad brother, Raymond. Today it's very trendy among adolescent girls, and this new religion has probably saved complexions almost as much as it has destroyed the family dinner. But the difficulty with teen-age veggies is that very few of them know anything much about nutrition. Eating well on a non-meat diet requires some thought, information and a lot more planning than pouring out yet another bowl of crunchy Granola and sprinkling everything with wheat germ.

Despite the calumny of the past few years, eggs are a splendid, cheap, versatile high-protein food. The cholesterol contretemps is in a state of flux, with doctors disagreeing on whether or not it has anything whatever to do with the incidence of heart attacks. Revisionism rages on whether eggs are, or are not, good for you. I love them, and have decided to go on eating them until the controversy is resolved—which will probably be *never*. I think too much meat (bulging with cholesterol, by the way) is a far graver problem in the national diet. Here is a formula to make meatlessness endurable—but it isn't much of an exercise in self-denial; it's too good.

SPINACH AND CHEESE SOUFFLÉ

Soufflés are not at all hard to make. They can even be made in advance and refrigerated until dinner time. And they take only 30 minutes to cook. About the only tricky thing is getting people to sit down at the table *before* you remove the soufflé from the oven. Soufflés do not oblige people. They won't stand up for anybody for more than a few minutes after they leave the oven. It is their nature to collapse. If for some desperate reason you cannot serve the soufflé immediately it is done, you can invert it on a hot plate and serve it unmolded—as if that was what you intended all along.

In the classic French soufflé the center is a little runny and provides a sauce for the more firmly cooked part of the soufflé. Overbaking makes a soufflé dry and tough, so try to educate your friends and family to the soft-centered soufflé.

Serves 4–6.

4 grade A "large" eggs,
  separated
3 egg whites
2 tablespoons softened butter
¼ cup finely grated Parmesan
3 tablespoons unsalted butter
4 tablespoons flour
2 cups hot milk
Pinch of salt

⅛ teaspoon cayenne
Grating of nutmeg
1 package frozen chopped
  spinach, thawed
¾ cup grated or shredded
  cheese (Jarlsberg; Gruyère, or
  imported Swiss Emmenthaler)
2 tablespoons minced scallions
½ teaspoon cream of tartar

Separate the eggs, breaking each one over a small bowl. Let the white drop into the small bowl, then put the yolk into a medium size bowl. Transfer the white to a very large, clean, dry mixing bowl. This way, if one egg should be less than fresh, or if a little yolk gets into the white, it can be discarded without ruining the whole batch of eggs. *Egg whites will not mount* if there is one speck of yolk in them, or the slightest film of grease in the mixing bowl or on the beaters. Scald the utensils and dry them with paper towels.

Butter a 2-quart straight-sided porcelain or Pyrex soufflé mold. Dump in the grated Parmesan and shake it all around the inside, especially the sides, so that the soufflé will have a rough surface to cling to as it rises—otherwise it will slide down the walls of the mold. Chill the mold while you proceed.

Preheat the oven to 375° F.

Melt the 3 tablespoons butter in a heavy 2-quart saucepan. Stir in the flour and cook over very low heat a minute or so. Pour in the hot milk all at once and beat smooth with a wire whisk. Cook, whisking constantly, about 3 minutes. Add the salt, cayenne and nutmeg. Remove from heat. Whisk in the egg yolks one at a time (it's easy to tip out one yolk at a time, but if two fall in, don't worry, it isn't important).

Drop the thawed spinach into boiling salted water for 2 minutes. Drain it and press out all excess juice. Add this to the yolk-enriched sauce base along with the cheese and scallions.

Purists claim the whites must be beaten in a copper bowl with a muscle-powered wire whisk. I have a copper bowl inset for my Kitchenaid electric mixer and it could beat air into mud. But not too many people have a special copper bowl for beating egg whites, so the cream of tartar supplies the acid that is present in copper. However, with any kind of rotary beater, electric, hand or giant electric balloon whip, or a plain hand-held wire whisk, anyone can make a perfectly marvelous soufflé.

Whip the 7 whites with the cream of tartar until they are stiff but not dry. Fold about ¼ of the whites into the lukewarm sauce to lighten the mixture.

Now comes the crucial step: Folding the sauce into the whites must be done lightly, passing a light plastic scraper across the top, down the sides and *under* the whites. Pour the sauce into one side of the beaten egg whites. Begin folding them together, working quickly and lightly. Do not overmix or the air structure will collapse and neither prayer nor curses can make your soufflé rise. It doesn't matter if there are some lumps of unincorporated egg white in your mixture.

Scrape the soufflé mixture into the mold, put the mold on a cookie sheet and place it in the center of the *preheated 375° F.* oven. Close the oven door and *immediately decrease the heat to 350° F.* Bake 30 minutes or until the soufflé has a well-risen and crusty, burnished "cap."

Alternatively, you may put the soufflé into the refrigerator for up to three hours before baking it. I must confess that this has always scared me a bit as it is a restaurant technique that I learned only recently. It amazes me when the porcelain dish doesn't break on contact with the hot oven. Another technique for "making ahead" that has no hazards at all is to make the sauce base with its flavoring—cheese, vegetable, fish, whatever—cover it and set it aside or refrigerate it until dinner time. When I am ready to bake, I whip the whites, warm the sauce base to tepid, and fold the two parts of the soufflé together. This technique may not be brave, but I've never lost a soufflé.

Now, if you can make this soufflé you can make dozens of others. Whatever you choose, minced mushrooms, flaked salmon, crab or lobster, the ingredient must be cooked, thoroughly drained, and either ground or minced very finely. Great chunks would sink to the bottom. (Soufflés baked on a platter often have whole fillets of fish or whole poached eggs—you just have to remember where they lurk.) Use about ¾ cup of your chosen ingredient added to the basic soufflé.

Soufflé-making takes more time to recite than it does to execute. With soufflés in your repertoire, you can always make a quick, elegant meal out of a few eggs and whatever the pantry yields up. Whether it's Lent or Ramadan or Yom Kippur, or just some nice spring day.

Index

ABOUT THE AUTHOR

MIRIAM UNGERER began her professional career as a journalist, was then a fashion editor and writer before deciding that food was an endlessly absorbing subject. She has lived and cooked in Texas, Tennessee, Montana, California, Florida, Pennsylvania and her native South Carolina before investigating the cuisines of France, Germany, Italy, Switzerland, Spain, England, Ireland and Canada. Smatterings of all of them have been incorporated into her food-writing and cooking over the years. Miriam Ungerer lives with her husband, Wilfrid Sheed, in the woods "surrounded by predatory deer" near the old whaling village of Sag Harbor, on the eastern tip of Long Island.